THE PRO WRESTLING HALL OF FAME

THE CANADIANS

ANDRÉ THE GIANT GETS A HUG FROM "THE CANADIAN
WILDMAN" DAVE McKIGNEY. PHOTO: OLIVER COLLECTION

THE PRO WRESTLING HALL OF FAME

THE CANADIANS

Nothing says Canadian wrestlers abroad like oversized beer mugs. Here Ben and Mike Sharpe enjoy Japanese hospitality. Photo: Sharpe Family

GREG OLIVER • ECW PRESS

Copyright © Greg Oliver, 2003

Published by ECW PRESS
2120 Queen Street East, Suite 200, Toronto, Ontario, Canada M4E 1E2

NATIONAL LIBRARY OF CANADA CATALOGUING IN PUBLICATION DATA

Oliver, Greg
The Pro Wrestling Hall of Fame: the Canadians
ISBN 1-55022-531-6
1. Wrestlers–Canada–Biography. I.Title
GV196.A1054 2002   796.812'092'271   C2002-902171-5

Edited by Michael Holmes
Cover and Text Design: Darren Holmes
Printing: University of Toronto Press

This book is set in Utopia and Akzidenz Grotesk

The publication of *The Pro Wrestling Hall of Fame: The Canadians* has been generously supported by the Canada Council, the Ontario Arts Council, and the Government of Canada through the Book Industry Development Program. Canadä

DISTRIBUTION
CANADA: Jaguar Book Group, 100 Armstrong Avenue, Georgetown, ON L7G 5S4

PHOTO CONTRIBUTORS

TONY LANZA — Montreal's Tony Lanza is probably Canada's greatest wrestling photographer and we are thrilled to have his participation in this book.

TUROFSKY BROTHERS — The Turofsky Brothers were the official photographers at Maple Leaf Gardens.

BOB LEONARD — As a photographer and promoter for Stampede, Regina's Bob Leonard has excelled.

L'IL AL — Chris Swisher is the proud owner of the L'Il Al Collection of photos primarily from the southeastern United States.

TERRY DART — London, Ontario's Terry Dart is a great fan and a great photographer.

OLIVER COLLECTION — Greg Oliver's personal collection of photos continues to grow.

MELBY COLLECTION — Minnesota's James C. Melby has one of the most amazing collections of photos around.

MIKE LANO — Dr. Mike Lano of California has been shooting wrestling for decades.

MAY COLLECTION — B.C.'s Vern May is a leading Canadian wrestling historian.

LEDUC COLLECTION — Quebec's Paul Leduc shared his archives without hesitation.

We would also like to thank the many fans, wrestlers and their families who shared personal photos with us.

PRINTED AND BOUND IN CANADA

ECW PRESS
ecwpress.com

*This book is dedicated to Wayne Cassibo (1945 – 2001),
who was a fan of pro wrestling both before and after
his long stint as Ontario referee Wayne Cashman.*

Acknowledgements

Despite what may happen in the ring, pro wrestling is definitely a team sport, with wrestlers relying on each other for protection, production crews to make them look good, and promoters and bookers to lay out exciting storylines. Writing a book like this is no different.

First off, my tag-team partner in life, Meredith, deserves a world title for putting up with all the wrestling stuff in the house. The fact that a photo of Abdullah the Butcher sticking a fork in my forehead is at the top of our stairs speaks volumes to her patience. My parents were in my corner too from the start of my writing career all those years ago.

The business itself has changed over the years. Back when I first started writing, learning the inside of the business was tough to do. My thanks go to Ontario mainstays like Ricky Johnson, Big Mac, Ron Hutchison and the late Wayne Cashman and his family for helping a young kid out.

But it's the fans that make this book worth doing, whether they're trusted, essential historians like J Michael Kenyon, Tom Burke, Vern May, and John Woods, or my buds with whom I can talk wrestling for hours. I'd like to especially mention Terry Dart, John Powell, John Molinaro, Jeff Marek, Terry Harris, John Dolin, Jon Waldman and Chris Schramm.

The friendships I've made with people in the business also mean a lot to me. The warmth of the Rougeaus, the Vachons, the Cormiers, and the Harts has always astounded me. The fun I've had talking to legends like Don Leo Jonathon, Gene Kiniski, and Legs Langevin again and again for stories is impossible to register. Believe it or not, some of the best stories have come from non-wrestlers — referees, managers, photographers. I'd also like to encourage everyone to join the Cauliflower Alley Club, an association for wrestlers and fans. Check them out at www.caulifloweralleyclub.org.

I also see this as a thank you to all my subscribers of *The Canadian Wrestling Report,* and to everyone who read what I did at SLAM! Wrestling. It's been a wild ride.

Contents

Foreword

Hi everyone, I'm Jacques Rougeau.

Maybe you've heard of me—but even if you haven't, perhaps my family name rings a bell. For a long time now, the name Rougeau has been part of wrestling tradition. For many, the name Rougeau is synonymous with technical, high-flying, tag-team wrestling. In Quebec, people remember my uncle, Johnny Rougeau, as fondly as the NHL's Maurice "Rocket" Richard. Wrestling in Canada, in the early days, was huge: in fact, more money was made at the old Montreal Forum at a wrestling event than from a typical hockey game, or any other form of sports or entertainment.

Eddy Auger, my great uncle, was the first of the family to become a pro wrestler—what a gentleman, everyone liked him. But maybe I should draw you a little family tree to better situate you within my story.

THE QUEBECERS, JACQUES ROUGEAU JR. (LEFT), AND PIERRE CARL OUELETT. PHOTO: PAUL LEDUC

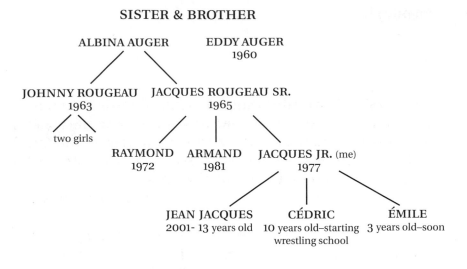

SISTER & BROTHER

ALBINA AUGER   EDDY AUGER
1960

JOHNNY ROUGEAU   JACQUES ROUGEAU SR.
1963   1965

two girls

RAYMOND   ARMAND   JACQUES JR. (me)
1972   1981   1977

JEAN JACQUES   CÉDRIC   ÉMILE
2001- 13 years old   10 years old–starting   3 years old–soon
wrestling school

There were many other families in the Canadian wrestling game: the Harts, the Vachons, the Baillergeons, the Cormiers and others. Something that always impressed me was the respect the fans would show us—especially when they realized you were related.

I guess blood is thicker than water.

But now that I've said my piece and briefly introduced the first families of Canadian wrestling, I should acknowledge that there's a much, much longer list of Canadian wrestling greats. My friend Greg, in this marvelous book, will tell you all about some of the best wresters in the world, giving you a Canadian Top 20 and outlining the impact of Canadian wrestlers, in general, in the process.

"My friend Greg" is Greg Oliver—the man behind this book. He's a person who's always trying to reach out to get the best out of you. Greg's been very generous with his time and he's given a lot of support to people who've had either a history or interest in wrestling. For me, personally, Greg's not only a friend—he's also a great writer.

Now, sit back and have fun learning about the history of pro wrestling in Canada.

Sincerely yours,

Jacques

Introduction

"As far as professional wrestling is going, Canada has really done its part. It seemed like over the years, at certain times in the evolution, Montreal was the town for a while, then they had that there gym in Hamilton that turned out a lot of people, then Stu Hart turned out a lot of guys."

— Don Leo Jonathon

What sets Canada apart in the history of pro wrestling isn't that we created so many wrestlers, it's that we created so many wrestlers that were so good. Population-wise, it's an amazing accomplishment, but one overlooked by the mainstream media.

Yes, pro wrestling is a fixed sport. So what? These entertainers have performed before more people than most NHLers or Canadian actors. Their names are better known internationally than any Canadian politician's. Wherever they have performed around the globe, they have taken a little bit of Canada with them.

It's time they got their due.

This book is by no means a complete list of Canadian wrestlers since the dawn of the modern era. It is instead a celebration of the best-known names, or the names that as a wrestling fan you should come to know. The succession lines are there to be followed: Jack Taylor to Earl McCready to Whipper Watson to Gene Kiniski to Roddy Piper to Bret Hart to Chris Jericho; Emil Maupas to Yvon Robert to Johnny Rougeau to Ivan Koloff to Rick Martel.

Understanding Canadian wrestling, however, requires a basic understanding of Canadian geography. The five major regions of the populated part of the country — B.C., the Prairies, Ontario, Quebec and the Maritimes — are also the five most important regions of Canada when it comes to wrestling. Here is a breakdown of the basic facts on each area and the territories associated with them:

BRITISH COLUMBIA: Geography has traditionally meant that any promotion based in British Columbia would have closer ties to the U.S. Northwest than to the rest of Canada. This is true with regular trading of wrestling talent from each side of the border over the years. Promoters in the B.C. area include Cliff Parker and Rod Fenton, Gene Kiniski and Sandor Kovacs, and Al Tomko. Wrestlers would often

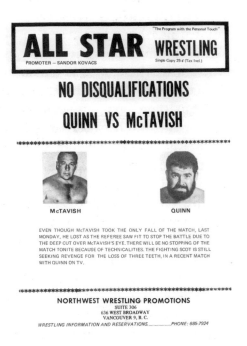

work in this area while on the way to or from Japan, Australia, New Zealand or Hawaii. Today, Extreme Canadian Championship Wrestling is the dominant promotion.

THE PRAIRIES: Since 1948, wrestling in Alberta and Saskatchewan has been Stu Hart's domain. Today, his sons are trying to keep the Stampede Wrestling name alive. The respect that promoters and wrestlers had for Hart meant that he could pick and choose talent. The local crew that was loyal to Hart was rough and tough and could have main-evented in many places. Hart also had a working relationship with Japan, which meant that wrestlers could make good connections while based out of Calgary. The road trips for Stampede were among the worst in the business. Besides the big cities of Calgary, Edmonton, Regina and Saskatoon, Stampede would rotate through smaller communities, including destinations in Montana and up into the Yukon and Northwest Territories.

Manitoba had its own scene, and its closest ties were to the south, with Minneapolis and the American Wrestling Association (AWA). Over the years, there were places like the Madison Club where wrestlers could learn the business, then perform in front of crowds once a week. Something in the water in Winnipeg must encourage bad blood between promotions; there always seemed to be two or three going at any one time, a tradition that continues to this day. In the 1980s, the AWA taped their television show at the Winnipeg Arena and the shows were aired on TSN. It would be remiss to talk about Manitoba without mentioning Tony Condello's "Northern Death" tours, which he has run for the last couple of decades. Condello would get a bunch of wrestlers together, put them in vans, and head to the Native reservations in northern Manitoba in the middle of winter, their driving time cut considerably shorter if they braved the frozen lakes.

ONTARIO: Being the most populated province, Ontario has always had a lot of wrestling. Larry "Babe" Kasaboski was the promoter in northern Ontario for years, bringing talent up to Sudbury, North Bay and Timmins, primarily as a summer promotion. In the 1970s, "Bearman" Dave McKigney would collect wrestlers and hit small towns all over the province.

TORONTO PROMOTER FRANK TUNNEY (LEFT) WITH RING ANNOUNCER NORM KIMBER AND REFEREE TERRY YORKSTON. PHOTO: TERRY DART

The Maple Leaf Wrestling promotion in Toronto was the dominant territory in Canada. Run by Frank Tunney and his nephew Jack from the 1950s until the 1980s, Maple Leaf centred on Maple Leaf Gardens, the mecca of pro wrestling in Canada. The Maple Leaf TV show was the first to go country-wide, and made a star out of Whipper Watson and his dastardly opponent of the week. Frank Tunney was an influential member of the National Wrestling Alliance board and his lobbying was a big reason why Watson had two NWA title runs and that the World title occasionally changed hands in Toronto. Tunney also controlled the rest of the province in many ways, divvying up pieces of it to friends. The promotion had a naturally close tie with whoever was running Buffalo as well. When the WWF took over pro wrestling, Toronto was still an important stop and TV tapings were done both at the Gardens and in Brantford.

With so many gyms around Hamilton, the wrestling scene thrived. Joe Maich was the promoter of the "bullshit" circuit around Steeltown, a starting ground for many of the men featured in this book.

Down around Windsor, various promoters ran shows, the most notable of which was George "Crybaby" Cannon with his Superstars of Wrestling program in the 1970s. The Windsor area always worked closely with Detroit.

Today, pro wrestling in Ontario is almost non-existent because arcane rules and stiff fees levied by the Ontario Athletic Commission discourage entrepreneuring promoters. Over the last number of years, promotions have started up with much fanfare only to disappear in a blaze of broken promises and bad debt.

QUEBEC: As with its history and politics, pro wrestling in Quebec has been somewhat different from the rest of the country. Catering to a French-speaking population meant that it was essential to have a French-speaking attraction on top of the card. Yvon Robert was the first major star, but others like Johnny Rougeau, Edouard Carpentier and Dino

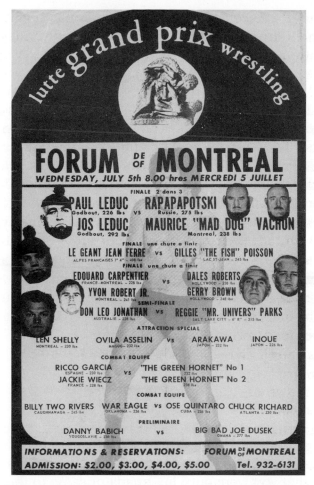

lutte grand prix wrestling

FORUM DE OF MONTREAL
WEDNESDAY, JULY 5th 8.00 hres MERCREDI 5 JUILLET

FINALE 2 dans 3

PAUL LEDUC Godbout, 226 lbs VS **RAPAPAPOTSKI** Russie, 275 lbs
JOS LEDUC Godbout, 292 lbs **MAURICE "MAD DOG" VACHON** Montreal, 238 lbs

FINALE une chute a finir

LE GEANT JEAN FERRE ALPES FRANCAISES 7' 4" - 408 lbs vs **GILLES "THE FISH" POISSON** LAC ST-JEAN - 245 lbs

FINALE une chute a finir

EDOUARD CARPENTIER FRANCE-MONTREAL - 228 lbs vs **DALES ROBERTS** HOLLYWOOD - 238 lbs
YVON ROBERT JR. MONTREAL - 241 lbs **GERRY BROWN** HOLLYWOOD - 248 lbs

SEMI-FINALE

DON LEO JONATHAN AUSTRALIE - 228 lbs vs **REGGIE "MR. UNIVERS" PARKS** SALT LAKE CITY - 6' 8" - 315 lbs

ATTRACTION SPECIAL

LEN SHELLY MONTREAL - 230 lbs **OVILA ASSELIN** MAGOG - 232 lbs vs **ARAKAWA** JAPON - 232 lbs **INOUE** JAPON - 226 lbs

COMBAT EQUIPE

RICCO GARCIA ESPAGNE - 230 lbs **JACKIE WIECZ** FRANCE - 228 lbs vs **"THE GREEN HORNET" No 1** 232 lbs **"THE GREEN HORNET" No 2** 238 lbs

COMBAT EQUIPE

BILLY TWO RIVERS CAUGHNAWAGA - 245 lbs **WAR EAGLE** OKLAHOMA - 226 lbs vs **OSE QUINTARO** CUBA - 226 lbs **CHUCK RICHARD** ATLANTA - 230 lbs

PRELIMINAIRE

DANNY BABICH YOUGOSLAVIE - 230 lbs vs **BIG BAD JOE DUSEK** OMAHA - 277 lbs

INFORMATIONS & RESERVATIONS: **FORUM DE OF MONTREAL**
ADMISSION: $2.00, $3.00, $4.00, $5.00 **Tel. 932-6131**

Bravo followed. In 1939, Eddie Quinn came up from Massachusetts and built Montreal into a powerful promotion. Quinn had a lot of sway in the National Wrestling Alliance (NWA) and acted as booking agent for stars-in-demand like Robert and Carpentier. When Quinn died in 1965, Johnny Rougeau stepped into the void with Les Etoiles de la Lutte. In 1972, Paul Vachon gathered up his friends to compete with Rougeau with Grand Prix Wrestling. Both promotions duked it out for four years, but neither survived. Wrestling was dead in Quebec for a short period until Frank Valois, André the Giant and Gino Brito combined to start International Wrestling in 1980. Brito kept that promotion going until 1989 when it proved impossible to compete with the WWF. Since then, there have been a myriad of small promotions in Quebec, the largest of which is Jacques Rougeau Jr.'s Lutte Internationale 2000.

THE MARITIMES: Nova Scotia, New Brunswick and Prince Edward Island have always been an attractive destination for tourists, and wrestlers were no different. Whether it was Len Hughes, Emile Dupré, the Cormiers or the current Real Action Wrestling promoting events out east, the wrestlers wanted to go there. Traditionally, it is a summer territory, which meant beautiful weather, lots of beaches and a relaxed lifestyle highlighted by short drives from town to town.

Wrestling in Newfoundland and Labrador has been hit-and-miss over the years. Because of the expense of getting the crew to the province, promoters would set up a tour, going from the main city of St. John's to the different outposts. The road between towns was long and hard.

The Criteria

Choosing who went into this book and who didn't was not an easy task. By this book's definition, being a Canadian wrestler meant that you were born in Canada or came to the country as an immigrant while still a youth. A wrestler's career-span, success record, name recognition, titles and influence also came into play. The Adopted Canadians section is for wrestlers who came to Canada as adults and chose to stay, or who made their start in Canada. Today's Stars are Canadians who are making a full-time living wrestling professionally.

The Top 20 Canadian Pro Wrestlers

1. WHIPPER BILLY WATSON

Gene Kiniski and Whipper Billy Watson were a perfect match in the 1950s. The rough and ready Kiniski was a braggart — a blowhard who wanted to make a name for himself. Watson was the established star, a Canadian legend who defended the honour of good people everywhere. He had, in the words of the late Toronto promoter Frank Tunney, a dignity to him even when being strangled. Above all, The Whip was an honest, capable, law-abiding hero.

The Kiniski-Watson battles were pure good vs evil, and with television starting to invade homes across the country, the timing couldn't have been better. They took their act on the road, headlining wherever they went. "I wrestled him so many, many times. I think I wrestled him in every city and village in Canada," said Kiniski. "In fact, the first time we met in Newfoundland, my God, you couldn't get near the airport. They had the largest crowd in the history of Newfoundland to welcome him."

Such was the power of Whipper Billy Watson, easily the biggest name in Canadian pro wrestling history. Others wrestlers were certainly better showmen (Killer Kowalski), better talkers (Kiniski), better wrestlers (Earl McCready), tougher (Mad Dog Vachon) and more popular in certain regions (Yvon Robert). But The Whip remains the one name

WHIPPER WATSON AND YUKON ERIC TEAM UP IN TORONTO IN 1955. PHOTO: MICHAEL BURNS

everyone knows, and to his eternal credit, Watson's name is associated with far more than pro wrestling.

Whipper Watson was a tireless fundraiser for charities across the country, both during and after his ring career. He didn't just lend his name to a cause, he threw himself into it, learning all that he could. Watson always said in interviews that he donated his time because he always got back more than he gave. When he had his own accident in 1971, which ended his wrestling career and left him requiring a cane the rest of his life, Watson's perspective changed and he gave even more. With a new understanding of the issues at hand, Watson campaigned for better facilities and funding for the disabled.

There will never be another like him.

Watson was born William Potts in East York, Ontario on July 25, 1917. His father was killed in France near the end of World War I and Billy was raised by his mother and stepfather, whom he resented. Young Billy was always a great athlete, whether it was softball, marathon swimming, football or hockey. At 13, he found the father figure that he had been looking for in Phil Lawson, a trainer at the local YMCA. Lawson taught him amateur wrestling skills, and was instrumental in getting Billy booked to wrestle in England in 1936, where lighter-weight wrestlers were appreciated. Lawson would later serve as Watson's business manager.

At 19 and weighing about 190 pounds, Watson boarded a cattle ship bound for Cardiff along with fellow young grapplers Al "Krusher" Korman, Ken "Tiger" Tasker, Tommy Nelson and their trainer Harry Joyce. They found no wrestling in Cardiff, sleeping in tents and even a chicken coop until finally making it to London.

The promoter there didn't think the name William Potts was going to fly in the ring, so he named him Billy Watson. The nickname Whipper came from the newspapers, adopted from his use of "the whip" in the ring, a move in which he would duck and throw an opponent over his head. In his first match, Billy made $20 for defeating Tony Bear.

The English promoters took liberties with the facts of Watson's life. For a 1937 Rotterham match against Charlie Green, Watson was touted as an "ex-rugger star and champion baseball player. The wrecker of champions! Light-heavyweight champion of Canada. The man who originated the Irish Whip and many other scientific wrestling holds. Watson is all action personified and thrills with his daring and sensational wrestling." Another poster billed him from America, and claimed a thumb jabbed into his left eye left him with 10% vision on that side.

While in England, Watson met his first wife, Patricia Utting. When World War II began, and the bombs started falling on England, Watson knew that it was time to head home. They started making plans to return home in April 1940, but didn't get on a boat until July, even though they had to be ready to leave on 12 hours notice at any point. The convoy of passenger ships were escorted to Halifax by British warships.

Watson had sent ahead a promotional package to Toronto ring boss Frank Tunney, but when he turned up at the mat office, he learned Tunney hadn't bothered to pick it up at the post office. Billy quickly explained what he had been doing over the previous four years and was offered opening spots on upcoming cards. It was an odd beginning to what would become a very profitable 30-year relationship.

As a main-eventer at Maple Leaf Gardens, Watson fought all of the top names and his favourite hold was the Canuck Commando Unconscious, a variation of the sleeper hold. He held the NWA world title on two occasions — beating Wild Bill Longson in February 1947, and losing to Lou Thesz two months later — and again in March 1956, beating and then losing to Thesz. Throughout his career, Watson would praise Thesz as the greatest he ever fought.

Thesz puts Watson and Quebec star Yvon Robert in the same category, not great wrestlers but stars in their territories. "They were both promoted very well, and really, really did a great job. They had a great deal of visibility, and they did well," said Thesz. "Both of them drew a lot of money for the promoters, and did very, very well."

Lord James Blears was another wrestler who fought Watson in main events. "He was a very methodical wrestler and he was a god in Canada," Blears said. "He didn't have a real flashy style like me, going around drop-kicking, that kind of stuff. But he was a good, basic wrestler. Tough. He was the King of Toronto."

Over time, Watson immersed himself in the details of the Toronto wrestling office, working hand in hand with Tunney. His opponents knew of his pull with the man signing the paycheques. "He was the boss, so if you didn't do exactly what he wanted, he would go back to the office. But I didn't give a damn, I didn't have to go to Toronto. I could go anywhere else. But I got along with him in a way," said the goose-stepping Hans Schmidt, who guesses that he fought Watson "about 1,000 times."

Watson had many ways to promote his name outside of his work with charities. He had his own lines of barbell

THE WHIP CARRIES KEVIN COLLINS, THE "TIMMY" IN 1976,
ON HIS SHOULDERS AT THE SPORTS CELEBRITY DINNER.
PHOTO: MICHAEL PEAKE, TORONTO SUN

equipment and soda pop, his Whipper's Safety Club boasted 50,000 members in Canada and the United States and he would speak at schools when he could. For *Matches with Whipper*, the official newsletter of his fan club, Watson would write updates on his career and his family life. A great friend and fan of John Diefenbaker, The Whip ran as a Conservative candidate for York East in the 1965 federal election, but lost. It all combined to create a huge fan base for him, a fact that was not lost on his opponents.

"He had a real loyal following in Toronto and (you always had) two fights with Watson. One with him, and then if you won, one getting out of the ring," laughed opponent Don Leo Jonathon. "The people, they loved him and they just hated to see anything go against his wishes."

Though Watson is best known for his work around southern Ontario, he did travel extensively through the U.S., especially during his runs with the World title. By the late 1960s, Watson's career had wound down, and he was only wrestling about 100 shows a year. He had a farm north of Toronto where he lived with his wife and three children, painted, and grew corn. His two sons, John and Phil, both got into pro wrestling for a time, though Phil's career lasted much longer than John's.

Having wrestled the night before in Kitchener, Watson was loading a fireplace screen into his trunk on November 30, 1971 when a car hit him, snapping his leg. It took five months to recover, and the accident left him requiring a cane for the rest of his life.

His ring career ended, Watson continued to make appearances on shows, promoting his protégés like Dewey Robertson. In 1978, a Whipper Watson Appreciation night was held at Maple Leaf Gardens, where he presented the Canadian title to Dino Bravo, who had beaten Watson's old rival Kiniski.

His hospital stay in early 1972 forced Watson to miss his first dinner/fundraiser for the Ontario Society for Crippled Children, where every year he carried "Timmy," a handicapped boy, to the head table. But a year later, Whipper was

WHIPPER WATSON.
PHOTO: TONY LANZA

back. Watson also served at various times on the Ontario government's advisory council on physical disabilities, the Canadian Rehabilitation Council for the Disabled, the Canadian Paraplegic Association, the Multiple Sclerosis Society, and participated in fundraising for countless hospitals. In 1974, Watson was made a Member of the Order of Canada. He has received Honorary Citizen Awards from cities across Canada, from St. John's to Vancouver, and in 1984, York University presented him with an honorary degree. Watson would pay for his own flights to most of these charity events.

Besides carrying Timmy and Tammy at dinners across the country, Watson's other big fundraiser was Snowarama, an Ontario-wide snowmobile pledge ride. When his weight ballooned to 350 pounds after his accident, Watson organized Pounds for People, where he lost weight and raised money at the same time.

"When he became ill and was no longer able to wrestle, I really got to know the individual," said his old rival, Kiniski. "He was a very, very caring person. He gave so much back to the community. He was just a phenomenal individual. I can't, to be honest, speak highly enough for him, about him."

Whipper Billy Watson died of a heart attack while in Florida on February 4, 1990. "He was a great, great asset to the world of professional sports," said Kiniski. "He was known worldwide, and of course his name, Whipper Billy Watson, is synonymous with wrestling in Canada."

2. YVON ROBERT

Yvon "The Lion" Robert and Maurice "The Rocket" Richard are two names that are forever tied because of their combined dominance of the Montreal sports market from the 1930s to the 1950s. Yet it is perhaps an unfair comparison. Richard was mainly known in North America; Robert had an international following through his trips to Europe. Robert also made far more money than any hockey player did during that era. Even today, more than 30 years after his death, his name is still known around the province.

But what made Robert so popular? It's a combination of things. Robert was young, good-looking, solidly built, French-Canadian and he oozed charisma. He knew the importance of promotion, whether it was talking with the newspapers, radio, or in later years, TV. Robert also made tremendous allies and business partners, the most important of which was Boston's Eddie Quinn, who would become the head promoter in Montreal from 1939 until his death in 1956.

Robert was born in Verdun, Quebec on October 8, 1914. School didn't interest him, and he considered apprenticing to be a blacksmith. Instead, he was encouraged by a coach at a local gym to seek out the legendary Emil Maupas and train as

YVON ROBERT TRAINS WITH TONY LANZA. PHOTO: TONY LANZA

"Le lion de Quebec."
Photo: Tony Lanza

a wrestler. Robert was to spend 10 months at Camp Maupas in the Laurentians, honing his body and learning the wrestling trade. After Camp Maupas, he went to Camp Riopel, run by Lucien Riopel, the Montreal promoter. There he furthered his knowledge of scientific wrestling and got to know stars like Henri Deglane, Raoul Simon and Frank Judson.

On April 9, 1932, a 6-foot, 240-pound Robert made his pro debut at Montreal's Mount Royal Arena, earning his first $25. He hit the road down to New England, wrestling around Boston. Two years later, he was pitted against Canadian star Earl McCready in Montreal, and the bout went to a draw. His accession was pegged by *Le Devoir* the next day; the newspaper wrote that Robert had never had as good a chance to prove himself as he did that night against McCready.

Having racked up the wins wherever he went, Robert was ready to challenge for the World title. In Boston, he cooked up a scheme with Quinn. The two were sitting at ringside in 1935 for a match between world champion Danno O'Mahoney and Frank Judson. Robert had his trunks on under his clothes, and between falls, he leapt into the ring, doffed his street wear and challenged O'Mahoney. The match was signed for Montreal in July.

The World title situation in the years before the formation of the NWA in 1948 was always up in the air, with many

YVON ROBERT JR. IS ACCOMPANIED TO THE RING BY HIS FAMOUS
FATHER IN HIS DEBUT AT THE MAURICE RICHARD ARENA IN
MONTREAL. PHOTO: TONY LANZA

wrestlers claiming to be the champ, and different jurisdic-
tions interpreting the rules differently. In winning the belt
from O'Mahoney in front of the masses in Montreal, Robert
laid claim to the belt recognized in New England. He would
lose and regain the same belt a half dozen times over his
career.

From today's perspective, it is somewhat difficult to
understand Robert's stature. Lou Thesz was one of those
World title claimants, and fought Robert many times. "Yvon
was a great attraction. The French-Canadians thought he was
a god," Thesz said. "Yvon was a good wrestler, not a sophisti-
cated wrestler. But he did very, very well financially, and they
kept promoting him, and they did a great, great job. He could

go the distance. If he had to wrestle a 90-minute match, and make it look like he couldn't beat a guy, he could do it."

Angelo Savoldi also fought Robert. "Yvon Robert was one of the tops," he said. "He was very clever and very scientific. He was champion-calibre."

For Verne Gagne, one particular match in Boston, before a packed house, stands out. "It was a very scientific match and as things went on, it was give and take, and finally I came off the ropes and hit him with a drop kick. He went down but before I could grab him, he would stagger up to his feet and I'd hit him again. And then I hit him again a third time, and he went down and I tried to pin him and he kicked out. He got up and I hit him with another one. The guy was tough! I just couldn't keep him down. I think I drop-kicked him 11 times, and finally the people were starting to boo me for doing that. I just kept going on him with these drop kicks. I just about wore out after 11 of them. I finally got him, but he was tough! That one stands out in my mind very vividly."

As one of the top heels of the 1950s, Gene Kiniski battled The Lion in Montreal and Ottawa. It was an uphill battle. "You were against the world and outer space wrestling him in places like Montreal! You're fighting for your life, besides watching him, you had to watch the fans," Kiniski said. "The fans loved to watch him wrestle. He was a very good technician in the ring. He could make the moves. Hell of a man."

Robert's best-known holds were the rolling short-arm scissors and the drop kick. He had many injuries over his career, including a broken leg in a match against Cliff Olson, graphically described in the fan book *Wrestling Scene*: "They both were going at it, in the fast, modern style and suddenly there was a slight plop as if a small paper bag had burst. Yvon Robert's face grew pale. A doctor hurriedly made a diagnosis — broken leg." During one of his hospital stays, Robert fell in love with his nurse, Leona, and would court her for eight years until they married.

During his career, Robert fought all the top names, men like Killer Kowalski, Don Leo Jonathon, Henri Deglane, Lou Thesz, Ed Don George and Bobby Managoff. In 1949, Robert and Toronto's Whipper Billy Watson duelled over the British Empire title, playing off the hot Leafs-Canadiens rivalry between the two cities. Later, he would team with Watson to win the Canadian Open tag-team title. His brother Maurice also wrestled for a spell, but was not in Yvon's league. Robert made three trips to Europe, becoming a star in Paris against grapplers like Deglane and Yvan Martison.

The TV show *Sur le Matelas*, hosted by Michel Normandin, was one of the highest-rated programs in the early days of Quebec television because of Robert. He is responsible for some of the largest crowds and gates at the Montreal Forum including epic matches against Primo Carnera and Gorgeous George.

Robert also deserves credit for not keeping the rising stars down. He was instrumental in the careers of Larry Moquin and Johnny Rougeau, taking both under his wing as his public protégés. He helped bring Edouard Carpentier over from France. By the time Robert's final match came in 1957, in a tag team with Rougeau, an heir apparent was already in place. Robert would manage Rougeau's career, and referee matches. He also helped his son, Yvon Robert Jr., break into the business.

Away from the ring, Robert was involved with a number of businesses, including a restaurant, and he had a hand in the Montreal wrestling promotion. He loved horse racing as well.

After his retirement, Robert suffered a series of heart attacks. He died July 12, 1971 at his home at Havre des Iles, Laval. A biography, *Yvon Robert: Le Lion de Canada francais* by Pierre Berthelet, came out in 1999, and was eight years in the making.

Rick Martel was one of the many wrestlers influenced by Robert though he never saw him wrestle. "He was the epitome of the wrestler here in Quebec. He was like a folk hero," said Martel. "I read a lot about him. In fact, I read his book."

3. KILLER KOWALSKI

Now in his 70s, Killer Kowalski shuffles along slowly, slightly hunched. He has a pair of classic cauliflower ears to go with the most amazing hooked nose on the planet. His long arms end in meaty paws that still seem more than capable of hurting an opponent.

Yet there's a duality to Wladek Kowalski that makes him even more fascinating. He was nicknamed "Killer" in the ring; away from it, he's a peaceful vegetarian who loves photography. In the ring, he was usually a heel, but a loved one well before "Stone Cold" Steve Austin made loving bad guys cool. Kowalski is quiet and contemplative until asked a question, after which he has been known to go on for hours.

He's a man happy with his life, the choices he made and the paths he took. "I traveled the world. Somebody asked me, if you were to live your life over again, what would you do, become an electrical engineer or professional wrestler? Travelling the world didn't cost me a dime. Long-trip plane tickets everywhere I went. And I enjoyed myself," said Kowalski.

Born and raised in Windsor, Ontario by Polish immigrant parents, Kowalski really did study to become an electrical engineer. At the same time, he had been sculpting his body at the Windsor YMCA, where he

KILLER KOWALSKI

became interested in wrestling. There was an amateur coach there who also wrestled professionally around the area. Kowalski asked for a lesson and got one. "[He] put a hold on me and I screamed," he said. Soon, Kowalski had graduated from the Y to Michigan and Ohio preliminaries. A foreman at work was getting tired of his requests for time off, and so when an offer came to go to St. Louis in 1947, Kowalski quit his job without hesitation.

In St. Louis, he was billed as Tarzan Kowalski and found a mentor in Lou Thesz. "He tested you to see how tough you really are," Kowalski said. At 6-foot-6, 280-pounds, Kowalski found it pretty easy to get booked, even if he wasn't winning every night. In Toronto, he challenged Whipper Watson for the British Empire title, coming clean in the newspapers with his Canadian — rather than Polish — heritage to ensure he had the credentials to wear the belt (he didn't win). Television further enhanced Kowalski's career, and he was featured in the first professional wrestling match to be televised in Canada in January 1953. Kowalski was a menacing heel, but photogenic and well-spoken on the microphone.

It was in Montreal, however, where his legend was made. Killer had been wrestling there for a while before an incident in the ring in 1954 created headlines. He was facing Yukon Eric, and had tied his leg to the rope so that he could perform his feared flying knee drop. As Kowalski launched himself off the top turnbuckle, the referee was trying to untie his opponent. "Coming down, Yukon Eric says, 'Holy, jumping Josephat!' He tried to pull his head away. I thought I missed him," Kowalski said. "My shinbone grazed his left cheek and I ripped his ear right off the side of his head." With Yukon Eric unable to continue, Kowalski was named the victor. Two days later, he was ordered to visit Eric in the hospital by the promoter. Kowalski saw Yukon Eric, his head all bandaged up, and thought he looked like Humpty Dumpty. He broke into laughter, giving the press in attendance fuel for their feud. The new nickname they gave him, Killer, stuck.

"Kowalski meant very much in Montreal," said Legs Langevin. "He was a very, very popular guy in the province of

Quebec. He was a heel but he was very, very popular." In Montreal alone, Kowalski held the promotion's version of the AWA/IWA World title eight times between 1952¹–1962. It was during his time in Montreal that he decided to take time off from wrestling, purifying his body and becoming a vegetarian.

The Killer always had the respect of his peers for his conditioning and his skills. "People thought the guy was a maniac, but really he was one of the nicest guys in the world," said Jacques Rougeau Sr.

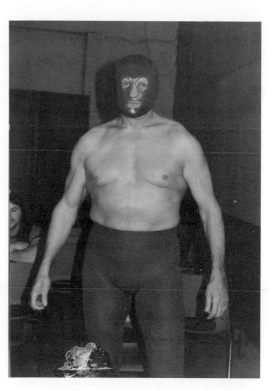

KOWALSKI UNDER THE MASK AS THE EXECUTIONER. PHOTO: TERRY DART

"He was a hard worker, always worked hard in the ring, always in good shape. You were always sure to get a lot of action with this guy. Never had a bad match." Gene Kiniski agreed. "Walter was always in great shape. He's another one that never got tired in the ring."

Besides his success in Montreal, Kowalski racked up many titles around the world, including belts in Texas, California, Hawaii and the WWWF. He loved Australia, and was the world champ there for a number of years. Kowalski found success as a tag team partner as well, winning gold with Hans Hermann, Gorilla Monsoon and even under a hood as part of The Masked Executioners, with protégé Big John Studd.

By the mid-'70s, Kowalski had settled in Salem, Massachusetts and become a U.S. citizen. He had already helped start the career of a few wrestlers, like Studd (John Minton), but some eager wannabe wrestlers at the Salem YMCA set up a ring and begged Kowalski to train them. "That was the first wrestling school of all in 1978," Kowalski said. "I start training guys and pretty soon they start writing it up. I was on the David Letterman show. And before David Letterman, I was on other TV shows. Word got out, there's a wrestling school."

One of his early students was Mike Shaw, who would go on to star as Makhan Singh and Norman the Lunatic. "Kowalski had a great school. He spent a lot of time with us," Shaw said. The Killer's association with New England promotions helped get his students booked, and later he ran some shows on his own. Among Kowalski's top grads wrestling today are Hunter Hearst Helmsley, Chyna (Joanie Laurer), Perry Saturn, and Albert/A. Train.

Kowalski is still sought out by many interviewers and fans. He is polite to all, and happy to talk. In February 2002, however, the Killer was left almost speechless when he was awarded the Iron Mike Mazurki Award, the Cauliflower Alley Club's top honour, named after the club's founder. The Killer now knows that he's gone from being hated to being loved. "I went through a lot, but I always ended up on top," Kowalski told the packed banquet hall. "I was a big, mean, mean guy in my career . . . but now they look at me as being an angel."

4. MAD DOG VACHON

During his farewell tour of Quebec in 1986, Maurice "Mad Dog" Vachon made the remarkable transformation from despised wrestler to beloved popular icon. Just as he was hanging up his boots for the last time, doors were finally opening for him. Interviews both in print and on the air praised his contribution to society. He was hired to hawk beer and chocolate bars. He wrote his autobiography, made a rap album in French, and most bizarrely, the veteran of more than 16,000 bouts over almost 40 years was tapped to be a restaurant reviewer.

MAURICE "MAD DOG" VACHON

A YOUNG MAURICE VACHON. PHOTO: LEDUC COLLECTION

The words "Canadian icon" have rarely suited a better man. The love that the public had for Vachon became even more apparent a year after his retirement when he was struck by a car while walking with his third wife Kathie in Des Moines, Iowa. Vachon had his right leg amputated below the knee. The story was carried by media across Canada, and he was flooded with letters from well-wishers.

The tale of Maurice Vachon would be amazing enough even without his accession into mainstream culture. Born in Ville Emard, a working class neighbourhood in Montreal, in 1929, Vachon was the second of 13 children. His father was a strongman who worked for the local police force. Teased about his name — "Vachon le cochon" — Maurice got into many scraps as a youth. At 12, his father started him training at amateur wrestling at the Montreal YMCA. Maurice dropped out of school at 13 to work various jobs, and pursue his athletic endeavours.

Encouraged by his father, Maurice took to wrestling quickly and made the Canadian Olympic team for the 1948 London Games. "When you walk into the Stadium at Wembley in London, there's probably 6,000 athletes there, King George VI is there, the Queen, and they play your national anthem — it gives you goosepimples," Vachon said. The Montrealer competed at 174 pounds and finished in seventh place, eliminated in the third round. Vachon also met future pro opponents Verne Gagne and Joe Scarpello at the Games.

Undeterred by his Olympic defeat, Vachon rebounded in 1950 to claim gold at the British Empire Games (the forerunner of the Commonwealth Games) in New Zealand. "When you wrestle professional, the money goes in your pocket," Vachon said. "When you wrestle amateur, the medals, they go in your heart."

Growing up, Vachon had always been a fan of the pro game, and upon his return to Canada, he wrestled a bit around Montreal before heading to Northern Ontario for the Kasaboskis, which was a summer territory. The 5-foot-8, 240-pound Vachon was a hit and other opportunities soon came along.

"Mad Dog had an instant reputation when he started wrestling professional because he had been a bouncer in a Montreal nightclub, he'd never lost a streetfight. He loved to fight," said his brother Paul.

Vachon was in Hawaii when he first met Portland promoter Don Owen, who invited him to come to his territory. Vachon attacked his opponent, the referee and a ringside

MAD DOG ENTERS THE RING. PHOTO: MAY COLLECTION

police officer before the bell in his Pacific Northwest debut and was disqualified, fined and suspended. Owen told him then that he looked like a mad dog, and the nickname stuck, as did Owen's decision to bill Vachon as hailing from Algeria.

For the next 30 years, Mad Dog carved out a reputation for himself around the globe. With his shaved head, and clipped moustache and beard, Vachon would drape himself in chains while growling through his interviews. As time wore on, and his larynx took more and more of a beating, his voice became better suited to his character.

According to Killer Kowalski, Vachon would carry that character with him outside the ring. "One time we went to a bar outside Minneapolis. Someone gave him a little flak and he beat the shit out of the guy. Took a jar, or something like that, and hit the guy over the head with it," he said with a laugh.

Vachon's biggest successes, by far, came in the AWA out of Minneapolis where he was well-matched against Verne Gagne, and in Montreal, where he ran the Grand Prix Wrestling promotion in the 1970s, partnering with his brother Paul, Yvon Robert Jr. and others.

He was also extremely well known for two tag teams. One was with his brother Paul "The Butcher," and together they held the AWA tag titles for a long time. The other was his teaming with Baron von Raschke, a partnership that had its heyday in Montreal. "Baron von Raschke was one of my best partners in wrestling. We were very successful together. Not to diminish the prestige of my brother Paul "The Butcher" when we were teamed together. As far as I am concerned, the Mad Dog and Baron von Raschke were the oddest, most explosive tag team in wrestling history."

Wrestling solo, Vachon had epic feuds with the likes of Gagne, Kowalski and Wild Bill Curry, and faced all the top talent from his era. In Montreal, the Vachons were forever feuding with the Rougeaus and the Leducs.

Over the last number of years, Vachon has continued to put in occasional appearances with various promotions, including a memorable ringside seat at a WWF pay-per-view event where his prosthesis was used as a weapon in the match. He lives in Omaha, Nebraska with his wife Kathie and manages to travel to Hawaii every year for a vacation.

Give credit where credit is due. Mad Dog knows how to be the Mad Dog, and lives it every day, continuing to dye his moustache and beard black. Loosely translated, the title of Vachon's 1988 autobiography, *Une vie de chien dans un monde de fous,* means "The Life of a Dog in a World of Crazies."

Vachon has also been the subject of an hour-long documentary on The Comedy Network called *Wrestling With the Past* where he told road stories and hammed for the camera. According to the series director John Dolin, Mad Dog's magic has never left. "When he gets into character and starts growling, it's hysterical. And it's still powerful. He is a strong, strong man still and he brings crazy energy at his age."

5. EARL McCREADY

Earl McCready is the most decorated amateur wrestler ever to turn pro in Canada. "The Moose" wasn't just a journeyman pro either, but a top-notch competitor throughout his 28-year career, working around the globe and fighting for the World title on numerous occasions.

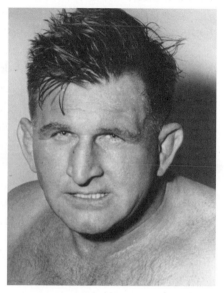

EARL McCREADY AFTER A MATCH. PHOTO: MELBY COLLECTION

Born in Lansdowne, Ontario in 1908, but raised on a farm near Amulet, Saskatchewan, McCready dreamed of becoming a doctor. Legend has it that he ordered a book called *How to Handle Big Men With Ease* and learned to wrestle from it. Working on the farm had already made him solid and tough. In high school in Regina, where he also wrestled, he was already over 200 pounds.

McCready went to New Westminster, B.C., in 1926, for the Canadian amateur wrestling championship. He took the heavyweight crown, but more importantly, impressed three grapplers from Oklahoma A&M University. They returned to their school and convinced their coach, the renowned Doc Gallagher, that the 220-pound Canadian was worth a look. McCready was offered an athletic scholarship, and accepted, with his medical dreams still on his mind.

Oklahoma A&M was a wrestling powerhouse, and was

made even moreso by McCready. He won every match he was in for three years for the school's championship team. McCready took the heavyweight title in each of the first three NCAA wrestling tournaments from 1928–1930. Back in Canada, McCready would win two more Canadian amateur titles and represent Canada at the 1928 Olympic Games in Amsterdam, where he was also the flag-bearer in the opening ceremonies. In 1930, he took a gold medal in freestyle at 100 kg at the first British Empire Games in

A POLISHED McCREADY IN A WARNER BROS. PUBLICITY SHOT. PHOTO: MELBY COLLECTION

Hamilton. While at Oklahoma A&M, McCready played football and worked part-time waiting tables and tending furnaces. McCready graduated with a degree in physical education.

Having triumphed in the amateur ranks, it was time for McCready to turn pro in late 1930. He was a quick study, taking what he could from mentors such as Jack Taylor. His reputation preceded him, and by 1932, McCready had a shot at the world title, held by Jim Londos.

Hamilton's Dano McDonald fought McCready on a couple of occasions. "He was a really smooth operator, a real fine gentleman. It was pleasant to know the guy and be around him," he said.

In Canada, McCready was an easy sell, despite not being the most colourful character on the circuit. *Maclean's* magazine, in a 1931 article, mentioned that McCready's arrival on the pro scene was a boost for Canadian content. "Hitherto the sport has prospered in Canada without much native talent. Earl McCready, Regina's representative on Canada's 1928

Olympic team, has proved his fitness for competition in the most select company." He fought all the top Canadian names — Whipper Watson, Yvon Robert, Stu Hart, Al Mills, John Katan — and defeated his mentor Jack Taylor for the Canadian and British Empire titles in April 1933.

McCready made his first of 13 trips to New Zealand and Australia in 1935. The wrestling there was different than the North American version, with eight rounds contested, with breaks in between. "McCready was the standard by which New Zealanders measured all men and he was a worthy criterion," wrote wrestler Paul Boesch in his autobiography.

Lord James Blears first met McCready in New Zealand. "They liked him down there. He was very respected," Blears said. "He'd wrestle with anybody. Some big bully figures he wants to be a wrestler, put him in with Earl McCready and he'd straighten him out. They started out at 5-foot-11, and they wound up 6-foot-6. He stretched them!"

Besides Oceania, McCready made trips to England, South Africa and Latin America.

In the early '50s, McCready was slowing down, and did less travelling, choosing instead to battle in the West for Stu Hart's fledgling Stampede Wrestling promotion between trips to New Zealand.

McCready retired from the ring after 28 years, and settled in Edmonds, Washington, where he worked as a massage therapist.

Outside the ring, McCready fought many battles as well, including diabetes for the last 40 years of his life. In 1942 when a train hit his car, McCready escaped with only bruises, though the car was totalled. Osteomyelitis claimed his left leg in 1964, forcing McCready to use a wooden prosthesis. His other foot was broken getting off a bus and complications led to its amputation as well.

The end came for McCready in December 1983, when he died of a heart attack in Seattle. But unlike many old wrestlers, McCready hasn't been totally forgotten. His many accomplishments are celebrated through his inductions into the Canadian Sports Hall of Fame, the Oklahoma Sports Hall of

Fame, the U.S. Wrestling Hall of Fame, the Saskatchewan Sports Hall of Fame, the *Wrestling Observer* Pro Wrestling Hall of Fame and the Stampede Wrestling Hall of Fame.

6. GENE KINISKI

"Stamina" is a word that describes Gene Kiniski perfectly. Whether it was a 90-minute championship match or a spirited rant on the microphone, "Big Thunder" never lacked for energy (or self-confidence), making his claim that he was Canada's Greatest Athlete all the more credible.

Even today, Kiniski is still big on making bold declarations. "Hey, I was always in great, great shape. I was never out

An enraged Gene Kiniski under the ring, hiding from Whipper Watson at Maple Leaf Gardens in 1957.
Photo: Turofsky Brothers

of shape. Hell, I'm 73 years old and I still work out five days a week," said Kiniski. "If my knees were good, I honestly, I really think I could still wrestle. Christ, it would be good to go work out with the Olympic team."

KINISKI'S SIZE 13 BOOT LANDS ON STAN STASIAK'S SKULL IN CALGARY. PHOTO: BOB LEONARD

The secret to Gene Kiniski's success was that he could back up his constant boasting and bragging. Too often, people refer to him as a football-player-turned-wrestler. But Kiniski got into grappling in his teens at Edmonton's YMCA and "got addicted to it." It didn't hurt that he was 195 pounds at age 15. Kiniski was a champion amateur wrestler both in Alberta as a youth and later at Arizona University. Football was a sideline for him, and he elected to play in his hometown of Edmonton rather than for the Los Angeles Rams simply because there was more money to be made at home. His parents, Nick and Julia Kiniski were well known in the community — Julia served as a city councillor for years and was involved in the CCF political party.

Kiniski played pro football only four years, before he was forced to retire from the game in 1953 because of a knee injury. He started wrestling professionally in Tucson, Arizona, for Rod Fenton. Kiniski had already met many pro wrestlers over the years. "When I was still at the University of Arizona, I used to work out with the pros like Tony Morelli and Dory Funk Sr.," he said. Kiniski dismisses the common assertion that Stu Hart trained him. "That's a fallacy," he spat, saying that he'd wrestled with Hart at the YMCA a few times, but that was it.

The transition to pro was relatively smooth, and Kiniski

CANADIAN OLYMPIC SKIING GOLD
MEDALLIST NANCY GREENE IS SWEPT
OFF HER FEET BY KINISKI.
PHOTO: BOB LEONARD

absorbed all the knowledge he could, in and out of the ring. "In my early career, I'd get in the ring with a guy like Lou Thesz. He could look at you and hurt you. He just had so many moves. Just going along, you learn as you progress. It's just like a carpenter having a lot of tools — what good is it if you don't know how to use them? So you just tried to perfect certain holds and moves that suited your style."

Kiniski's style might best be described as a 6-foot-5, 275-pound freight train barrelling down the tracks, knocking obstacle after obstacle out of the way with a loud growl. Lord James Blears often tagged with Kiniski in the '50s in California, and recalled the hatred he elicited. "He was a big, rugged bastard. He'd go plowing into 50 people. We were attacked every night. In California, Gene and I, I'm not kidding you, had to fight our way out of the ring. We couldn't get out. The fans wanted to kill us."

Kiniski's ring accomplishments could fill an entire chapter. Kiniski held titles everywhere he went and became a true wrestling superstar. Though best known for his three-year NWA World title reign from 1966–1969, many forget that he also held the AWA World title in 1961 and the WWA World title in 1965. He is still revered in Japan today, and goes on a tour there at least once a year.

Both of Kiniski's sons, Nick and Kelly, became pro wrestlers for a short period as well, but not before they were

well-grounded in the fundamentals of amateur wrestling
like their dad had been. "They
wrestled all their lives. Nick
wrestled at Simon Fraser. Kelly
went to West Texas State."
According to Nick, the
amateur background helped
get him out of many in-ring
jams caused by his father.
"Sometimes I'd get in the ring
and guys would try to wrestle
with me — 'Your father used to
do this to me!' and try to rub
my face in the mat or something," Nick recalled with a
laugh. "I just had such an
extensive background in
wrestling, wrestling against
world champions, Olympic
champions, that they're not
going to do too much with me."

Lord James Blears (left)
and Kiniski. Photo: Mike
Lano

"Big Thunder" Kiniski was a natural self-promoter,
comfortable on the air under any circumstances. He loved
politics, and would read the local newspapers in the towns he
visited to learn what was going on, and what buttons to push
with the crowd. He was a quote-machine. Kiniski still has
people asking him to say his sign-off catch phrase, made
popular during his years and years in the Vancouver All-Star
Wrestling promotion, which he co-owned. "I'd like to take this
opportunity to thank my fellow Canadians and American
viewing audience for allowing me into their TV, and as usual
Ron, you did a superb job," he would say, as host Ron Morrier
struggled to get a word in edgewise.

Kiniski's last match came in 1992, after almost 40 years in
the ring. He still makes media and charity appearances from
his home in Washington State, near the Canadian border. With
his close-cropped hair, cauliflower ears and big grin, he's still

recognized almost everywhere he goes. He doesn't mind. "God, I go down the street, or I go to these sports dinners, Christ, it's like I never left the scene. Like I said, I was always smart, I could always exploit myself. Hey, I had a product to sell and it was Kiniski. And I sure as hell did a good job, I thought."

7. RODDY PIPER

Over the years, in countless interviews, media kits and web sites, Roddy Piper's story has been told again and again — and it's been different every time. He's loud, outspoken, funny, and sometimes totally off the wall. Perhaps that's what makes him such a fascinating figure, and the reason that he was hated (and loved) as one of the greatest wrestlers of the last 25 years.

The basic facts aren't hard to come by. He was born Roderick Toombs in Saskatoon in November 1956. His father worked for the Canadian National Railway as a police officer, and they moved to many different outposts over the years: The Pas for his first year at school, then, Dauphin Port Arthur, Dawson Creek, Winnipeg, Montreal, Toronto, not to mention Glasgow, Scotland and Melbourne, Australia. "We moved all the time. I was always the new kid on the block. I was always getting beaten up," said Piper.

Young Roddy and his father clashed and he was out on his own at 13 (or was it 12? — the numbers never agree). Among the places he lived as a street kid was Toronto.

In 1972, Roddy drifted into the life of Tony Condello, who was just starting up a wrestling school in Winnipeg. "He was 17 years old; this kid approached me and said he wanted to be a wrestler. I taught him. I gave him that name and that gimmick that he holds," Condello said. "He was with me until 1974-75 at least. His first match was June 5, 1973." Piper recalled that first match was pretty short, and that he was soundly defeated by "The Axe" Larry Hennig, who outweighed him by 150 pounds. The Piper surname came about because the ring announcer couldn't remember his actual last name, and Roddy was playing the bagpipes on his way to the ring, a skill he had been practicing since age five.

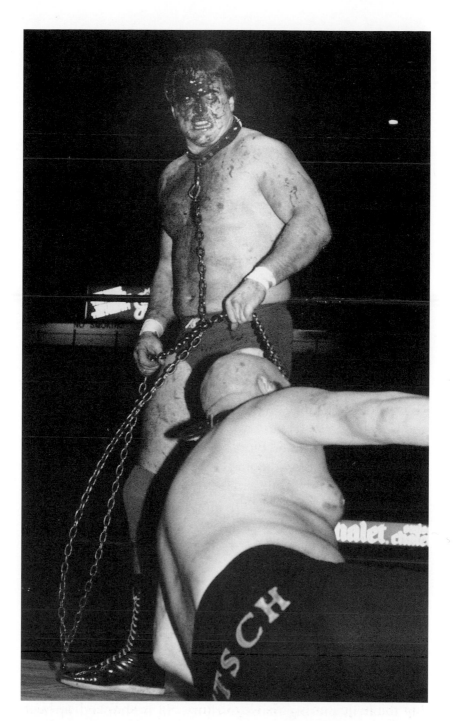

A BLOODY RODDY PIPER HAS A CHAINED ALEXIS SMIRNOFF WHERE
HE WANTS HIM IN 1980 IN TORONTO. PHOTO: MIKE LANO

During at least part of his two years in Winnipeg, Piper said he actually lived in Al Tomko's gym. "He had me paint all the weights. So what I did was take a 45-pound weight and paint '30 pounds,' and messed all the weights around. Great entertainment there for myself."

Some of what was to make Piper a big star was already in evidence in Winnipeg, Condello said. "I knew he had a lot of potential. I knew he was pretty good yapping. I figured one of these days, this kid will hit. He had something about him that nobody else in the club had. Of course, I never knew he was going to be such a big star."

He took his act on the road, to Kansas City, Portland, Texas and eventually to southern California in 1975, where Gene and Mike LeBell turned him into a superstar who dominated the territory, winning both singles and tag titles.

Piper has had too many mentors to credit. "When I got into wrestling, I went from having nothing to having 100 fathers," he said. "These guys taught me the ways of life, brought me up." As the young rookie on the totem pole, Piper had to do what he was told.

"I owe my whole career to everybody but myself," he said. "The structure by which I was taught. You need to keep your mouth shut at all times, write nothing down, keep everything in your head, shut your mouth and give it your all at all times."

One story concerning a match with Mad Dog Vachon illustrates his point. "I'm wrestling Mad Dog. I'm on the floor and he picks up the stairs as you climb into the ring, and he throws them down on my head. It hit me on the jaw, and just went, 'kwooong!' I know 'Don't give up.' I've been taught, just go back in there."

Vachon came looking for Roddy in the dressing room. "Here comes Mad Dog. 'You, cocksucker!' I didn't know that was a nice name for me! He said, 'You, you travel with me.' And the reason was that I didn't quit."

After a stint in Portland, Piper had a first go at the WWWF in 1979, but was deemed too small at 6-foot-2, 235 pounds to be a star in the big man's territory. So he hooked up with Georgia Championship Wrestling, which was just beginning

A ROOKIE PIPER IN WINNIPEG. PHOTO: TERRANCE MACHALEK

to be noticed on Ted Turner's TBS Superstation. Both there, and subsequently in Charlotte when the promotion merged with Jim Crockett Promotions, Piper was a superstar. He could talk and talk and talk, whether it was as a colour commentator beside Gordon Solie or cutting a promo for a feud. Most importantly, he could back up his words in the ring.

That ability to rile a crowd with words and actions would shoot Piper to superstardom in the WWF in 1984. He arrived just as the wave broke, sending pro wrestling into mainstream consciousness. In fact, by booting Cyndi Lauper and setting up the first Wrestlemania, Piper wasn't just there — he kick-started the Rock 'n' Wrestling connection.

"WrestleMania was basically an accident. The War To Settle The Score was the big one," he explained. At War, which aired on MTV, "a lot of stuff happened that wasn't going to happen, like the New York City police jumping into the ring, and also I got to tussle with them . . . . Next thing I know, I see something blonde coming out, and I turned and kicked. You can see it, I tried to pull the kick. Field goal! Cyndi Lauper! Oh, and it exploded."

Piper was on top in the wwf until his "retirement" match against "Adorable" Adrian Adonis at the third WrestleMania at the Pontiac Silverdome. But he would return on many other occasions, including a run with the Intercontinental belt — his only wwf title.

The main reason Piper took time off from wrestling was to start an acting career. Best known for his starring role in John Carpenter's *They Live*, Piper has done numerous other flicks, including *Jungleground, No Contest, Marked Man* and *Hell Comes to Frogtown*.

In 1996, Piper was signed by World Championship Wrestling and quickly resumed his legendary feud with Hulk Hogan. With their roles now reversed, the babyface Piper was unable to wrest the wcw World belt from the heel Hollywood Hogan, though he came very close on many occasions.

Since disappearing from the wcw scene, Piper has acted in various roles, written his autobiography and worked on various business ventures, including a stab at promoting small shows. He lives in Oregon with Kitty, his wife of more than 20 years, and their six children.

8. SKY LOW LOW 8¹/₂. LITTLE BEAVER

To those who knew the midget superstars, Sky Low Low and Little Beaver were almost opposites outside the ring. Sky was moody and could get violent when drinking; Beaver was a fun-loving joker. Yet inside the ring, they were *the* two greatest midget wrestlers ever — pure box-office gold. Their careers are so intertwined that it is impossible to write about one without talking about the other.

They definitely had the respect of the larger wrestlers. "Sky Low Low and Little Beaver, they must have worked a thousand times together. These guys were out of this world," recalled Jacques Rougeau Sr. "They had their match down pat

Sky Low Low has his world turned upside down by Little Beaver. Photo: Tony Lanza

SKY LOW LOW LOOKS RIGHT AT HOME
IN AN ANTIQUE AUTO AS STU HART
(LEFT) AND PAUL BAILLARGEON
LOOK ON. PHOTO: BOB LEONARD

so well that everything was timed perfect."

Sky Low Low (Marcel Gauthier) was almost ten years Beaver's senior. Born in Montreal, he was 3-foot-8 and weighed 86 pounds. Little Beaver (Lionel Giroux) was from St. Jerome, Quebec, weighed 60 pounds and was 4-foot-4. Both got into wrestling under Jack Britton, the wrestler-turned-promoter who first came up with the idea of midget wrestling after World War II.

Britton had the word out that he was looking for midget talent to compete with Sky Low Low, who was among the first into the business. He headed up to St. Jerome to visit the Giroux family, as Lionel was only 15 at the time. According to Britton's son, Gino Brito Sr., it didn't go well at first. "They talked to his father and at first they said no," said Brito. Eventually, the family relented. Giroux grew up quickly, said Brito. "He didn't know nothing, but he learned fast. Three years later, he wasn't the same man anymore."

Little Beaver was an immediate hit with fans, wearing a huge Indian headdress that covered his Mohawk haircut. For a time, he even took a de-scented skunk with him to the ring.

Of course, every great hero needs a great villain. With his bald head and mean look, Sky Low Low was Beaver's arch-rival for the younger man's whole career. They took their act around the world many times, including performances for royalty like Queen Elizabeth and King Farouk of Egypt.

"If you're going to look at the work of wrestling, Sky Low Low is number one," said Brito. "There's nobody that could do what Sky could do in the ring, not Beaver, not anyone. He was the guy who made Beaver look great."

It was a combination of factors that made Sky great. "Acrobatics, timing, the faces he made to get the people going. That's why Beaver, who had the gimmick that the people bought, they bought into Little Beaver, but they also bought into Sky. There were three midgets that people bought, to me, the most. Sky Low Low, Beaver, not necessarily in that order, and Fuzzy Cupid. . . . Oldtimers, when they talk about the midgets, those are the three that come up. The others, they don't even know their names. These three, they remember."

The next name on the list of great midgets would likely be Lord Littlebrook, though he didn't get to North America to wrestle until almost a decade after Beaver and Sky. Littlebrook (Eric Tovey) learned a lot from Sky, and said that he was the best. "He was a wrestler, that's what he was. He was in it for the business. He loved the business," Littlebrook said. "He was very witty, fast-thinking and just a tough little bugger, that's all I can say! He's the type of guy that never said no, no matter how much you hurt him, he never said no."

Veteran grappler Angelo Savoldi was good friends with both Sky Low Low and Little Beaver. "The matches I watched with Beaver and Sky Low Low were the most scientific matches I saw from two little midgets. They were great. The admission was well-paid for," he said. One of the highlights for Savoldi was seeing Sky Low Low and André the Giant walk down the street to attract attention for the evening's card.

Nicknamed "The Little Atlas of the Wrestling World," Sky Low Low could stand on his head without using his hands for balance. One of his gimmicks was an open challenge to any midget wrestler for $100 in a two-out-of-three fall match.

During World War II, Sky served fixing rivets in the tails of aircraft bombers. Outside the ring, he loved to golf, fish and go horseback riding. His stories of drinking and carousing are legendary. "Once he had a few drinks, he was pretty obnoxious," said Littlebrook. "He became Mr. Tough Guy."

Once he was old enough to drive, Britton assigned his son Gino the task of shepherding the midgets from territory to

ANDRÉ THE GIANT TOWERS
OVER LITTLE BEAVER.
PHOTO: BOB LEONARD

territory. "That was a job in itself. You had to have a lot of patience. I was young and I didn't," said Brito. He often had to go looking for Sky Low Low. "You had a carload of four midgets and bags. Then we'd be looking for him. Let's say we're staying at the Harlem Hotel in New York, and we have to make Philadelphia TV in the afternoon. You're looking for him and he's out with some broad somewhere and you can't find him. And you're responsible for him. All of a sudden, you spot him and you've got one hour to go from New York to Philadelphia. He says, 'She's coming with me! I'm marrying her.' The broad, the next day, she made him for $700."

Though the midgets could command over $1500 a week, and at times 15% of the gate at the arena, Brito was instructed to give them just $100 advance each day. For Sky Low Low, it was never enough. "Most of the time, they'd come back, like two in the morning, I'd be sleeping. Let's say we're in New York, and he'd be at the Copacabana with Dr. Jerry Graham. He'd come knock on my door and say, 'I need a couple of hundred bucks more.'"

On November 6, 1998, Sky Low Low died from a heart attack. He was 70.

Little Beaver and Lord Littlebrook didn't get along very well, in part because both were often in the role of babyfaces, but Littlebrook isn't shy about praising Beaver's abilities. "In the ring, he was a great little wrestler," he said. "He and Sky were pretty well-matched. Sky was definitely a better wrestler.

I would say that Beaver was maybe the better showman because he had the gimmick."

Gino Brito Jr. grew up with the midget wrestlers tromping through his house. It was great fun for him as a child to play with adults his size. "Little Beaver was a very quiet, very jokey guy. He used to always pull jokes and try to have fun with you," he said.

When he got older, Brito Jr. got into wrestling himself for a few years, and had a better appreciation for the skill of the midgets. "If you go with the phrase *timing*, I'd say Little Beaver had very, very good timing and a sense of people and everything. Although Sky Low Low was a little better acrobat, a little better showman, maybe. They both had their good qualities in that sense. He'd really pop the people, Little Beaver. The other one would do it with his jests, spin on his head, so on and so forth."

Little Beaver's last ring appearance was at age 52 at 1987's WrestleMania III at the Silverdome in Pontiac, Michigan where he suffered a legitimate back injury at the hands of King Kong Bundy. The actual match featured Hillbilly Jim, Little Beaver and Hatii Kid vs. King Kong Bundy, Little Tokyo and Lord Littlebrook, with Hillbilly's team winning. It's one of Bundy's most memorable moments. "I remember Little Beaver popping me with that moccasin and that thing stung like a son-of-a-bitch. So I was a little hard on the Beaver that night, know what I mean? But he deserved it," Bundy said before turning quieter. "But, you know, I hope I wasn't responsible for his early demise. I wouldn't want that on my conscience."

After six months in the hospital, Little Beaver died on December 4, 1995 of chronic emphysema in Saint-Jerome, Quebec. He was 61.

Sky Low Low and Little Beaver were simply the best. "It's funny, they were among the first midgets," said Brito Sr. "My dad went through maybe 30, if not more, but nobody ever came up to these two, no one even came close to these two.

Canada's Multitude of Midgets

Besides the Big Two of midget wrestling — Sky Low Low and Little Beaver — Canada can lay claim to a number of pint-sized entertainers.

Leading the pack is Lord Littlebrook (Eric Tovey) who came over from England and married a Canadian girl, settling in rural Havelock, Ontario. "It was so peaceful. I was born right in the middle of London, I've lived in a big city all my life, and to get out in the country, it was beautiful for me," said Littlebrook. They lived there almost 13 years. On the farm, Littlebrook trained wrestlers both big and small, including Frenchy Lamont, Tiny Tim and Cousin Billy Williams. Now in his 70s, Littlebrook lives in Missouri, training wrestlers and following the wrestling career of his son, Beautiful Bobby.

THE MIDGET STARS RETURN TO QUEBEC FROM AUSTRALIA. FROM LEFT: PROMOTER BOB LANGEVIN, SKY LOW LOW, TINY TIM, LITTLE BRUTUS, LITTLE BEAVER. PHOTO: LEDUC COLLECTION

After training with Littlebrook, Frenchy Lamont (Roland Barriault) made his debut in 1963. He quickly made his way onto the circuit, drawing raves for his strength. In 1982, he started touring Canada with Phil Watson's Half-Pints midget basketball team, as well as wrestling. His son "Karate Kid" Chris Dube (Leon Demaranville) also got involved in the mat wars.

Little Farmer Pete is another veteran of both the ring and Watson's hoops team. The Hamilton native wrestled primarily around Ontario, and still gets in the ring when he's not on the court.

Major Tom Thumb (Billy Bowman) came to Canada from England at age 12. His family settled in Brantford, Ontario. He worked as a truck driver, a pro swimmer, a weightlifter, and a comedian-on-skates with a carnival before becoming a wrestler. His 20-year career took him across North America, Europe, Japan, South American and Australia. Thumb retired from the ring in 1962, and moved back to Brantford. He died at 65 in October 1981.

Farmer Brooks (Clifford Fraser) was the greatest midget wrestler from Atlantic Canada. Born in New Glasgow, N.S., he got into pro wrestling in Toronto at the encouragement of Whipper Billy Watson. Brooks stopped wrestling in 1992.

Little Brutus (Jean-Jacques Girard) is another French-Canadian wrestler, and one of the stars from the '50s. He's out of the business now, living in Iberville, Quebec.

Calgary's Cowboy Lang gave up his dream of becoming a truck driver in the '60s to become a wrestler. At 16, he travelled to Toronto to learn the sport. Now in his 50s, Lang still dons the tights on occasion.

Tiger Jackson (Claude Giroux) is the Canadian midget wrestler best known to today's fans. Jackson got

FRENCHY LAMONT.
PHOTO: GREG OLIVER

involved in wrestling through Little Beaver. Sky Low Low and Little Brutus taught him the ropes. He was featured prominently in the wwf as Dink the Clown, second to Doink the Clown (Matt Borne). "I had a good time," said Jackson of his days as a clown for the wwf. As Dink, he attended over 200 shows a year. Jackson still wrestles around Quebec, and runs a landscaping business outside of Montreal.

=====

9. BEN & MIKE SHARPE

In 1936, a 20-year-old Ben Sharpe went to London, England as an oarsman for the Canadian Olympic rowing team. He carried the flag in the parade of athletes and shook hands with Adolf Hitler. Sharpe could tell that a war was brewing and wrote home to warn his family.

At home in Hamilton was his brother Mike, six years younger, but just as good an athlete. When war was declared, Ben Sharpe enlisted in the Royal Air Force and was stationed in England as a physical fitness instructor. At 6-foot-5, he was too big to get into the cockpits of the planes he dreamed of flying.

Mike followed his brother into the Air Force when he was old enough, and like his brother, he was too big to fly and his uniform had to be custom-made. Ben had not seen his brother in four years, and could not believe that he had grown bigger than him. During his time in England, Ben had seen many wrestling exhibitions while on weekend furlough and thought his brother had what it took to compete. It took some convincing, but soon Mike was wrestling and Ben was his manager.

"That's how they made money during the war. He said the grandest time he ever had was during the Second World War," said Karen Sharpe-Grubert, daughter of Ben.

One of the people Mike fought was Englishman Jan Blears, who was in the British Merchant Navy. "I wrestled Mike Sharpe in Middlesborough. Great, big raw-boned guy. Jesus!

MIKE AND BEN SHARPE AFTER ANOTHER WIN IN SAN FRANCISCO
IN 1951. PHOTO: SHARPE FAMILY

Big, tough son-of-a-gun," said Blears, who would face the
Sharpes many times during his career as Lord James Blears.

When the war ended, an English promoter offered both
Mike and Ben a chance to stay and wrestle, but they declined,
heading back to Hamilton, where their father was a policeman. Ben Sharpe quickly realized he didn't want to continue
with his pre-war job designing elevators, so he strong-armed
his brother into wrestling again.

The brothers headed to San Francisco in 1950, where
legend has it they were walking down the street when the
local wrestling promoters, Joe and Frank Malcewicz, saw
them and signed them up.

Ben and Mike Sharpe would dominate the San Francisco
territory for the next 15 years, claiming its version of the tag
titles more than a dozen times, along with singles belts.

THE FORMER OLYMPIC ROWER BEN SHARPE GIVES POINTERS TO
HIS BROTHER MIKE ON THE HAMILTON WATERFRONT IN 1947.
PHOTO: SHARPE FAMILY

Don Leo Jonathon met the Sharpes while he was stationed
with the Navy at the Alameda base near Oakland. The brothers would frequent Jonathon's father's gym. "Mike, he was all
about the workout and for the business. He was really, really
dedicated. Ben, he was a little older, and he was more looking
into other businesses besides wrestling," said Jonathon.

Bob Orton Sr. was working as an usher at the wrestling
events when he first met the Sharpe brothers. "The Sharpe
brothers were real serious wrestlers. You believed them as
men and wrestlers," he said. "I looked up to them and really
respected them."

Unlike most top names at the time, the Sharpes did not
travel much. They wrestled here and there over the years,
including around southern Ontario when visiting family, but
never had long runs anywhere else. Japan was a short hop
from San Francisco, and they did do tours there, with their

legend being made in 1956 when they exchanged titles with Rikidozan and Kokichi Endo.

In San Francisco, Lord James Blears and Gene Kiniski were one of the top teams they faced. "We wrestled them a hundred times. If you put Gene and I against the Sharpes, it was a sell-out, without even knowing what was underneath the card. I'm not boasting, it's true," said Blears.

"They were a good, good team. They painted a good image. Those two men always kept themselves in great, great shape. They were a hell of an asset to wrestling," said Kiniski. "Joe Malcewicz had them pretty well tied up. He wouldn't let them go anywhere.

"They had just a different array of wrestlers coming in, and kept feeding them different talent. That's why the longevity hung in there," Kiniski said.

The Sharpes were very well known around the Bay Area, which was difficult at times for their children. "When I was playing college football and wrestling in college, my buddies would come over and he'd just amaze the guys that I knew," said Digby Sharpe, son of Mike. "Sometimes, when it's your father, you really don't pay too much attention. It's like, 'Oh, that's my dad.' Well, everybody wanted to come over and visit with and talk to my father. And I was like, 'What do you guys want to come over to my house for? Let's go somewhere else.' Then finally when you hit about 30, you realize, 'Hey, you know what? This is pretty special.'"

Away from the ring, Ben Sharpe was the owner of Copperwood Lodge, a restaurant and bar in Colma. For the last 14 years of his life, he was in a wheelchair as a result of all the bumps from wrestling — yet he still worked out. In late 2000, his body weakened, he developed an infection in his leg and died in November at 85.

Mike's wrestling career lasted a little longer than his brother's, and his name was kept alive by his first-born son, Mike Sharpe Jr. After his last match was in 1964, Mike worked as a brewer for Anheuser-Busch in Van Nuys, CA. He died in August 1988 of a heart attack, while on the way to his sister-in-law's funeral.

10. STU HART

At this point, the story of Stu Hart has grown beyond fact and entered the land of myth. No man could possibly have done so much for wrestling and his city. No man could possibly have inflicted so much pain. No man could possibly have had a hand in training so many superstars. No man could possibly have suffered so much publicly.

Yet Stu Hart has experienced it and more. And in 2001, he was finally recognized for it, by his peers, with the Iron Mike Mazurki Award, the Cauliflower Alley Club's highest honour, and by his country, with his appointment to the Order of Canada.

Stewart Edward Hart's story comes out of the depths of the Depression in rural Alberta. Living in poverty gave him a determination to succeed in life, and he chose to start amateur wrestling in Edmonton in 1930. Athletics was a way out for him, and he succeeded in baseball and football too, playing for the Edmonton Eskimos.

Stu Hart loves to tell stories of his early days learning the skills of submission wrestling. "[I] went through three or four years of being a guinea pig, where the good wrestlers would grab me and shove my head between my knees and pull my knees up over my head and knock me out if they could and rub my elbows together behind my head. Sometimes my forehead was down touching my belly button and make my neck three feet longer than it was. And see how many times I could get twisted around. Finally, after three or four years, the world started turning, and I was directing traffic a little bit. Finally I got to the point where the boys who used to use me as a practice dummy, I was using them."

When World War II broke out, Hart enlisted in the navy. He was used to entertain the troops with wrestling exhibitions against the likes of Sandor Kovacs and Al Korman. Hart was always in tremendous shape. In 1946, he walked into a restaurant in New York City: "There was a big guy sitting there with cauliflower ears. I went by him and he looked up. 'You've got a big neck on you, kid.'" The guy was local promoter Toots

Mondt. "'I thought maybe you'd wrestled with that neck on ya. I'd like you to come work for me.' I told him I couldn't right now. I had to go back to the service. He gave me his card then and told me to get through the Navy, come down and join him." When the war ended, Hart headed back to New York and started his pro career.

STU HART IN HIS PRO-WRESTLING PRIME. PHOTO: GLENBOW ARCHIVES

As a pro, Stu Hart was rough and tough, as was expected from Prairie stock, but he was also an attractive young man who caught the eye of many a female fan, including his wife, Helen Smith, who he met and married in New York City. Angelo Savoldi fought Stu Hart "many, many times" around the American northeast. "He was a good, good wrestler," Savoldi said. "He was good right from the beginning. I think he was just born a wrestler."

Hart wasn't a top competitor in the wrestling ranks in New York, so he headed west to improve his standing. In the Dakotas, he really started to learn the behind-the-scenes of wrestling, and in 1948, began promoting matches in Edmonton. The promotion was initially called Big Time Wrestling, then Wildcat Wrestling, and, when Calgary became the base, Stampede Wrestling. Hart would wrestle on a regular basis until the 1960s, and later, when needed, he would still don the tights.

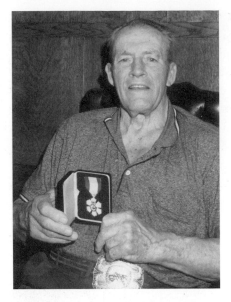

STU SHOWS OFF HIS ORDER OF CANADA. PHOTO: BOB LEONARD

Stampede Wrestling had its ups and downs as a territory, but Stu's reputation as a trainer never flagged. Soon, "The Dungeon" in the Hart House became a badge of honour for those who survived. "That was a tattoo that you got. That was a learning deal that you went through that nobody ever went through. If you made it through Stu Hart's school of learning up there and came out of that thing, you were known to be a product, a quality product," said Blackjack Mulligan.

Again pain is a theme in Stu Hart's life. "He used to take those pro ball players at the end of the season. They were in fair shape, played ball all season. He'd take them out there, and they didn't even know what they were getting into. They just couldn't believe. He'd take them down and stretch them and you'd hear them squealing for half a mile," said Archie Gouldie.

Soon promoters were sending raw talent to Hart for training. Montreal stars like Rick Martel and Jacques Rougeau Jr. were both in Stampede before they were old enough to legally have a drink. Second-generation grapplers like Greg Valentine and Jake Roberts were sent north by their famous fathers. The list of the graduates of Hart's finishing school is not as long as the list of those who quit, unable to withstand the grip of Old Man Hart.

In 1984, Hart caved to the expanding WWF and sold Stampede Wrestling. He had planned to retire and take it easy, but was soon back promoting, running the new Stampede until 1989. Though Stu has not been the main trainer in the Dungeon for the last number of years — the task having fallen to his sons Bruce, Ross and Keith — he still heads down on occasion to stretch some hapless wannabe. "Submission wrestling is not that spectacular. I could demonstrate submission wrestling on you now, and I wouldn't have to be turning somersaults in the air. I just keep my body close to yours and when I finished, your head would be close to ass and you'd be saluting me when you went by." Even at 86, one still has to salute Stu Hart.

11. ABDULLAH THE BUTCHER

In the late 1960s, Larry Shreeve was the fourth of seven children in a Windsor, Ontario home. He had a contract for the upkeep of the Vic Tanney Gyms around town, and taught karate as well. Wrestlers-in-training like Frankie Lane, Gino Brito and George Cannon came into the gym at various times and encouraged him to consider the mat wars. Perhaps if they knew that Shreeve would one day be "The Madman From The Sudan," Abdullah The Butcher, carving up foreheads around the globe, they might not have tried so hard to convert him.

"I don't know if it was us that convinced him. He knew we were wrestlers," said Brito. "In those days, there was an old church there with a basement. We used the basement, put a ring in there, we have a gym. We'd invite guys to come over and work out in the gym." Soon, a fit, athletic Shreeve was wrestling around Detroit for Brito's father Jack Britton.

It took a while for the character to come together, but everything was in place when he hit Calgary's Stampede Wrestling. Abdullah the Butcher would go through the roster one by one, making his way to the top of the cards. "I can't say anything but good about Abdullah the Butcher," said Stu Hart. "He worked for me here and I never had an empty house while he was with me."

In fact, the praise is similar from many different wrestlers. Apparently the price one paid for wrestling Abdullah — bleeding, getting poked with an arsenal of foreign objects — was worth it when your wallet was full.

Jacques Rougeau Sr. was one of those who made out big

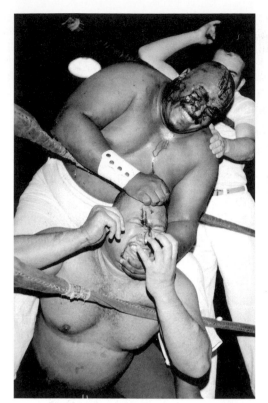

ABDULLAH THE BUTCHER GOUGES TOR KAMATA IN ONE OF STAMPEDE WRESTLING'S BLOODIEST FEUDS.
PHOTO: BOB LEONARD

against Abby. "I must have wrestled him 50 times," Rougeau said. "The guy liked to have blood in every match. He was probably the only guy that would bleed so much. You'd just touch him, and he'd cut open right away. He'd ask you to do it. 'Gimme a good punch' and cut himself open. He'd start bleeding and go like a wildman. It was something new, an attraction."

Once his act was established, enhanced further by wrestling magazines and television, The Butcher took his act from territory to territory, country to country. He knew the act could wear thin quickly, though "thin" would never be a word used to describe Abby's midsection. During his tours, The Butcher was managed by many different people, including Eddie "The Brain" Creatchman, The Great Mephisto, Scandor Akbar and even Cactus Jack Mick Foley, who brought Abby in for a short mainstream run in wcw in the late '80s. It wasn't Abdullah's job to talk; he was there to create mayhem, shrieking in his blood-lust.

Conversation with Abdullah can be frustrating. He is short with his answers, still protective of his past and his business. His favourite opponents? "Me and Bruiser Brody. And Carlos Colon." Favourite foreign object? "A fork." How did you get

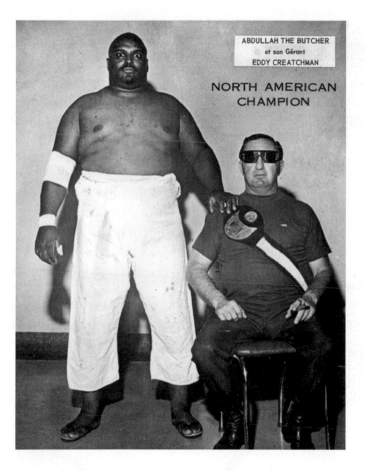

ABDULLAH THE BUTCHER
et son Gérant
EDDY CREATCHMAN

NORTH AMERICAN
CHAMPION

OCCASIONALLY, ABBY WOULD EVEN WIN A TITLE.
HERE, HIS MANAGER EDDY CREATCHMAN WEARS THE
NORTH AMERICAN TITLE. PHOTO: CREATCHMAN
FAMILY

started in wrestling? "I was hungry. You ever been hungry before?"

Success followed Abdullah wherever he went. He held a surprising number of titles during his career, often coming in to topple the lead babyface and be a transition champion. On many occasions, he was the catalyst for turning a hated heel into a fan favourite.

In Japan, where he was known as Kuroi Jujutsushi (Black Wizard), Abdullah was one of the international superstars of the '70s and '80s, along with fellow Canadian Tiger Jeet Singh. "Singh became a cult figure there and superseded The Sheik from the standpoint of the wildness, and so did Abdullah," said Johnny Powers. "They built unique personas over there. You'd have to be there actually to appreciate how huge they were. Their wildness and uniqueness and exoticness for the Japanese really caught on. They became huge stories."

Now in his 60s, Abdullah still laces up the curled boots, puts the fork in the waistband and jumps in the ring periodically. He runs Abdullah The Butcher's House of Ribs & Chinese Food in Atlanta, Georgia, and has settled into community life, sponsoring sports teams and raising money for charity.

12. JOHN & CHRIS TOLOS

From the 1950s to the 1970s, there was only one was to spell wrestling — "T-O-L-O-S!" It is also an excellent alternate way to spell Family, a theme that runs throughout the careers of the Canadian Wrecking Crew, Chris and John Tolos.

The interviews of "The Golden Greeks" were punctuated with, "Isn't that right, brother Chris?" — "That's right, brother

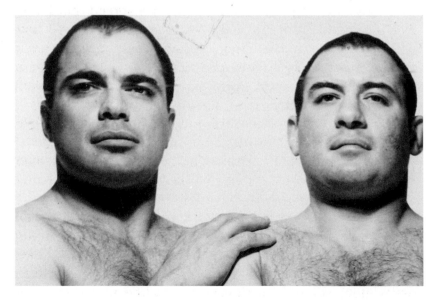

JOHN & CHRIS TOLOS. PHOTO: OLIVER COLLECTION

John." As a tag team, the brothers would stop at nothing to defend each other; their fanatical devotion knew no bounds. In the 1970s, Chris Tolos took himself off the road to look after his elderly mother Evangelina and his sister Mary in Hamilton.

In the 1988 book, *Drawing Heat*, author Jim Freedman described his visit to the reclusive Tolos household and found the family to be genuine. "Their home was authentic, made charming and warm by the undiluted sentimentality of immigrants securing each other's past and future. It was hard not to notice this, and I blurted out my appreciation when leaving. I told Evangelina how comfortable I felt in a house where there was a close family," Freedman wrote.

JOHN TOLOS.
PHOTO: MIKE LANO

Don Leo Jonathon had known both Chris and John since the 1950s, and also visited their home. He agreed that family was important to them. "I think they were very good boys when it came to their mother," he said. When he later met up with John on the road, and asked about the whereabouts of Chris, Jonathon recalled being told that he was home taking care of family business.

Wrestling was good to Chris and John Tolos. Chris was the older sibling, and broke into the business in the early 1950s. A few years later, he helped train his slightly bigger and heavier brother for the ring. Their cousin, the late Steve Bolus, would soon follow.

Like many Hamilton wrestlers, the Tolos brothers were known for their roughness. "They had a tough stomping style," said Don Curtis, who often teamed with Mark Lewin against the Toloses in New York State and Florida. "They were pretty much equal in the ring, and really had good timing and thought very much alike."

Four legends are all smiles at a Cauliflower Alley Club reunion. From left: Red Bastien, John Tolos, Ray Stevens, and Killer Kowalski. Photo: Mike Lano

The list of tag team titles they held is remarkable: The Pacific Coast belts in 1953; the WWWF U.S. tag titles 1963, knocking off Killer Kowalski and Gorilla Monsoon; the NWA World tag championships in both Florida and Detroit in 1964; the Canadian and World tag belts in Vancouver in 1967; the International belts in Toronto.

Wrestling journalist Bill Apter was a fan when he first saw the Tolos brothers in the early '60s. Later, he came to appreciate what they meant to wrestling. "Back then, tag teams were something very special. Tag teams never split up, sort of like they do today, with interim tag teams," Apter said. "They were one of the core groups of people who kept the lineage of tag-team wrestling going."

Though it's John Tolos that most remember as a singles star, both Tolos brothers were great on their own. In the late '60s, Chris "The Body" Tolos feuded with "Iron" Mike Dibiase in Omaha. He also had a few NWA World title shots. When he returned to Hamilton in the '70s, Chris wrestled around Ontario for Frank Tunney and "Bearman" Dave McKigney.

Described by many as "reserved" compared to his brother John's "outgoing" personality, Chris Tolos wrestled until 1980.

The singles career of John Tolos was much more memorable than that of his brother. California and the Pacific Northwest seemed to agree with him best, though he also did stints through the Midwest and WWWF.

In Los Angeles in the early '70s, no one was hated more than John "Mr. California" Tolos. He was a magnificent interview, starting off quietly before becoming a raving madman, stripping off his finely tailored suit to prove his point. He was hardcore before hardcore was a word, using all kinds of foreign objects to make his opponents bleed, from chairs to two-by-fours and even a boa constrictor.

There are many classic moments that fans will recall, but none ever surpassed his actions on May 8, 1971, when he blinded a returning Freddie Blassie with "Monsel's Powder." Blassie fell to the ground screaming and was taken to the hospital. Weeks later it was announced that Blassie's career was finished. When Blassie made his inevitable return, the Olympic Auditorium wasn't big enough for his match against Tolos, so the show moved to the L.A. Coliseum. Over 25,000 saw Blassie get his revenge, plus thousands more on the first ever closed-circuit broadcast of wrestling.

John Tolos would have other monumental feuds during his career as both a hated heel and a loved babyface. Fans particularly remember battles with Killer Kowalski, Pork Chop Cash, Al Madril, Chavo Guerrero Sr., Great Goliath and Black Gordman. Kinji Shibuya was one of the foes he traded the Beat the Champ TV title with. "He had a great attitude. He had a positive attitude. He was a good wrestler," said Shibuya.

When his ring career ran down in the 1980s, Tolos stayed out of the business for a while in California before being lured back as a manager of Cactus Jack and Bob Orton Jr. in Herb Abrams' UWF promotion. He would follow that with a brief run in the WWF as "The Coach," with "Mr. Perfect" Curt Hennig as his main star.

Chris and John Tolos have both moved back to Hamilton again, having lost their 101-year-old mother Evangelina in

February 2001. According to Dutch Savage, John Tolos was always frugal on the road. "He saved his shekels. He retired. He played the stock market. He and Chris both, they're not hurting for anything."

13. STOMPER GOULDIE

THE STOMPER ENDS A MATCH AGAINST DAVEY BOY SMITH WITH A BOOT TO THE HEAD. PHOTO: BOB LEONARD

Beyond a shadow of the doubt, Archie "The Stomper" Gouldie was the biggest home-grown star ever in Stampede Wrestling and one of the greatest talents to survive the training in the Hart Family Dungeon. But his story is much more than just that. It's the story of a small-town boy from tiny Carbon, Alberta (pop. 600) who made it big at home and abroad as the vicious Mongolian Stomper.

Growing up in the 1950s, pro wrestling looked good to him. Gouldie would go to the matches on a regular basis, and started to talk to the wrestlers and promoter Stu Hart, begging him to begin training. Eventually, Stu relented.

No one expected to see the strong, lanky, 6-foot-2 kid with a junior football background back at the Dungeon the day after his first stretching, but he returned again and again. "I wanted to make it. I didn't want to fail," said Gouldie. "I just wanted to do it, and I figured the only way I could do it was to keep going because Stu was such a persistent person that if you did lay out — I've seen a few guys lay out for a week or two and he'd just give up on them. So I just kept going."

The journey to the Hart House was almost as bad as the training. "I didn't have a car. I used to walk out to that old gym, that old pit every day. Sometimes it'd be 20 below and snow, but I'd

THE MONGOLIAN STOMPER WITH THE SOUTHERN HEAVYWEIGHT TITLE. PHOTO: BOB LEONARD

keep going — until he hurt me so bad, I couldn't go. Take a couple of days off, and I'd go back. My mother used to say I was crazy, but I kept going."

Being crazy helped Gouldie during his career, and from today's perspective, he looks back and shakes his head at some of the things he did. The one that stands out the most was letting Jos Leduc hit him over the head with sledgehammer to break a concrete block on his head while they were working in Knoxville. "Stupidest thing I ever did in my life. My neck's never been the same. I've got arthritis in my neck so bad from that." Gouldie's counterstrike on Leduc sent the Quebecer to the hospital.

After starting out in Calgary for a few years, generally as a preliminary talent learning the ropes ("Stu never put me over"), Gouldie headed to North Carolina to work for Jim Crockett Sr. Gouldie worked there for three months, then injured his back and was let go. He hopped on a bus to Alabama, then ended up in Amarillo, Texas, working for Dory Funk Sr. "He started me out refereeing, then started me out wrestling," said Gouldie. "He made me Sputnik Monroe's bodyguard. Sputnik was the champion in Amarillo. That was a real trip. Sputnik would go into bars, throw beer in somebody's face, and say, 'Talk to my bodyguard about it!' I finally went to Dory Sr. and said, 'I can't handle this no more.' He took me out of those duties."

Gouldie got his first big break in Kansas City in 1964. Former world champ Pat O'Connor was a co-promoter there, and had seen Gouldie work in Texas. It was O'Connor who dubbed Gouldie "The Mongolian Stomper." "He said he wanted a gimmick-type character in Kansas City; he had just bought the promotion. I went along with it and it stuck with me. It worked well so I stayed with it."

As The Mongolian Stomper, Gouldie terrorized the southern U.S., winning belts in Kansas City, Texas, Georgia, Florida, San Francisco, Tennessee and Puerto Rico. He figures that he went to Japan almost 20 times, and did three tours of Australia. He was meant to be a mysterious figure. "With The Mongolian Stomper, I always had a manager, so they didn't want me to talk. They didn't figure that it would go along with the gimmick, me talking and being Mongolian," he said.

In 1968, Gouldie returned to Calgary and would transform the territory. As Archie "The Stomper" Gouldie, he was allowed on the microphone and delivered intense promos that brought new fans into the arenas. According to longtime Stampede photographer and promoter Bob Leonard, Gouldie's work ethic and intensity "made believers out of so many people, even those normally uninterested in wrestling."

Gouldie would win the North American belt in Stampede eight different times ("that belt meant a lot to me"), and had an amazing run against a vast collection of opponents. "Cowboy" Dan Kroffat is proud of the matches they had together. "We set some records that have never been broken" in the old Calgary Corral, Kroffat said.

Besides being close to home, Gouldie enjoyed his local celebrity and place on the cards. "The good thing about working Calgary was that once a year, you got to wrestle the world champion," he said. Over the years, Gouldie took on the likes of Terry Funk, Dory Funk Jr., Harley Race and Ric Flair, though not all in Calgary.

Conditioning and physique have also been a major part of

Gouldie's life. "I started training and working out and just sort of kept it up," he explained. "I enjoy it. I was fortunate enough to meet a few people across the country who helped me out." He still works out, going to the gym, playing racquetball, and riding his bicycle on average 100 miles a week on the hills near Knoxville, TN.

Gouldie once set a record for the number of sit-ups done in an hour while wrestling in Dothan, Alabama. "I'd mentioned it to the promoter down there at the time that I wanted to do it. I used to do a lot of them anyways. He said, 'We'll do it while the wrestling show is on for 60 minutes. Can you do them that long?' I said, 'Yeah, I think I can.' So they put me on an isolated camera in the corner of the screen as the matches were going on. I'd done 1,800 in 60 minutes, non-stop. I had a chair with a bottle of baby oil beside me. That was the worst thing that was happening — these blisters were building up on my rear end, they kept building up and break-ing. They'd start smarting and stinging, so I just swash this baby oil on to keep it slippery there. 'Course it was live. They had a couple of hundred people there in the studio. You didn't want to quit anyways, you just kept going. Couldn't sit down for two or three weeks. Laid in the bed on my side or my belly."

Another legendary tale often told about Gouldie was an angle in Stampede where Bad News Allen attacked Gouldie's "son," piledriving him on the cement and sending him out on a stretcher. It was so violent that announcer Ed Whalen quit and the promotion came to a standstill as the media attention raged. "It really went overboard. It didn't just arouse the fans, it disgusted a lot of them. Ed quit, and Ed was a fine person. I didn't like it. Of course, it was too late then," Gouldie said. "I didn't think it would come out like it did."

Gouldie continues to wrestle on occasion around his Knoxville home, primarily on charity shows. His last run in a territory was with Jim Cornette's Smokey Mountain promo-tion. Currently, he works in the guard shack at a prison. Before that, he ran the paddy wagon for three years until he "got tired of hauling drunks." The Mongolian Stomper is still recognized quite a bit. "I think there's more fans in prison than there are in the street," he chuckled.

14. BRET HART

As far as catch phrases go, Bret Hart's, "The best there is, the best there was, the best there ever will be" is great, if a little misleading. The "Hitman" certainly lays claim to being one of the best of his generation. He was there to step up to the plate when Vince McMahon's WWF was in the middle of a steroid scandal and wanted to push a great athlete rather than a 'roid monster. But in the annals of Canadian pro wrestling, Hart can hardly claim to be the best ever.

He can, however, say he's the best-known Canadian wrestler, in large part because of the increased world-wide exposure of the WWF. Hart flew the Canadian flag proudly wherever he went, and was never shy of cameras or reporters. During his last big run in the WWF as the leader of the Hart Foundation, he turned the patriotism up another notch, in an

LEO BURKE IS TRAPPED IN BRET'S ABDOMINAL STRETCH. PHOTO: BOB LEONARD

attempt to be a heel in the U.S., and a babyface in the rest of the world. Add to that his now-infamous "screw-job" in Montreal, where he had the WWF World title taken from him, and his brother Owen's tragic accidental death, and it's easy to see why the Hitman is so well known.

Bret Hart was groomed in Calgary by his father Stu Hart to be an amateur wrestler, but he had other ideas. He took one year of broadcasting at Mount Royal College with the dream of one day becoming a movie director. But destiny called, and Hart began training with some of the wrestlers on the Stampede circuit, where he debuted in 1978. Being a fan favourite came easy to him. "Well,

BRET IN HIS ROOKIE YEAR.
PHOTO: BOB LEONARD

Bret is one of the most popular wrestlers I know and he's been popular ever since he was in high school," Stu Hart said. "He was a good athlete in football and high school sports."

In Stampede, Bret feuded with the likes of Archie "The Stomper" Gouldie, The Dynamite Kid and Bad News Allen. He won the promotion's North American title, British Commonwealth lightweight belt, and the tag straps with his brother Keith. Besides western Canada, Hart also worked in Puerto Rico, Japan, Germany and England.

When Stu Hart sold the Stampede promotion to the WWF in 1984, Bret, Davey Boy Smith, Jim Neidhart and Dynamite

Kid were all part of the package deal. Initially, Bret was a curtain-jerker for the WWF, working opening matches to little response from the crowd. After passing on a "Cowboy" Bret Hart gimmick, the Hart Foundation, with Neidhart and manager Jimmy Hart, was created and quickly took off. The team would hold the WWF's tag belts on two occasions, both as heels and faces, and had great matches with the British Bulldogs, Killer Bees, Rougeaus, Demolition and Nasty Boys.

In 1991, Bret began competing as a singles wrestler. He took the Intercontinental title from Curt Hennig in August, dropping the strap to The Mountie Jacques Rougeau Jr., who in turn lost to Rowdy Roddy Piper. Hart and Piper went back a long way, and the match-up of two babyfaces at WrestleMania XIII was memorable, with Hart winning. But it was only a sign of things to come. In August 1992, the Hitman faced Davey Boy Smith, his sister's husband, for the I-C title in a huge match at SummerSlam. Hart still feels the match was his crowing glory, despite what was to come.

"My favourite memory has to be Wembley Stadium in England where I fought my brother-in-law in front of 82,000 people in what I feel was the greatest match of all time," Hart said. "Even though I lost, it was the first true sign that bigger and better things lay ahead for me. Hence, winning the world championship from Ric Flair six weeks later."

Hart's WWF World title win over Flair in October 1992 was a little unexpected, given that it was at a non-televised house show in Saskatoon. Hart would go on to hold the WWF belt on four other occasions, but his last reign, and his last moments in the WWF still stand out. Hitman had signed with WCW and was preparing to leave. Despite having other chances to remove the title from Hart, the WWF kept the belt on him until November 1997, at the Survivor Series in Montreal. Hart didn't want to lose his WWF title to Shawn Michaels in Canada, and exercised a clause in his contract giving him reasonable creative control during his last days in the company. WWF boss Vince McMahon agreed with Hart, and a DQ finish was planned. In a shocking turn of events for the cast and fans, Michaels put Hart's Sharpshooter move on the Hitman and the referee, Earl Hebner, immediately called for the bell. The new champion, Michaels, bailed out of the ring quickly as Hart confronted McMahon, spitting on him. Backstage, Hart would punch McMahon before leaving the wwF forever. More remarkably, most of what transpired was captured with the film crew for *Wrestling With Shadows* in attendance, and it proved that the facts were firmly on Hart's side.

In wcw, Hart would immediately step into the main-event mix, headlining a pay-per-view against Ric Flair. But the established wcw guard of Hulk Hogan and his allies felt threatened by Hart and kept him down card for much of the rest of his stay. During the Mayhem ppv in Toronto in November 1999, Hart captured the wcw World belt in a tournament final against Chris Benoit. It was a last hurrah for the Hitman, who was injured by a kick to the head during a match with Bill Goldberg in December 1999 and never wrestled again.

Outside the ring, Hart has dabbled in acting, and is involved with many different charities. Though he is no longer a part-owner, Hart continues to be a huge supporter of the Calgary Hitmen junior hockey team.

After leaving wcw, Hart made occasional appearances for the fledgling wwA promotion, attended autograph signings, worked on his autobiography and wrote weekly columns for the Calgary *Sun*. In the summer of 2002, he fell off his mountain bike and suffered a mild stroke.

15. JACK TAYLOR

It is hard for today's fan to understand the importance of a wrestler like Jack Taylor in the 1920s. He was *the* wrestling star in Canada. Newspapers would run articles on upcoming matches weeks in advance, hyping both the local star (both Winnipeg and Calgary claimed him, though he was born in Regina) and the incoming foe.

A cynic might say that the newspapers and the local wrestling promoter were in cahoots to build up Taylor and sell tickets. "Although Taylor has shown fans that he is a mighty good wrestler, still he is not yet in a class to dictate to a man like [John] Freberg (who is a challenger to the world's title) just what terms he must accept," wrote the Winnipeg *Tribune* on December 5, 1922. Taylor would upset Freberg in the match on December 15 in two of three falls. "Loud cheers greeted the Canadian champ and he advanced a step further in his quest for a match with the world's champion," said the *Tribune*, suddenly onside again.

Taylor got into wrestling in 1903 and came from an athletic family of Scottish descent. He worked his way around western Canada, moving up cards and proving his toughness in a not-yet-completely fixed wrestling game. The legendary Farmer Burns took the strong Taylor under his wing for a time as well. Taylor worked out of the prestigious New York office, but couldn't crack the top of the cards there.

Back in Canada in the 1920s and early '30s, he was the headliner on many, many shows. Stu Hart was a youngster

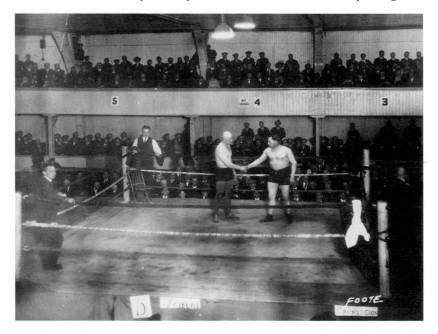

JACK TAYLOR (RIGHT) SHAKES HANDS WITH PAUL MARTINSON BEFORE A BOUT IN WINNIPEG IN APRIL 1923. PHOTO: PROVINCIAL ARCHIVES OF MANITOBA

who worshiped Taylor, and remembers watching his idol wrestle in Calgary in 1932.

"Jack was an impressive big man, huge cauliflower alley ears on him, a big square face and a 20-inch neck, maybe," said Hart. "I was wrestling amateur and Taylor, he was kind of above us." Taylor and Hart would later work out a bit together.

The toe-hold was Taylor's speciality, and when angered by an

JACK TAYLOR.

opponent, he would let fly a series of rabbit punches. He weighed in anywhere from 210 to 225 pounds during his long career, which included bouts against big names like Wladek Zbyszko, Charley Cutler, Leo L'Heureux, Reginald Siki, Ed "Strangler" Lewis and Ed Don George.

Like many greats, Taylor knew when it was time to pass the torch. He helped break Camrose, Alberta's Al "Murder" Mills in the business, but it's Earl McCready he is most often credited with starting off in pro wrestling. With his amateur career and degree finished, McCready sought out Taylor to train.

On April 20, 1933, the two Canadian stars going in opposite directions met in Calgary, and McCready snatched the Canadian and British Empire championships from his mentor. Wrestling had changed over the years, with showmanship given greater emphasis, and Taylor was booed by the crowd, who favoured the young, good-looking McCready. "The fans ran true to form in receiving Jack with an assortment of salutations which rolled off like peas off a duck's back.

They booed lustily and Mrs. Taylor's husband bowed in satiric acknowledgement," wrote the Calgary *Herald* after the fight.

After 1933, Taylor fades from the record books, and much of the rest of his life remains unclear. Gene Kiniski knew Taylor when they were both living in Edmonton. "Jack was very, very tough. Jack, he always had a couple of these balls in his hand, or in his pocket. He'd be walking along and he'd be squeezing them. He had a pair of forearms on him like a guy's thighs. He was a really, really tough wrestler. He could pretty well have handled anybody," said Kiniski. "He was very, very reserved. In fact, in his latter years he was a bouncer in a gambling club — an illicit gambling club in Edmonton. He spent his final years in Edmonton."

To Kiniski and other fans of old-time wrestling, it's disappointing that Taylor and McCready are not celebrated like others from the pre-war era. "Nobody would even know them. They don't realize how great they were," said Kiniski. "Unless you saw them both then, I don't think you'd appreciate what they accomplished."

16. JOHNNY ROUGEAU

In the 1970s, a real-life feud developed between Johnny Rougeau's Montreal promotion and the upstart Grand Prix Wrestling run by the Vachon brothers. Rougeau tried his best to keep the Vachons out of the Montreal Forum, but his efforts were in vain. So for a number of years, there were competing promotions in Montreal, duking it out for fan affection.

Thirty years later, Paul "The Butcher" Vachon has no problem talking about his foe. "You know who was one of the greatest Canadian wrestlers? Johnny Rougeau. Without a doubt. He was an asshole but he was one of the greatest wrestlers, for professional." Pro wrestlers are notorious for holding grudges through the years, so it was somewhat of a surprise to hear "The Butcher" speak so highly of his rival. "Rougeau was quite a professional. He was good. I don't mind saying that."

There is certainly lots to say about Johnny Rougeau. His impact on Quebec's wrestling scene is undeniable, but what sets him apart is his work outside the ring with politics, hockey and various business ventures, including his wrestling promotion. He was a celebrity and a hero to many.

Inspired by his uncle Eddie Auger, who was a mid-level pro, best known around Quebec, Johnny Rougeau entered the mat wars as an amateur in 1943, training at the Palais Nationale. Rougeau had little success in Montreal, and got his first break travelling with his uncle to Detroit. There the

JOHNNY ROUGEAU
PHOTO: TONY LANZA

youngster was re-christened "Handsome" Johnny Rougeau, and was portrayed as a ladies' man.

According to his brother Jacques Rougeau Sr., Johnny fell under the sway of "The Nature Boy." "Buddy Rogers took him under his wing and took him to Columbus, Ohio," Rougeau Sr. said. "From there, Johnny went all over the place."

Settling back in Montreal on the advice of famed CBC announcer Michel Normandin, and raising a family, Rougeau climbed the ladder quickly. He became a protegé of the great Yvon Robert. In 1959, he took a trip to Europe and was main-eventing in Paris. Johnny was the star, "Because he had charisma. He was a good-looking guy. He knew how to talk.

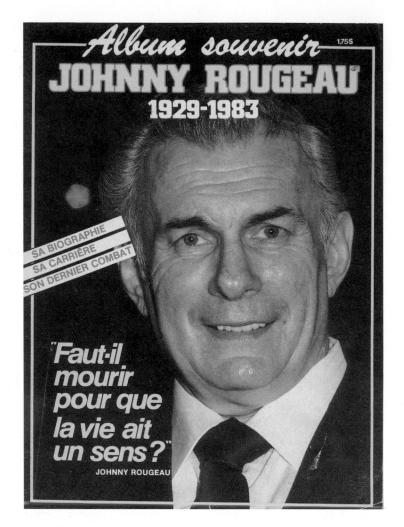

Album souvenir 1,75$

JOHNNY ROUGEAU
1929-1983

SA BIOGRAPHIE
SA CARRIÈRE
SON DERNIER COMBAT

"Faut-il mourir pour que la vie ait un sens?"
JOHNNY ROUGEAU

He could take a mic and talk for half an hour, and do it well," remembered Jacques Sr.

Despite his fame, Rougeau always had his eye on other businesses, things he could perhaps do after his career was over. In 1956, he bought a hair salon, then a garage with his brother Jacques. He also had a public tryout with the Montreal Alouettes, but balked at the low pay compared to his wrestling wages. From 1961 to 1965, Johnny owned the Mocambo night club in Montreal, and lived it up night after night with top talent and big stars. For much of the early '60s, Rougeau only wrestled sporadically.

In 1960, he briefly ran a clothing store, but it burned down. It was there, however, that he first met René Levesque, an influential young politician for whom Rougeau was soon working, both as a bodyguard and as a political organizer.

When Montreal wrestling promoter Eddie Quinn died in 1965, Rougeau saw another opportunity. Attendance was down and wrestling was almost dead. He started a new promotion, got a TV deal and got back in the ring himself in 1967. He had a big retirement match in August 1971, ceremonially passing the torch to his nephew Raymond, but less than a year later, he was back in the ring.

Hockey was the other big love of Rougeau's life. He was the goalie on "Sur Le Matelas," a hockey team of wrestlers in 1969 that included Ivan Koloff, Jacques Rougeau, Toni Angelo, Gino Brito, Paul & Joe LeDuc, Larry Moquin, Antonio Baillargeon, Len Shelly, les Masques, Lionel Robert, Butch Morgan, Hans Schmidt and others. Eddie "The Brain" Creatchman was the coach.

In the 1970s, Johnny invested in a junior hockey team, and later went on to coach the Laval Nationals, with a young Mike Bossy in the lineup. In 1981, Rougeau was made president of the Quebec Major Junior Hockey League.

When he died in 1983 of cancer, more than 7,000 people attended the funeral. Rougeau's legacy lives on in a number of ways. In the ring, his nephew Jacques Rougeau Jr. is now a promoter and his promotion has the Johnny Rougeau Memorial Tag Team Titles. An autobiography, *Johnny Rougeau*, was written on his deathbed, and published in 1983.

17. DON EAGLE

Don Eagle, a Mohawk from the Kahnawake reserve in Quebec, deserves recognition as one of the greatest box office attractions of the early days of televised wrestling. He followed in the footsteps of his father, War Eagle, who was a light heavyweight wrestler in the '20s working the Montreal-Detroit corridor.

Don Eagle (right) with his father Chief War Eagle.
Photo: Melby Collection

"He was the pioneer in wrestling as an Indian person," explained Don Eagle's protégé Billy Two Rivers. "Combined with his natural abilities, the colourfulness of ourselves in costumes, and I guess the curiosity, he was a boon to wrestling, but also he was a role model for a lot of Indian people."

After a few years as an iron worker, Don Eagle debuted in the ring at 20. His father was his manager, and they worked out of Columbus, Ohio, travelling from territory to territory in a big, long Cadillac with a 20-foot canoe on top.

DON EAGLE.
PHOTO: MELBY COLLECTION

Six-time world champion Lou Thesz remembered Don Eagle as a "very colourful" performer. "He did the little dance. The people were kind of Indian-oriented at that time, and everything was pro-Indian," said Thesz, whose career began well before Eagle's and lasted into his 60s. "It was wonderful because he was a good attraction. But when we're speaking about an attraction, and we're speaking of wrestling, we're speaking of two different ballgames."

On May 23, 1950, Don Eagle beat Frank Sexton in Cleveland, Ohio, in a best-of-three-falls match for one of the versions of the AWA World title. But Eagle held the title for just three days, falling victim to a double-cross in a televised match against Gorgeous George in Chicago. The betrayal hurt Don Eagle, and he soon decided to take time off to heal his aching back — and train Billy Two Rivers.

Don Eagle was never the same, and he retired in 1963. On March 17, 1966, he died at age 41 from an apparently self-inflicted gunshot wound.

According to his good friend Don Leo Jonathon, Eagle made a difference outside the ring, as well as in it, helping Canadians better understand the Native population. "Besides the fact that he was a good wrestler, a scientific wrestler, I think he gave the white people, or the rest of Canada, a better look at what the Native people were like."

18. JOHNNY POWERS

A young Johnny Powers.
Photo: Oliver Collection

To be a big star in wrestling is to have your name on the marquee. However, very few ever got to the next step — having a TV show named after you. For six years in the late '60s and early '70s, *Championship Wrestling With Johnny Powers* came out of Buffalo, proclaiming its Hamilton-born star (and part-owner), Johnny Powers, as the star of stars.

Born Dennis Waters in 1943, he broke into the business by working out at Jack Wentworth's Hamilton gym. Initially, he worked around Detroit at 17 and 18 under the name Lord Anthony Lansdowne. After he became disenchanted with geology at McMaster University, Waters took to the ring full-time and never looked back.

In 1963, he made his way to Pittsburgh and the WWWF-affiliated promotion there. Waters took the name Johnny Powers and quickly moved up the cards. "My break came when I wrestled Bruno Sammartino in Pittsburgh," Powers said. His power-move-based style worked well against the Italian strongman. "I did a lot of ground work. I evolved a figure-four leglock into something that was called a Power-lock. I had a lot of success with that. So, I worked strongly on the ground and strongly at the top."

Yet main-eventing wasn't enough for Powers, who yearned for more. "By the time I was 22, I was bored with the wrestling side, so I was interested in the marketing aspects, the promoting aspects," he said. Powers bought the rights to promote in a few Ontario towns, including Sutton ("Took me three maps to find it at that time"), then Galt. Following the advice of Toronto

JOHNNY POWERS AS NWF WORLD CHAMPION. PHOTO: JOHNNY POWERS

promoter Frank Tunney, Powers purchased part of Pedro Martinez's operation in Buffalo. "We took it actually from a standstill that was a quasi-dormant territory, and when we finished, it was really moving. That organization had everybody from Johnny Valentine to The Sheik to Bobo Brazil. There was a lot of quality talent at that time."

The Buffalo territory ran from western New York to Cleveland, and Powers soon became a star. He also worked with Martinez to change the way wrestling was marketed, taking the newly christened NWF and syndicating the TV shows around the world. Clients included the Armed Forces Television Network, Telesystema de Mexico, and the Japanese Television Network. "Within reason, I guess, I was a pioneer at international syndication, and I ran that as a part of National Sports Television in Buffalo."

Besides the wrestling, Powers got involved in promoting musical events — mostly rock-and-roll revival shows — and the Harlem Globetrotters. Powers's idea of the spectacle led to a major show in Cleveland's Municipal Stadium, where there were 50 wrestlers on the card, with three rings going simultaneously, set up at home, first and third base.

The expansion of the NWF's reach helped Powers tremendously in Japan. He had already done a tour there, but as his fame grew, he was in demand. It also coincided with the beginning of the career of Antonio Inoki and his New Japan promotion. Powers went to Japan as the NWF World champion. "The national magazines started picking up the NWF as a viable federation," he said. "That's what caught the interest of Japan, and it got taken over there. They weren't able, at that time, to get the champions — NWA, and the newly-coined WWWF — over there."

In Japan, Powers exchanged the NWF World belt with Seiji Sakaguchi and battled Inoki countless times. It was the first world title won by a Japanese wrestler, and in 1973, New Japan bought the NWF. "They bought, quote, the franchise, the rights to the National Wrestling Federation Association," Powers said. "The baton got turned over to Inoki and his association. So the titles got turned over, and the association got turned over."

At that time, no one came close to Powers on an international scale. "There is actually nobody that has the international exposure as a Canadian that I had for the period of time that I had it. Nobody in that era, the '60s and '70s, was going to Japan as much as I was or was doing Singapore and stuff like that." In all, Powers guesses that he did over 30 tours of Japan.

In the late '70s, Powers began to wind down his wrestling career, retiring for good in 1982. "I had done 20 years in the business, and I was getting tired of it," he said. Powers ran a wrestling school with Sweet Daddy Siki in Toronto for a time, and got involved in many other ventures.

The wrestling business was a wonderful learning opportunity for his next career. "I use my marketing side and my deal-making experience that I garnered from the wrestling business to carry me over," he said. "I learned how to sell tickets, in other words. From a public persona standpoint, and also from a deal-making standpoint, and that has been a solid understanding."

Powers has distanced himself from his old occupation. "When I retired, I said I was going to step away from the business," he said. When the Japanese Wrestling Hall of Fame wanted to induct him, it took them two years to find him.

Yet Powers has no regrets about his past. "For the time, and for the moment in its context, I achieved what I wanted to achieve. From the east-end of Hamilton, going up through a sport and ending up on top for a while, both as a competitor and as a businessman."

19. RICK MARTEL

From his debut in 1973 in the Maritimes until he walked out on Tito Santana, his partner in Strike Force, Rick Martel was a huge fan favourite. Good-looking, personable and well-spoken, Martel was the ultimate babyface and a major success around the world. But when he turned heel on his partner, and was dubbed "The Model," he heard the boos for the first time in his career — and loved it.

"I remember the first day I came back, after WrestleMania where I walked out on Tito. I wrestled in Rochester, New York," recalled Martel, whose real name is Richard Vigneault. "After I walked out, people started booing me. Whoa, what a different feeling. And, funny enough, it felt pretty good. I walked in there and they started booing me. . . . My career took off from there as a different kind of style."

Martel's brother Michel had started wrestling as a pro in 1968. Knowing that his younger brother was interested in the sport, Michel brought Rick along for a two-week tour in Stampede Wrestling to learn about the road. Rick was hooked, and when a desperate call came from the Maritimes where

MICHEL MARTEL HOISTS HIS BROTHER RICK'S ARM EARLY IN HIS CAREER IN CALGARY. PHOTO: BOB LEONARD

they needed an extra wrestler, the 17-year-old hopped on a plane as fast as he could.

During his early years, Martel got frustrated by the Montreal scene. Johnny Rougeau was the main promoter, and had his own young, good-looking star in his nephew Raymond. Martel was encouraged to hit the road, which paid amazing dividends. "I was able to see a lot of countries, met different people and saw different wrestling styles," he said. "It helped me a great deal because I matured outside, overseas."

Martel was a major success in New Zealand and Australia, did numerous trips to Japan, and held tag titles in Hawaii and the Pacific Northwest. He drew his first big media attention from the wrestling press when he entered the WWWF, and quickly won the tag titles with Tony Garea. The two were a terrific tag team, the youthful fire of Martel a good complement to the veteran ring-savvy of Garea.

He jumped to the AWA, and was in the right spot at the right time when Hulk Hogan left the promotion. Martel ended up taking the AWA World belt off Jumbo Tsuruta on May 13, 1984, and held the title for a year and a half before dropping it to Stan Hansen. "Stan, I'll be honest, is the toughest man I've ever met in wrestling. No doubt," Martel said.

With the WWF taking off in popularity, and frustrated with

AWA honcho Verne Gagne, Martel jumped back to New York. He brought Tom Zenk with him, and the Can-Am Connection took off. The duo were eerily similar. "When I saw him in the ring, I said *Wow*, because it's so strange. He really was so similar to me. Later on I found out that Tom had been watching me a lot and kind of copied my style and did a lot of the moves that I was doing." But Zenk bailed out on his partner and the WWF, quitting the business for a time. Martel, left out to dry, was paired with Santana. The chemistry wasn't quite as good, but Strike Force did hold the WWF tag belts for awhile.

Then Martel's heel turn, "The Model," became a memorable WWF character, spraying his Arrogance perfume into the eyes of his opponents. In the end, though, Martel's career petered out and he began exploring real estate as another career in his hometown of Quebec City.

In 1997, Martel returned to pro wrestling after a couple of years absence, fighting in WCW. Although he was probably in the best shape of his career, he suffered a knee injury during a TV title match against Booker T and never made it back into the spotlight. Now done with his wrestling dreams, Martel has returned to working in real estate. His nephew Kevin Martel now wrestles in Quebec.

RICK AS HAWAIIAN CHAMPION. PHOTO: BOB LEONARD

MARTEL PREENS AS THE MODEL. PHOTO: TERRY DART

20. WALDO VON ERICH

Waldo von Erich was easily one of the most hated wrestlers Canada ever produced. Born Wally Sieber in Toronto in 1933, he grew into a 6-foot, 265-pound monster who learned from the success of Fritz von Erich's German gimmick, and became his "brother" to instant success.

WALDO VON ERICH LISTENS CAREFULLY TO MANAGER FREDDIE BLASSIE WHILE IN THE WWWF IN 1974. PHOTO: MIKE LANO

Sporting a wwii helmet and riding crop, von Erich's famed finishing move was the Blitzkreig — a kneedrop off the top rope and a yell to go with it. He was also great on the microphone, mercilessly picking on the babyfaces and announcers.

As a single, von Erich peaked in wwwf World-title matches against Bruno Sammartino at Madison Square Gardens in New York. He also held the Buffalo-Cleveland version of the world title in the early '70s — feuding with Johnny Powers — as well as countless other belts. "I'm not blowing my own horn, but I guess I was the hottest heel in each territory I was in," he said.

For runs in other territories, von Erich would don a mask to hide his identity. His

DRESSED FOR MAYHEM.
PHOTO: L'IL AL COLLECTION

various aliases included The Great Zimm, Wild Man Zim, The Great Hornet, El Tigre and Mr. M.

Von Erich first tried to retire in 1973, but stuck around until 1979. He has also helped train wrestlers at a school in Cambridge, Ont. Outside of wrestling, he is well-known for creating a chair to help alleviate back problems, especially those caused by athletic injuries.

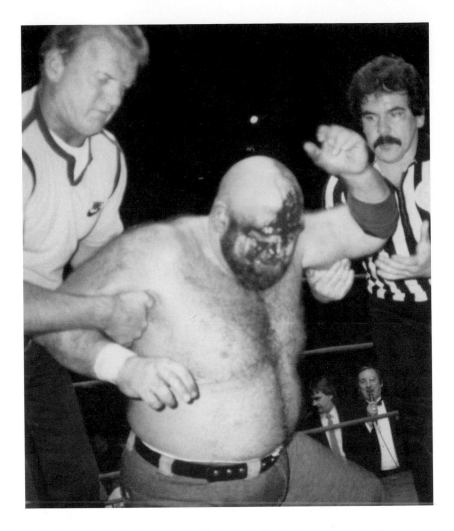

Jos Leduc is helped up by Jacques Rougeau and ref Adrien
Desbois. Photo: Tony Lanza

The Announcers — An Essential Element

Television and pro wrestling go hand in hand. Wrestling was one of the early successes on television and it continues to this day.

But aside from the wrestlers, it's the announcers the fans remember. They were the front line, agreeing or disagreeing with the wrestlers, arguing with the colour commentator or saying hello to all the "shut-ins at home." The fans could identify with the announcers, who were usually dwarfed by the size and ego of the men they worked with.

"I have come up with a complete generation of people," *All-Star Wrestling* announcer Ron Morrier told the Vancouver *Sun* shortly before his death in August 1981. "I've lived in their living rooms, their bathrooms, their bedrooms. You know, they've grown up with me. They always say, 'Jeez, Ron, I hate to call you Ron, but I feel like I know you so well. It's recognition, and I enjoy it."

Some of Canada's greatest announcers include:

MICHEL NORMANDIN

Possibly the greatest name in Quebec sports broadcasting history. Normandin covered everything from Canadiens hockey to the Royals baseball team to football, and also served on city council. To wrestling fans, he was the one that brought *La Lutte de Mercredi Soir* to them every Wednesday, broadcasting the early matches live in the 1950s. He died in November 1963.

STAMPEDE ANNOUNCER ED WHALEN
(CENTER) IS IGNORED BY THE ARGUING
STU HART (LEFT) AND ARCHIE "THE
STOMPER" GOULDIE. PHOTO: BOB
LEONARD

ED WHALEN

The reach of *Stampede Wrestling* always amazed Ed Whalen. He loved to tell stories of tribes in Africa watching the show, or of getting mobbed in Antigua. He was host of the program for 27 years, leaving in a huff over the violence on a couple of occasions. "In the meantime, and in-between time, that's it for another edition of *Stampede Wrestling*," "Ring-a-ding-dong dandy," and "Malfunction at the junction" are his best known catch phrases. He was also the announcer for the NHL's Calgary Flames and a columnist for the Calgary *Sun*. Whalen died in December 2001 of a heart attack.

RON MORRIER

In many ways, Morrier is best remembered for standing silently as Gene Kiniski went off on another rant, thanking him for his role. "As usual, Ron, you did a great job interviewing me," Kiniski would deadpan. Morrier was impartial in his call of the action — always calm, cool and collected. He also had many other roles on BCTV. He would end the shows with, "Be the good Lord willing, we'll see you next week." He was the host of *All-Star Wrestling* until his death in August 1981.

BOBBY AND RUDY KAY ARE INTERVIEWED BY MIKE MCMAN AND
BILLY RED LYONS ON THE MAPLE LEAF WRESTLING SHOW.
PHOTO: KEVIN HOBBS

BILLY RED LYONS

More of an interviewer than an announcer, Billy Red wasn't
scared to stand up to the heels or take a bump. "Dontcha dare
miss it!" was his catch phrase for whatever card the Tunneys
had put together for Maple Leaf Gardens.

LORD ATHOL LAYTON

On TV shows in Toronto, Cleveland and Detroit, Layton had a
great gift for gab. His extensive vocabulary would often
confuse and provoke the wrestlers he was interviewing.

MILT AVRUSKIN

Avruskin was the announcer for George Cannon's *Superstars of
Wrestling*, Gino Brito's *International Wrestling* and later, his

own co-promotion with Angelo Mosca called *Pro Wrestling Canada*. He fell into the gig with Cannon by accident and just kept working. He currently lives north of Toronto and is involved in television syndication.

The Families

ANTONATION

Out of a family of 20 in Rossburn, Manitoba, came three brothers who gained success as wrestlers in the Prairies. Trained by well-known Winnipeg mainstay Bobby Jones, Lloyd, Orest and Bill Antonation all had spells in the pro game, achieving different levels of success.

Lloyd was the first to start wrestling in 1953, and was one of the top heels in Winnipeg. He worked into the 1970s. "Bashin" Bill was second into the ring, starting in early 1959. Orest is the best-known Antonation brother, both under his real name, and as "Buffalo" Bill Cody, the moniker he used in Stampede. He started as a pro in 1959 and wrestled into the early 1990s. Orest also made numerous appearances for the AWA.

BAILLARGEON

French-Canadians are often identified as traditionally rural people, comprised of farmhands and lumberjacks. The celebration of physical prowess was a natural one, based on the hardships of their lives. Louis Cyr and Victor Delamarre are still revered today for their amazing feats of strength, but at the top of the evolutionary chain of strongmen is the Baillargeon family from Saint-Magloire, Quebec.

In the late 1940s, the six Baillargeon brothers — Jean, Charles, Adrien, Lionel, Paul, and Antonio (Tony) — were the Ice Capades or Harlem Globetrotters of their day, taking their strongmen act from town to town. Dressed in a weightlifting singlet (with a maple leaf and a beaver adorning the front) to

THE BAILLARGEONS IN 1948. (FROM LEFT): CHARLES, PAUL, ADRIEN, LIONEL, JEAN, ANTONIO. PHOTO: MELBY COLLECTION

show off their impressive physiques, the Baillargeons wowed crowds. Charles would pull a bus with his teeth, Paul would lift a horse, they would make human pyramids with Jean or Paul at the base, supporting three or four people above. They brought in acrobats to complement their act.

By 1949, all six brothers had grown tired of having to arrange their own shows across North America. When the opportunity arose for them to train as wrestlers in Massachusetts, they took it. Their established fame was their in-ring calling card. "Their feats of strength have been recorded by the newsreel cameras and no doubt you have seen them in your local theaters," wrote *The Ring* magazine in April 1950.

The Baillargeon wrestling careers didn't actually last very long, averaging 12 years. Tony, the youngest, wrestled the longest, from 1949 until 1976. Jean wrestled 15 years, Adrien eight years, Lionel nine years, and Paul 11 years. Charles wrestled only six years, a car accident cutting his career short.

Both Edouard Carpentier and Paul Leduc recalled a trio of matches between Paul Baillargeon and former NWA world champ Yvon Robert. In Quebec City, Baillargeon went over. In Montreal, where Robert was spoken of in the awed tones usually reserved for Rocket Richard, Baillargeon lost. A third match at the neutral site of Ottawa was a draw. "He was one of the best strongmen I ever saw," said former world champ Carpentier. "Everybody was afraid to wrestle him" because of his strength.

Paul was the businessman of the family, and ran a very successful hotel in Quebec City, named, of all things, Hotel Paul Baillargeon. Maritime promoter Emile Dupré wrestled Tony Baillargeon on a dozen occasions, and became friends with Paul too. He stayed with Paul at his new hotel, just after Baillargeon had bought it. According to Dupré, it "wasn't much . . . a rinky-dink little place," but years later he stayed there again, after many renovations. "He really brought up that place like a class act," said Dupré. Paul Baillargeon was also a long-term president of the Quebec Hotel and Restaurant Association.

When talking about Tony Baillargeon, both Leduc and Raymond Rougeau mention his Citroën. "Nobody wanted to drive with him," recalled Leduc. "It was horrible to look at." To Rougeau, who broke into the business in the early '70s, Tony Baillargeon was "a fun guy, always joking around, always in a good mood."

Adrien Baillargeon changed the wrestling scene in Louisiana forever when he arrived. "Us little Cajun guys had never seen anybody that big before, or that strong, and best of all, he spoke French just like us! For the next several years, Adrien Baillargeon owned French-speaking Southwest Louisiana," said fan and promoter John Lester.

Jean Baillargeon died March 2, 1994. Adrien Baillargeon died May 9, 1995. Lionel Baillargeon died June 19, 1982. Paul Baillargeon died in October 1999. Tony Baillargeon died March 14, 1997. Charles Baillargeon is in his 80s.

BRITO / BRITTON

GINO BRITO JR. (LEFT) AND HIS
FATHER GINO SR.
PHOTO: THE BRITO FAMILY

The contributions that the three generations of the Acocella family made to pro wrestling can't just be measured in the ring. They were promoters and trainers, and paved the way for the popularity of midget wrestling in the 1950s.

Of course, this being wrestling, the name Acocella was hardly appropriate: too hard to pronounce, too ethnic. Instead, fans know the family under a variety of other names — Lou Kelly, Jack Britton, and Gino Brito, Sr. and Jr.

The sons of an Italian-born doctor who had immigrated to Montreal, Luigi and Gabriel Acocella started wrestling in the early 1930s. Luigi was the first into the ring wars, starting in Boston for promoter Paul Bowser. "There were a lot of Italians there, and Paul Bowser, he said, 'Listen, I'm not running shows just for Italians!'" laughed Gino Brito Sr., son of Gabriel Acocella. So Luigi became Lou Kelly, to capitalize on the Irish community around Boston. His brother started a short while later, taking his ring name, Jack Britton, from an old boxer.

As both Lou Kelly and later, Jacques Bernard, Luigi did well in the mat game. The various weight classes in wrestling at the time made it easy for smaller men like the Acocellas to find work. They made trips to Europe and Mexico to fight. Angelo Savoldi knew both Kelly and Britton right from the

JACK BRITTON REFEREES THE MIDGETS IN JAPAN IN 1962.
PHOTO: THE BRITO FAMILY

start in Boston, and offered his comparison of the two. "Jack was the business brains and Lou, I think, was a little better wrestler," said the veteran grappler.

In Detroit, the brothers worked for promoters Bert Ruby and Harry Light. After World War II, Britton, Ruby and Light started the midgets wrestling. Britton was in charge of booking up to two dozen midgets at a time around the world. Of them, Sky Low Low, Little Beaver, Lord Littlebrook and Little Brutus became superstars.

The midgets became Britton's work. "Once he started the midgets, wrestling was not a priority anymore. He would wrestle as a fill-in, he would referee his own midgets. He did a tour of Europe and he was the referee for the midgets. Then he went to Detroit, and he didn't wrestle anymore. By the time he was 38 years old, he had stopped wrestling," said Brito Sr.

In the late 1950s, Britton moved the family to Windsor, Ontario, where they stayed until 1967. Britton continued to book

LOU KELLY. PHOTO: THE BRITO
FAMILY

the midgets into the '70s, but the popularity had waned. "By then, midgets were not what they were," explained Brito Sr. "Some of them got old and quit. Others, they weren't making that good of a living anymore because they weren't the sensation that they were back in the late '40s, '50s and early '60s."

Brito Sr. began training as a wrestler at 19 in Windsor with George McArthur, who later gained fame as Crybaby Cannon. His father soon had him taking the midgets from territory to territory, and it helped Brito Sr. quickly learn the mat game. "Just staying around Detroit, since I didn't have the experience starting out, I was getting one, two, maybe three bookings a week at the most. So the midgets, every night I'd go into a town, sometimes they didn't even know [me], they'd just put me on the card. They could call me Joe Blow, they could call me any name they wanted." Brito quickly found the promoters knew who he was and work was easy to come by.

At 5-foot-10, 240 pounds, Gino Brito Sr. was hardly a monster specimen by wrestling standards. But he found success in many places, including the wwf, where he held the tag titles with his best friend Tony Parisi wrestling under the name Louis Cerdan (the last name taken from another old-time boxer).

In the late 1970s, Britton began to promote in Montreal's Paul Sauvé Arena, and in northern Ontario. When he died in 1980, his son took over. The International Wrestling promotion took off when it secured a TV deal that aired the show from the Maritimes to Ontario. With Dino Bravo, the

Rougeaus and Rick Martel on top as the faces, and heels like Abdullah the Butcher, the Destroyer and the Masked Superstar brought in to oppose them, International Wrestling was a hot territory until the WWF took Bravo and the Rougeaus, and Martel went to the AWA. Brito made the mistake of trying to fight the WWF, and was out of business by 1987. For four years after that, he worked as the local promoter for the WWF in Montreal.

In 1983, Gino Brito's son Dino Acocella decided to become a pro wrestler too, and became Gino Brito Jr. He was already familiar with wrestlers. "It was normal to me to see all these wrestlers walk in and out of the house. At that time, there was Jos Leduc, who my dad used to hang around with a lot, Giant Jean Ferre, and all those guys. So it became something normal, even the midgets." As a child, Gino Jr. remembers wrestling the likes of Sky Low Low and Little Beaver both around the house and in the ring.

Brito Jr. wrestled for his father's promotion for five years, but never reached the heights of his predecessors. "I really enjoyed that five years. It was a lot of new experiences for a guy who was about 19 when I started on the road."

These days, family is equally important. Brito Sr.'s brother-in-law runs a large Subaru dealership near the old Montreal Forum, and both Brito Sr. and Jr. work there. It's been tough for the senior Brito to be away from wrestling. "My life was wrestling — all my life. I wrestled 25 years as a pro, then promoted another 10 years. It was hard getting out of it, but there was nothing there for me anymore. I tried a few local, little promotions after that. Every promotion I would drop two, three grand because you weren't drawing 300, 400 people."

CORMIER

From a farm in rural New Brunswick came four brothers who headlined wrestling shows around the world. The Cormiers were big stars under their various aliases — The Beast (Yvan, the oldest), Rudy Kay (Jean-Louis), Leo Burke (Leonce) and Bobby Kay (Romeo, the youngest).

The Beast was the first into the business. He had done various jobs as a teen, including working in the woods, shoeing horses, and driving heavy equipment. He was very strong. "When I was 17 years old, I could pick up the backend of a half-ton truck," he claimed. In 1957, the Beast-to-be met up with Maritime wrestler Emile Dupré. "One spring, I just came out of the woods and I had long, curly hair and a big beard. He looked, and he said 'Would you like to wrestle?' So I said I'd try it, and I trained a little bit."

A few years later, in 1962, he went to Indianapolis to train seriously, and started as a regular pro wrestler the following year. He wrestled as Ivan The Lumberjack until he was christened The Beast by Jim Crockett Sr. a short while later.

It was only natural that Cormier's brothers would want to follow him. What is perhaps more surprising is that only four

THE CORMIERS ALWAYS STAYED TRUE TO THEIR RURAL NEW BRUNSWICK ROOTS. FROM LEFT, IT'S RUDY AND BOBBY KAY, LEO BURKE AND THE BEAST. PHOTO: COURTESY THE CORMIER FAMILY

of the 13 kids in the Cormier household in Memramcook became grapplers. Apparently everyone was big and burly from the hard work on the farm, dealing with three dozen head of cattle and a few horses.

Rudy Kay was next into the business, in 1964. He started as a pro boxer at 14, but quickly realized the chance to wrestle more often would lead to more money. He trained with The Beast and Maritime wrestlers like Dutchie the Spinner, Dupré and Don Jardine. He was dubbed Rudy Kay by a

HOCKEY PLAYERS WERE AMONG THE FEW ATHLETES IN CANADA WITH BIGGER REPUTATIONS THAN PRO WRESTLERS. HERE, THE CORMIER BROTHERS CLOWN AROUND WITH HALL OF FAME GOALTENDER GUMP WORSLEY. PHOTO: BOB LEONARD

booker in Indianapolis who thought he was a dead ringer for a Chicago mat star of the same name from a decade earlier.

Both Beast and Rudy knew it was only a matter of time before another brother followed in their footsteps. "When Leo got a little older, it was a lot easier, because we started training them quite young," Rudy said.

"I lived, ate, drank wrestling since I was six years old," explained Leo Burke, six years younger than Rudy. "Of course, I have two older brothers in the wrestling profession who made me want to follow in their footsteps. This is why I chose the name Leo Burke. For no other reason — I didn't want to do it on my brothers' reputations. I needed to do it on my own or not at all." Leo borrowed the last name Burke from a friend who was a boxer.

Bobby Kay came next, and took the same surname as

Rudy. "I sort of fell in love with [wrestling] through my brothers," he said. "I was the youngest one to start. Rudy and The Beast were all over the States doing their little thing, and I sort of got into it by watching them. Then Leo got into it, and he's the one that dragged me around. When The Beast found out I was interested, I was only about 17 years old, he took me to Calgary. The old man, Stu Hart, took me under his wing and trained me. I refereed for a little while to get experience. I got into it from there."

The Beast is proud of his brothers, but also wants a little bit of credit. "They had it easier than I did," he said. "I brought them with me. I had a new car and some money — it was different when I first started! So, they came with me and I made sure they had a nice hotel to stay in, travelled good."

According to Rudy, helping his brothers wasn't just out of loyalty — he knew they were skilled. "We weren't afraid to talk to a promoter. As a matter of fact, we brought Leo with us to Calgary the first time. Beast and I went up there, seen what they had, and knew that he could do just as good or better than some of the guys they had there."

Over the years, the brothers all went their own ways. The Beast had a lot of success in Japan and Australia. Bobby and Rudy Kay formed a tag team for years. Leo Burke also went overseas quite a bit, but was top of the card in Stampede Wrestling. While the Cormiers's family relationship was acknowledged in a few promotions, they never made a huge deal of out it.

In fact, the Cormiers aren't ones to brag. "You start from nothing, a country boy here. You've got nothing. It's only a dream. We were watching wrestling at the time," Rudy Kay said. "When I started saying that I was going to make it into professional wrestling, they'd say, 'You're crazy. Everybody weighs over 200 pounds and you can never make it.' It goes to show that when you have something in your mind and you really want to do it, you're going to wind up doing it.

"We just didn't make it into wrestling, we wrestled just about all over the world, plus in main events for world championships and stuff like that. Which is just not saying 'Well,

I'm a wrestler and I was on the card and tried to look up my name.' We went to a lot of places besides the Maritimes where we were main attractions."

HART

Canada's first family of wrestling is the Harts. No other family has done so much for the sport over the years. Of course, the sheer number of Harts has helped their domination of the Canadian scene.

By now, the story is familiar to most Canadians. Stu Hart, a poor Albertan, becomes a pro wrestler in New York City, and meets the stunningly attractive Helen Smith, the daughter of U.S. Olympic miler Harry Smith. They married on New Year's Eve 1947, and as they would often joke, were snowed under from then on.

The Harts had eight sons and four daughters, the first being Smith, about a year after they married, and the last being Owen in 1965. "By the time I was born, my parents had

BACK ROW (LEFT TO RIGHT), WAYNE, KEITH, HELEN, STU, BRUCE, SMITH; MIDDLE ROW, DEAN, ELLIE, GEORGIA, BRET; BOTTOM ROW, OWEN, DIANA, ROSS, ALISON. PHOTO: STU HART

pretty well run the gauntlet with their kids," Owen joked in 1988. "The novelty had kind of worn off by the time the 12th child was born. I was lucky to get fed and changed, picked up and taken to school."

In 1948, Stu started promoting wrestling in Edmonton and soon had all of Alberta under his belt. His promotion was dubbed Stampede Wrestling and it proved to be an excellent place to school his children in the ways of the world. At their huge house outside Calgary, wrestlers of every shape and size would tromp through. Wrestling bears would hibernate under the porch steps. People were made into human pretzels in the Dungeon training room.

Stu Hart handled the wrestling end of the promotion, and Helen did the record-keeping, advertising and accounting. The cooking and cleaning were also Stu's responsibility, and industrial-quality appliances were installed. The kids would help at the shows setting up the ring, selling programs or cleaning up.

It was never calm around the house, and Ross Hart credits his mother for keeping things on an even keel: "She and my dad did a pretty good job raising us. It wasn't easy raising 12 kids in the '60s and '70s in a big household, running several businesses. They had a lot of ups and downs with their finances, but for the most part, we all turned out pretty well."

The Hart kids are:

Smith Hart: He wrestled occasionally and is now involved with a wrestling school in Cambridge, Ontario.

Bruce Hart: After Owen and Bret, Bruce is the best-known Hart. He was a tremendous middleweight wrestler and had a keen eye for talent. During the last 25 years, it has been Bruce who has been the primary trainer in the Dungeon. He hit his peak in the late '80s teaming with Brian Pillman as the tag team Bad Company.

Keith Hart: He wrestled for a while and teamed with Bruce to start an official Hart Brothers school of wrestling. Keith also trained Chris Jericho.

Wayne Hart: He was a referee for Stampede.

Dean Hart: He never really got involved with the wrestling end, but instead tried promoting rock shows around Calgary. Dean died in 1990 of kidney failure.

Elizabeth (Ellie) Hart: Married Jim 'The Anvil' Neidhart.

Georgia Hart: Married bodybuilder, gym owner and sometime wrestler B.J. Annis. Her son Teddy Hart is a promising next generation talent who was on a WWF development contract for a time.

Bret Hart: One of the greatest Canadian wrestlers ever.

Alison Hart: Married wrestler Ben Bassarab.

Ross Hart: He wrestled for a time, but found his niche behind the scenes with TV production and training.

Diana Hart: Married wrestler Davey Boy Smith.

Owen Hart: Was a solid WWF star until his accidental death in May 1999.

In many ways, the sheer fame of Stu, Bret and Owen has meant that important contributions by other members of the Hart family were never acknowledged. Bruce was running the Stampede promotion during its last legs, and recently teamed with his brother Ross to keep the business alive. The Dungeon still gets students applying from around the world. "For the most part, guys from the last 25 years all had their training with Bruce or Keith or even myself," said Ross Hart. "Stu would occasionally come down and show a lot of the submission-style wrestling, and the shooting moves."

When Stampede was running, the Harts would open their house to the wrestlers. Weekly dinners became a ritual. Jacques Rougeau Jr. was just a 17-year-old when he was sent out to Calgary to learn more about wrestling. Stu met him at the airport and made him feel at home. "I had dinner every Sunday with the cats and the Harts," he said.

Jack Brisco travelled to Calgary as the NWA World champion. "I thought Stu Hart was a great guy and a great character. I always enjoyed wrestling in Calgary. It was a high spot of my career. I got to visit his home and meet his wonderful wife and all his children. We had dinner on a mountain overlooking Calgary. Stu always treated me with great respect. He always drove me to the towns in his Cadillac. Everything was good about Stu but his driving."

The Calgary Stampede rodeo and fair in July was the peak of the wrestling promotion. The world champion would come in to defend the title, and the Stampede wrestlers would get to be in the parade. Archie Gouldie laughs at the memories:

"He put wheels on the ring in the cornerposts, and he put the guys in the ring, and would pull it along. Well, he'd always be late for the parade. You know that parade's got 150,000 people lined up to watch it, and it's a big thing. They give you a position to be in, two weeks before the parade. He'd end up there and he wouldn't know where his position was. He'd be 20 minutes late, the parade's already going. 'You're supposed to be in here!' And he'd try to weasel into the parade where he wasn't supposed to be. Oh Lordy, it was a cartoon if you ever seen one."

The last few years have not been happy ones for the Harts. Matt Annis, the 13-year-old son of Georgia and B.J. Annis, died of flesh-eating disease. Then on pay-per-view in May 1999, Owen Hart fell to his death in a ring stunt gone wrong. In late 2001, the family was rocked by the death of Helen Hart, followed soon thereafter by Stampede announcer Ed Whalen. In mid-2002, Davey Boy Smith died in British Columbia at just 39, and soon after, Bret fell off his mountain bike and suffered a mild stroke.

The outpouring of love over the death of Owen Hart was expected because he was so well known. Ross Hart was surprised at the response his mother's passing got. "It's amazing how well known my mother was. We had calls and emails from everywhere," he said. "She was more in the background, not too much of a public figure in wrestling, but she was really a charming first lady, of the family and the promotion. It was gratifying that she was so well received by wrestlers, by other promoters, by dignitaries, by politicians."

The final chapter on the Harts is hardly closed — in fact, at the rate the books about them are coming out, it may never be. But the next generation is waiting for their chance to shine. Teddy Hart, Natalie Neidhart and Harry 'Bulldog' Smith have all have been involved in wrestling promotions around Calgary. "I hope there will be a legacy of new names," said Ross Hart. "I think they've got a lot of potential to become the next big stars. They've grown up with wrestling, and they just have a real natural aptitude for it."

KASABOSKI

The Kasaboskis sent three brothers into the squared circle. Besides Alex "The Pitiless Pole" and Larry "Babe" Kasaboski, brother Vincent refereed in northern Ontario when Larry was a promoter.

Born into a large family of Polish immigrants in Renfrew, Ontario (near Ottawa), the Kasaboskis learned early they would have to fight for everything they wanted.

Alex, the oldest brother, was the first into the ring, beginning his career in Toronto before setting up shop in California. He wrestled from the 1930s right up

ALEX KASABOSKI.
PHOTO: MELBY COLLECTION

until 1950. He died in 1952 at age 41 from blood clots in his lungs — he had taken a kick to the chest wrestling against doctor's orders and died three days later.

Larry idolized his older brother and followed him into the mat game. In the 1930s, he excelled at amateur wrestling and turned pro in 1934 with his brother's encouragement. He started in the U.S. around Detroit, Cleveland and Chicago, wrestling the likes of Paul Lortie, Don "One Man Gang" Evans, Tony Tarelli, and Dory Funk Sr. For a time, the Kasaboskis wrestled as a tag team.

When he left the ring at 66, Larry took up promoting in north-eastern Ontario under the Northland Wrestling Enterprises banner. He retired to his farm in 1979 and passed away in 1985.

LARRY KASABOSKI.
PHOTO: MELBY COLLECTION

LORTIE

When the old-timers talk about Montreal's Bob and Paul Lortie, they make sure to differentiate between the two. "Paul was a good wrestler. Bob was just a second," said Tony Lanza, an opinion echoed by Jacques Rougeau Sr. "Paul was a real good wrestler. He probably would have been a big star if it had been 20 years later. Bob was not as clever."

Both Lorties started in the 1930s. Paul was the first into the business, and had serious amateur credentials. At 5-foot-11, 218 pounds, he was shorter than his brother, but about ten pounds heavier. In 1940, Paul held the Canadian Junior Heavyweight title, and held a version the world junior title a year later. Together, they were a rugged, aggressive tag team that found a lot of work in England and Europe.

Three of their nephews got involved in pro wrestling as well, and all trained at the Palais Nationale, a noted hangout for amateurs and pros. Andre and Paul (who was sometimes known as Ray) started before their cousin Donald, but their careers didn't last very long. Wrestling was not a priority for the brothers, said Don Lortie. "It wasn't too much of an issue for them. They used to have some good scores, but it wasn't the same."

After turning pro in 1951, Don Lortie grew in size and confidence. "I started at 180 in Montreal. . . . I did a lot of workouts. I gained some weight. I go up to 190, 200, 220. I stopped at 220," he said. After spending the early part of his career in Montreal, he hit the road. In 1962, he was paired with Tony Gonzales as The Masked Medics tag team that competed in Tennessee, Texas, and the Gulf Coast territory. In all, Don's career lasted 14 years. He's retired now and living in Louisiana, having worked as a longshoreman after his wrestling career ended. Don Lortie is unsure what happened to his cousins, and said that his uncle Bob committed suicide. Paul died from an appendix that ruptured while he was wrestling Harry Madison. "Paul Lortie was a great wrestler and he burst his appendix. Wouldn't go to the doctor and died," said Paul "Butcher" Vachon. "Tough, they were tough. They were tough guys, just for the sake of being tough."

ROUGEAU

Lutte Internationale 2000, the Montreal-based wrestling promotion run by Jacques Rougeau Jr., proudly offers family-orientated action, without the hardcore antics common on other shows. Family is a word that is strong within the Rougeau clan.

Rougeau Jr. is able to offer up his 12-year-old son J.J. as a performer, the fourth generation of Rougeau grappler, at the same time he is talking his brother Armand into suiting up after 16 years on the injury shelf. In 1999, he even convinced his father Jacques Sr. that teaming up with Raymond and Jacques at 69 years of age was a logical thing to do.

"There have been many family acts in wrestling in the past, but I don't believe any family has attained the standards set by the Rougeaus," said WWF honcho Vince McMahon in August 1994 in the Toronto *Sun*. "Both inside and outside the ring, the Rougeaus are wonderful human beings, which is the highest compliment you can pay any competitor."

Eddie Auger started the wrestling ball rolling, competing for 28 years, starting in the 1940s. As uncle to Johnny and

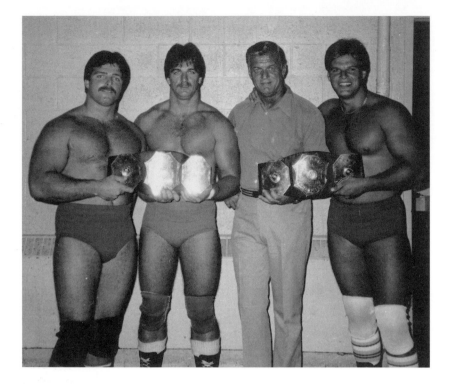

THE ROUGEAUS: (FROM LEFT): RAYMOND, ARMAND, JACQUES SR., AND JACQUES JR. PHOTO: ROUGEAU FAMILY

Jacques Rougeau, he was instrumental in their careers, both as someone to look up to and someone to help with the training. In his autobiography, *Johnny Rougeau*, Johnny calls Auger a second father, uncle and older brother with a heart of gold. Auger wrestled right up until his last match against Frank Valois, just days before his death from pancreatic cancer in December 1973. The funeral was attended not only by everyone in the Quebec wrestling scene of the day, but also Jean Beliveau, Rocket Richard, Reggie Chartrand, Leo Rivet and other prominent Quebecers.

Johnny Rougeau turned out to be the best-known of the Rougeaus, a Quebec superstar both in and out of the ring. At one point, he was receiving more than 400 letters a week through his fan club. Thankfully, he had his younger brother Jacques around to help with the replies.

THE FAMILY IN ST. SULPICE. (FROM LEFT): VIRGINIA AND
HUSBAND JACQUES SR., RAYMOND, 17, JOANNE, 15, ARMAND, 13,
DIANE, 7, JACQUES JR., 11. PHOTO: ROUGEAU FAMILY

Jacques turned pro not long after his brother in 1955, but
didn't do very well. "I wasn't making any money. I was starving
to death," he said. So Jacques went to work as a doorman at
Johnny's Mocambo night club, and made better money. When
the club was sold in 1965, Johnny started up a wrestling
promotion and wanted his brother to be involved.

As the main star of the promotion, it was Jacques who
would battle the imported monster heels like Abdullah the
Butcher and Ivan Koloff. His career highlight was taking on
The Sheik (Ed Farhat) at Montreal's Jarry Park in front of
26,000 fans. Away from Montreal, Rougeau found the most
success in the Buffalo-centred NWF promotion, where he held
their version of the world title. After losing a finger on a saw
while working for his cousin building benches, Rougeau
dropped wrestling and went into business for himself. He sold
lawn furniture for five years, then moved to Florida to sell
mobile homes. Today, he lives the life of a retired snowbird,
spending summers in Quebec and winters in Florida.

As a teen, Raymond Rougeau loved to work out, and by 16,
he was lifting 350 pounds on the bench press. His father asked

if he wanted to try wrestling. Raymond gave it some thought and agreed, entering Luigi Macera's school. "We had a couple of Mexican guys that were wrestling here in those days," recalled Jacques Sr. "Those guys were acrobats. So I used to bring the two Mexicans to the gym too every morning with Macera, and that's where we taught Raymond. First thing you know, the kid became good and was real good. The kid learned fast."

Raymond made his pro debut in 1971 in Joliette at age 16. He soon hit the road to learn more about the business. Tagging with his younger brother Jacques Jr., the Rougeau brothers had a couple of great runs in the WWF, almost winning the tag team titles on numerous occasions. Shortly after debuting in the WWF in 1986, the brothers realized they weren't being appreciated by the fans in the U.S. so they turned heel as the Fabulous Rougeau Brothers. As Ray told the Montreal *Gazette* in 1993: "After working as crowd favourites our entire careers, we were getting death threats. It was great." After retiring from full-time wrestling, Raymond worked as a commentator on WWF broadcasts, both in English and in French. He still suits up occasionally for his brother's shows. "Personally, I think my time has passed. I'm still in great shape. But, I'm not 20 anymore," Raymond said. "I'm doing it to help him out, basically. That's it, because I don't want to wear the tights anymore. I'm done."

Jacques Jr., five years younger than Raymond, followed in 1977, though no one really expected him to enter the mat wars. As a teen, he was tall — 6-foot-4 — and skinny. But he bulked up to a fighting weight of 240 pounds and started pro at age 16 for Stampede Wrestling. His father credits the family barn. "I had a ring put in the barn and that's where we started to teach Jacques to wrestle. He worked out for about six months too, and then went to Calgary to work for Stu Hart. That's where he broke in."

Jacques was the reason the Rougeaus disappeared from the WWF scene in 1989, wanting time off. His brother made the jump to announcing, and after a year, Jacques came back as The Mountie, truly one of the best characters from Vince

McMahon and the WWF. The gimmick even managed to work up the actual RCMP, and it was eventually ruled by the courts that Jacques Jr. couldn't portray The Mountie character in Canada. After another sabbatical in 1992, Jacques joined with Pierre Carl Ouellet to become The Quebecers, and finally won the WWF tag titles that had always eluded him and Raymond. Later, in WCW, they were known as The Amazing French Connection. He dabbled in promoting over the years, including a WCW show at the Montreal Forum where he pinned Hulk Hogan. "He respected the Rougeau family and me enough to come up here and make me look like a king," Jacques Jr. said of Hogan. Today, Jacques Jr. runs a wrestling school and promotes shows every couple of months.

RAYMOND ROUGEAU DEBUTS IN 1971 UNDER THE GUIDANCE OF UNCLE JOHNNY.
PHOTO: LEDUC COLLECTION

Armand, 16 months older than Jacques, began wrestling in 1982. He trained with his brother Raymond, but never really made it big. Armand was injured in 1986, had disks removed from his spine, and was forced to retire from the mat game. After retiring he took to running a garage. In December 2001, Armand returned to tag with his brothers, though it was a one-off deal.

Joanne, sister to Raymond, Jacques and Armand (the other sister is Diane), was a very successful bodybuilder for a number of years until joining the WWF in 1995 as a marketing specialist and promoter for Quebec and the Maritimes. She worked with the WWF until 1999. For a time, she was married to wrestler Denis Gauthier. Their son, Denis Gauthier, is an NHLer with the Calgary Flames.

As the oldest of the Rougeau clan, Jacques Sr. is content with the family's legacy, though quick to downplay it as well. "The Rougeaus were always well known here in Quebec. Outside Quebec . . . the Cormiers were very popular in New Brunswick, but if you went into northern Quebec, like Quebec City, that would be the Baillargeons. We were always very popular here, starting with Johnny. We were always the top names here as far as wrestling goes."

VACHON

PAUL "THE BUTCHER" VACHON.
PHOTO: L'IL AL COLLECTION

When the careers of Maurice, Paul and Diane Vachon are assessed, it's important to add some colour. As Mad Dog, The Butcher and Viviane Vachon, respectively, the siblings were three of the greatest wrestlers ever to come out of Canada. The next generation, Mike Vachon, son of Maurice, and Luna Vachon, daughter of Paul, didn't fare quite as well in the pro game, but are still well worthy of their surname.

When their sister Diane started to show interest in a wrestling career in the late 1960s, older brothers Maurice and Paul Vachon were immediately supportive. "She used to work in an office, and she used to hate that. She tried to work manual labour — brick, shovel, and work like a man. She was strong like a man anyway," said Maurice. Diane said that she wanted to try wrestling, so Maurice called up Lillian Ellison — The Fabulous Moolah — to begin her training.

VIVIANE VACHON.

The brothers were her biggest supporters. "My sister was a beautiful woman, highly intelligent," said Paul. "She could do anything. She was a model. But she wanted to wrestle so she could travel." He recalled offering her some advice — always be feminine. "She reminded me, year after year, 'You always told me that and I always dressed nice and smiled.'"

While the Vachon brothers ran the Grand Prix Wrestling promotion in Montreal during the 1970s, a feud developed with the Montreal Athletic Commission, who didn't allow women's wrestling within the city limits. It was okay for Viviane Vachon to perform in the suburb of Verdun, but not in Montreal itself, in its famed Forum. It gave Mad Dog an idea one summer day. "I said, 'Tomorrow morning, Viviane, I want you to wear beautiful shorts, red shorts, and a nice top and I'm going to make you a sign 'Equal rights for women wrestlers.' I want you to go 100 feet in front of city hall, in front of the mayor's office in Montreal, and protest because you're not allowed to wrestle in your hometown.' So we sent her to do that at 9 o'clock in the morning and she did that all day. We sent all our friends from the newspaper around, all the TV people. She made the headlines everywhere. She got more publicity than anybody you can think of." The rule against women wasn't changed immediately, but it didn't matter. The media attention made Viviane an even bigger star.

Besides the wrestling, which she excelled at, Viviane was also a talented singer, releasing a few records in Quebec. She was married to wrestler Buddy Wolfe for a time, and was the subject of a documentary film made in the late 1970s, *Wrestling Queen*. Viviane was killed at age 40, along with her nine-year-old daughter Julie when their car was struck by a drunk driver in August 1991.

LUNA VACHON, RIGHT, WITH HER PROTÉGÉ ANGEL IN FLORIDA IN 1984. PHOTO: MIKE LANO

At 17, Paul "The Butcher" Vachon decided to follow in his older brother's footsteps. More than four inches taller than Mad Dog, he'd had a decent amateur career before turning pro. Paul was initially billed as a Russian before re-assuming the family name. It was a big role to fill. "The first year I was in the business, Mad Dog and Johnny Rougeau had been having some feuds," said The Butcher. "Mad Dog left for Texas, and I had just started. The promoter had the ads in the newspaper read, 'Rougeau versus Vachon.' Then I show up!"

Paul wrestled from 1955 to 1986, and travelled the world. He was able to be a star with his brother Mad Dog, his fictional brother Stan Vachon, and on his own, especially overseas. Like his sister, Paul found his way into films, except his were made in India. The Butcher had befriended wrestler Dara Singh in Canada, and when they met up again in India, Singh, who was a movie star at home, had Paul act as a villain. Since his retirement from pro wrestling — after running the massive Mad Dog Vachon retirement tour in 1986 — Paul has worked as a salesman, first for gym equipment and now for magnetic health products.

The first of the kids to turn pro was Mike Vachon, who wrestled for only a few years in territories like Portland, Texas and Minnesota. "He was good, but he was not big enough," said his father.

"He was actually a pretty good little wrestler," said his uncle Paul. "I say *little*. He was almost as big as his dad. You want to be careful around Mad Dog when you say *little*. He didn't have the stick-to-itiveness that his father had."

Born in the United States, but raised in Montreal while her father and uncle ran the Grand Prix promotion, it's no surprise that Gertrude Vachon wanted to be a wrestler. "She could have done anything. She was a beautiful girl and very intelligent — smart, good-looking, of course, like her dad," said Paul with a laugh. "All she ever wanted to do [was wrestle]. Her idol was my sister, Viviane, who was a wrestler. She had been watching her ever since she was four or five years old. That's all she ever did. I told her she was a lunatic because all she wanted to do was wrestle."

As a teen, Paul showed her the ropes while he worked for the WWF, arriving early in the arenas. "We'd get up in the ring and I'd show her a few moves. Then some of the guys would start coming in and they'd help me start putting her through some paces." Gertrude was sent to work out with Moolah, who dubbed her Angel Vachon, then Paul hooked her up for a tour of Japan.

Her big break came in 1986 when Kevin Sullivan was leading a demonic cult-type group in the Florida promotion, and she was dubbed Luna, half of The Daughters of Darkness. Since then, Luna has had a few major runs through the big promotions, including two stints with the WWF. With her gravelly voice and crazy antics, it's easy to draw comparisons to her famed uncle. She is married to wrestler Dave Heath, better known as Gangrel.

THE GARVIN 'BROTHERS' (FROM LEFT), TERRY, JIMMY AND RONNIE. PHOTO: L'IL AL COLLECTION

Managers to the Stars

EDDIE CREATCHMAN

For all the great wrestlers that Canada has put out over the years, there have been very few great managers. The Montreal territory, however, was an exception because it needed someone to convince the French-speaking population that their English-speaking charges were evil in either language.

The greatest of them all was Eddie "The Brain" Creatchman.

Best known for his cigar, sunglasses and Star of David, Creatchman was a long-time manager on Quebec's circuit. He achieved his fame managing The Sheik and Abdullah the Butcher throughout the province. In fact, he was so successful managing The Sheik, that there was a riot at the Montreal Forum in 1970. Of course, that impressed The Sheik, and he brought Creatchman to Detroit to manage him.

"The Boss" Creatchman started out as a referee in the late 1940s. When necessary, he would fight in the ring as well, though he was never a top wrestler. Besides The Sheik and Abdullah, The Brain also managed Tarzan "The Boot" Tyler, Don Leo Jonathan, Gilles "The Fish" Poisson and Crybaby George Cannon. Outside the ring, Creatchman owned a scrapyard — evidently a business lucrative enough to provide him with a Cadillac to get around in. He died in March 1994 at 66.

Some other managers of note:

J.R. FOLEY

The most devious of managers in Stampede Wrestling from the late '70s to the mid-'80s, John Foley was a legitimately tough old wrestler from England. Foley's Army, consisting of

EDDY CREATCHMAN (LEFT) WITH MONTREAL PROMOTER LUCIEN
GREGOIRE AND THE SHEIK. PHOTO: CREATCHMAN FAMILY

the likes of Archie Gouldie, Duke Myers, Kerry Brown, David
Shultz, The Viet Cong Express and Dynamite Kid, made life
miserable for the Hart boys. With his constant interference,
run-ins, sneak attacks, and introduction of foreign objects,
Foley was always helping his wrestlers win titles. He died in
1988 of lung cancer.

ABU WIZAL

Beruit's Milad Elzein came to Canada and befriended Ross
Hart. Selling programs at the Stampede shows eventually led
to a gig as a manager. Despite being only 5-foot-2, Wizal made
himself visible throughout his stay in Stampede in the late
'80s. Today, Elzein is a property manager in Calgary.

J.R. Foley and
Dynamite Kid.
Photo: Bob
Leonard

Floyd Creatchman and the Great
Samu. Photo: Creatchman family

"PRETTY BOY" FLOYD CREATCHMAN

The son of "The Brain" was a manager in the late '70s and '80s in Montreal. He actually started out as a wrestler before turning to managing. His stable included Hercules Ayala, Sweet Daddy Siki, Pretty Boy Simms, The Great Samu, Richard Charland and Shiek Ali (Stephen Petitpas). At one point, he had a feud against his father's stable of grapplers.

FRENCHY MARTIN

The retired Martin managed fellow Quebecer Dino Bravo in the WWF in the mid-'80s. The Quebec flag he always waved proved to be a good weapon.

TARZAN "THE BOOT" TYLER

Having retired from active wrestling, Tyler tried to replace "The Brain" Creatchman in Montreal in the mid-'80s. His impressive stable included Sailor White, The Masked Superstar, Mad Dog Lefebvre, Rick Valentine, King Tonga, Richard Charland and Jos Leduc.

JOHN TOLOS

He had a forgettable stint in Herb Abrams' UWF promotion, managing Cactus Jack and Bob Orton Jr. led John Tolos to a brief run in the WWF as "The Coach", where "Mr. Perfect" Curt Hennig was his main star.

ABU WIZAL WITH VOKHAN SINGH (GARY ALBRIGHT), LEFT, AND MAKHAN SINGH (MIKE SHAW). PHOTO: MILAD ELZEIN

Roll Call

KENNY ACKLES

Nova Scotia's Kenny Ackles worked as a successful junior heavyweight from the 1930s to the 1950s before shifting into movies and television. A bodybuilder, he got into wrestling in Boston, and carried 215 pounds on his 5-foot-11 frame.

KENNY ACKLES.
PHOTO: MELBY COLLECTION

Ackles had long runs in some of the territories that used a lot of junior heavyweights — Los Angeles, Oklahoma, Houston, Columbus and Boston among them. He was best known for the use of the abdominal stretch, a move that a fan book from the 1950s claimed had "been barred in many states."

"Blonde, good-looking, and extremely supple . . . almost to the point of being double-jointed," was how wrestling historian J Michael Kenyon recalled Ackles. "He worked in the old, upright manner, almost slowly transitioning from move to move, as though he were demonstrating holds to the audience."

By the late 1950s, Ackles had all but retired from wrestling for acting. Among his credits are *Bodyhold* (1949), *L'il Abner* (1959), *Death Wish* (1974) and *Night of the Juggler* (1980). He also appeared on the TV programs *Edge of Night* and *Guiding Light*. Ackles died in November 1986 in Houston.

JOHN ANSON

JOHN ANSON.

John Anson was a real dual personality. On the West Coast, he was Handsome John Anson, a well-liked babyface. Everywhere else, he was known as Karl von Shotz, an evil German heel.

As von Shotz, the Vancouver-born Anson had multiple reigns as the Detroit version of the NWA tag team champs, with Kurt von Hess. As a single, his greatest success came in Stampede Wrestling, where he was a two-time North American champ in 1976. He also held titles in Hawaii, Portland, Newfoundland and Japan.

During his 13-year career, Anson went across Canada and the U.S., Hawaii and Japan and wrestled more than 6,000 matches. "I was one of the few Canadians that went international," explained Anson. "I did a lot of travelling."

OVILA ASSELIN

Tony Lanza discovered Ovila Asselin working out at a beach near Montreal. The 6-foot-1, 225-pound Asselin had been Mr. Canada at 17. Lanza took the bodybuilder under his wing and trained him for his debut in 1948.

Asselin was a mid-level star, known for his drop kicks and Irish whip, along with his sculpted

OVILA ASSELIN.
PHOTO: TONY LANZA

physique. "He didn't wrestle with the light heavyweights, but he was more that type. He didn't go out very much. He stayed in Quebec," said Bob "Legs" Langevin. One of Asselin's best friends was Eddie Auger, the uncle of Johnny and Jacques Rougeau.

Asselin worked into the early '70s before calling it quits. He then bought a hotel and restaurant outside of Montreal. He passed away a few years ago.

BOBBY BASS

Dennis Baldock can laugh now about his start in professional wrestling. It was never a dream, his family wasn't made up of wrestlers. Instead, it was a newspaper ad that changed his life.

"My father, he's reading the paper. . . . He said, 'Son, there's an advertisement in here for Whipper Billy Watson's School of Wrestling.' He lowered the paper and said, 'I think you're big and ugly enough to do that!'"

The story tells one a lot about Baldock, who was best known during his career as "No Class" Bobby Bass. For one, he's got an excellent sense of humour, but

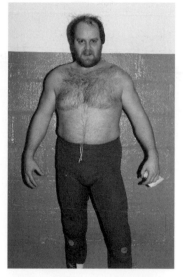

"No Class" Bobby Bass.
Photo: Bobby Bass

he's also comfortable with his place in wrestling lore. Never a big-name international superstar, even though he competed across North America (not to mention Japan, Germany, England and Australia), Baldock made an excellent living travelling from territory to territory, wreaking havoc as a heel wherever he went.

Whipper Billy Watson's School of Wrestling was actually run by The Whip's son Phil Watson, a.k.a. Whipper Watson Jr. Phil was "an excellent, excellent teacher" said Baldock, who trained with him for about a year. "He said I was ready after six months, but I always wanted to be a bump-taker, a jobber. That's what I wanted to be. But things turned out different," explained Baldock.

The nickname "No Class" was given to him by the late Stampede Wrestling announcer Ed Whalen after Baldock and Len Denton threw a midget into the air. "Little Louie, I think it was. . . . We threw him too high and he hit the light and broke it. 'No Class' Bobby Bass has stuck ever since."

Besides that pseudonym, Baldock was also Bobby Kincaid and "Texas Outlaw" Bobby Bass — pretty funny considering he was born in Nova Scotia and spent his youth in Toronto. He retired from wrestling in 1990, but recently got involved with the fledgling Real Action Wrestling promotion in the Maritimes.

SAMMY BERG

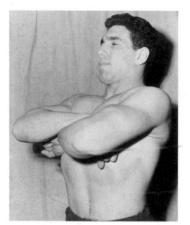

SAMMY BERG.
PHOTO: MELBY
COLLECTION

After winning the Mr. Canada bodybuilding contest in 1948, Sammy Berg Jr. turned to pro wrestling, learning the new skills from Tony Lanza and from the crew at Camp Maupas in the Laurentians. He had also been both an amateur wrestler and a swimmer at McGill University.

At 6-foot-4 and 238 pounds, Berg was one of the bigger wrestlers of the 1950s. He was a babyface around Quebec, but when he hit the road to Los Angeles, New York City, Texas or Boston, he was a heel. In October 1951, he lost an NWA title match to Lou Thesz in Memphis.

Still, "Slammin'" Sammy Berg is best remembered for his physique. "He had a hell of a body on him," said Jacques

Rougeau Sr. "He made it pretty good, except I think that his head was a little too big and somebody put him in his place and he quit." In the 1960s, Berg appeared in a few films as Samson Burke, including *The Adventures of Ulysses*, *Death Trip*, *Kill Me With Kisses*, *Five Into Hell* and *The Three Stooges Meet Hercules*.

Blood & Guts: Canada's Wrestling Flick

Canada has produced many great wrestlers over the years, but it has also produced one of the most unique wrestling movies.

Blood & Guts was made in 1978 and was a true product of Canadiana, directed by the Liverpool-born, Canadian-raised Paul Lynch (later known for *Prom Night*) and filmed in Hamilton.

DANNY O'NEILL (WILLIAM SMITH) AND JIM DAVENPORT (BRIAN PATRICK CLARKE), RIGHT, HOIST LUCKY BROWN (MICHELINE LANCTOT) IN THE AIR. PHOTO: TORONTO SUN

The Toronto *Sun* review called *Blood & Guts* "a wonderful worm's-eye-view of second-rate wrestlers on the tryout circuit, most of them destined to travel backroads forever. The action (and there's plenty of it) is fast, funny and often outrageous, a unique blend of sport and vaudeville that suggest what might have happened if Roman gladiators had to play Poughkeepsie."

William Smith (*Rich Man, Poor Man*) was the star of the flick, but for Canadian wrestling fans, the real joy comes in seeing all the Hamilton-based, small-time wrestling talent throughout the movie. Murray Cummings is a TV announcer, Reggie Love, Brian Mackney, Vic Rossetani and Bob Markus are all there. Cool Cat Jackson (Vincent Bright) has the biggest role of the bunch as Vince. Bull Johnston and his sons Danny and Randy all appear as well.

Danny Johnston explained how it all came about. "Everything kind of fell into place perfect because we had everything," he said. With his brother, Johnston ran a gym in Hamilton where they trained wrestlers. The production people were in awe when they first came to the gym. "They said, 'Oh my God, everything we need is right here.' So they signed us."

"It wasn't an . . . award-winning movie," Johnston joked. "You know what the best is? We got everybody involved that we knew. All the wrestlers, all the guys from around town got involved. We got friends involved as extras. We had friends of ours involved in fight scenes in bars. We even had the mayor of Stoney Creek as a referee! It was perfect, because we figured this might be a one-time thing, so we grabbed everybody we could, just to make Hamilton, just to put it on the map."

BRUTE BERNARD

Brute Bernard got his start in pro wrestling thanks to Mad Dog Vachon, who discovered a 350-pound, 6-foot-2, 13-year-old Jim Prudhomme working out in a Montreal gym. Vachon convinced him to try wrestling, and he whipped himself into shape. "I've never seen anybody work so hard in all my entire

BRUTE BERNARD (LEFT) AND SKULL MURPHY. PHOTO: L'IL AL COLLECTION

life. He lost about 100 pounds," Vachon said. Bernard debuted around Quebec for promoter Jack Britton, but he was to make a bigger name for himself elsewhere.

As a tag team, Bernard and Hamilton's Skull Murphy are probably Canada's greatest all-time non-related duo. They were world tag champs in Australia, the WWWF and Florida, and could scare fans with ease, putting on credible exhibitions of mayhem. "Brute Bernard and Skull Murphy were both very versatile in their ability. They could wrestle, they could fight, they could brawl," said Bernard's long-time manager Gary Hart. In 1970, Murphy died of an overdose of sleeping pills and Bernard was forced to go out on his own.

Bernard's thick French accent prevented him from being a star on the microphone, so he heightened the "Brute" part of his name, grunting on TV, swearing at fans, acting like a wildman. "Bernard would pick up anything, I don't care what it was, and hit anybody — timekeeper, announcer, referee, anyone," Hart said. "My job mainly was just taking shit away from him that he was going to hit people with."

Bernard wrestled into the 1980s, and found success both as a singles and tag team, particularly with "The Missouri Mauler" Larry Hamilton. He was married to female grappler Betty Jo Hawkins. Penny Banner, friend and tag partner of Hawkins, said that Bernard killed himself accidentally in July 1984. "Brute shot himself accidentally target practicing in his backyard. Someone told him the bullet was a 'hollow point' and he thought that meant blank and put it to his head."

DINO BRAVO

There was a time in 1986 when Dino Bravo was bigger than Hulk Hogan. The two were scheduled to wrestle each other in the main event at the Montreal Forum when, at the last minute, fearing a heel reception for Hogan, the bout was changed to two matches against separate opponents. The fallout from the match lead to Bravo leaving the WWF for a time, until returning as a full-fledged heel over a year later.

A YOUNG DINO BRAVO. PHOTO: OLIVER COLLECTION

So it was front page news in Montreal in March 1993 when Bravo, 44, died in a hail of gunfire at his apartment in an apparent mob-style hit. It was a terrible end to a great career.

Bravo, whose real name was Adolfo Bresciano, started wrestling in Montreal in 1970 under the guidance of Edouard Carpentier, Gino Brito and Luigi Macera. He quickly moved up the ranks in Quebec, usually teaming with Carpentier or Brito. In the late '70s and early '80s, Bravo set out on the road and improved his skills, even winning the WWWF tag titles with Dominic

BRAVO DURING HIS WWF DAYS. PHOTO: TONY LANZA

Denucci in 1978. In 1981, Bravo invested in the Montreal-based International Wrestling promotion, and became its top star.

In 1985, he entered the WWF, initially as Canadian champion. After his non-match with Hogan, Bravo came back with bleached-blond hair and teamed with Greg Valentine, and later Earthquake. He had bulked up considerably since his earlier days.

A devotion to working out is one of the things that his friend Rick Martel will always remember about Bravo. "I liked being around him. He was a good influence in the gym. We'd go work out together and he was really good to work out with. He would push me a lot."

BULLDOG BOB BROWN

Bulldog Bob Brown has to be listed among the greats of Canadian Pro Wrestling. Not only did he wrestle for 33 years, but he worked as the booker for Stampede Wrestling, Grand Prix Wrestling and West Four Wrestling Alliance, and was a key component in the resurgence of Vancouver's All Star Wrestling from 1969 to 1974.

BULLDOG BOB BROWN. PHOTO: TERRANCE MACHALEK

Born in Winnipeg, Brown became a police officer after high school. Alex Turk, a local promoter, told Brown to give wrestling a try. After putting in time in the Winnipeg clubs, Brown trained with Verne Gagne in Minneapolis on weekends. Soon, he was noticed by Bob Geigel and Pat O'Connor, who signed him to a deal and invited him down to Kansas City. It would become his home territory for the rest of his career.

At 6-foot-1, 227 pounds, with a less-than-chiselled physique and a bad brushcut, Brown didn't really stand out in any way physically. At the microphone and with ring psychology, however, he was a wizard, inciting or pleasing the crowds at will. In fact, he was so good at talking that numerous promotions gave him work as a colour commentator as well.

Brown's son David worked in Stampede as referee David Putnam, and his nephew Kerry Brown had a short, but successful wrestling career in the 1980s.

Brown's last big run was in Tony Condello's West Four promotion in Winnipeg in the late '80s, where he helped develop the careers of Chris Jericho, Lance Storm and Cyrus Don Callis.

In 1996, Brown suffered a massive heart attack, and was pronounced dead twice before being revived. That ended his wrestling career. The following February, another heart attack stopped the Bulldog for good at age 57.

CRYBABY CANNON

GEORGE CANNON.
PHOTO: OLIVER COLLECTION

Though best known to wrestling fans as a manager, TV announcer and promoter for the Windsor-based *Superstars of Wrestling* TV show in the 1970s and early 1980s, George "Crybaby" Cannon had a decent ring career as well.

Born George Arnold in Montreal, he took up pro wrestling in 1953, learning the trade in Japan for a couple of years before returning to Canada. For a while, he went as "Man Mountain" Cannon, an ode to his rather significant girth. At one point on the *Superstars* show, he even had a "Big Splash Competition" with the even more massive Haystacks Calhoun. The event saw each competitor flopping on top of one another in the ring to see who had the most lethal finishing move. His "Crybaby" nickname came from his unique ability to wipe the sweat from his eyes so it looked like he was crying.

In the late 1960s, Cannon's natural gift of the gab helped him land the hosting gig on a variety TV show in California. In 1970, he moved back to Windsor, Ontario and turned to managing. Cannon's big break came as manager for the Fabulous Kangaroos. The Superstars of Wrestling promotion was formed shortly thereafter, running shows in southern Ontario through to the Maritimes. Cannon died in July 1994 from cancer. He was 62.

TONY CONDELLO

It could be argued that no one was more important to the Winnipeg wrestling scene than Tony Condello, first as a wrestler, then as a trainer, and finally as a promoter, Condello shaped the business there.

Condello came to Canada from Italy as a child with his parents. He enjoyed working out, competing in amateur wrestling at the local YMCA. At 17 years of age, he got invited along by some pros to an AWA TV taping in Minneapolis. After initially declining, Condello was talked into getting in the ring by

"TORPEDO" TONY CONDELLO. PHOTO: TONY CONDELLO

AWA promoters Wally Karbo and Verne Gagne. The youngster was to face Lars Anderson. "I didn't know anything about pro wrestling," confessed Condello. "I was fighting for my life. Then he started to lead me into the match. He said 'Hey kid, it's not what you think it is. Just follow me, and you'll be fine.'" His payoff was $75 for the match, but he lost his amateur status at home.

Condello began working around Winnipeg, and continued to tour with the AWA, usually putting over better-known talent. In 1972, given the lack of work for local wrestlers because the AWA primarily promoted their own talent in town, Condello decided to open a wrestling school to the public — one of the first anywhere — and start a promotion. His best-known graduates are Roddy Piper, Ron Ritchie, Kerry Brown and Buddy Lane.

As a promoter, Condello ran tours around Manitoba, including the infamous "Death Tours" of northern native reserves. Besides promoting on his own, at various times Condello had deals for shows in Winnipeg with Stampede, the WWF, the NWA and even Bill Watts's UWF. He controlled a TV time slot on a local station, and would air whatever promotion he was building at the time. In the late '80s, Condello's *West Four Wrestling Alliance* was on TSN across Canada as well, replacing the defunct *Stampede Wrestling*.

To this day Condello continues to be instrumental in the Winnipeg wrestling scene, now running shows under the IWA banner.

VICTOR DELAMARRE

VICTOR DELAMARRE
PHOTO: CANADIAN
SPORTS HALL OF
FAME

The incredible strongman Victor Delamarre turned to wrestling in 1931 when the world seemed not to care any more about feats of strength. He wrestled an estimated 1,500 bouts during his career, but the Lac St. Jean, Quebec, native never put more than 165 pounds on his 5-foot-4 frame.

"He was a terrible, terrible wrestler, but he was famous as a wrestler," admitted Paul "The Butcher" Vachon. Delamarre's fame came to him early in life. A poor student, he concentrated on his physique. Some of his more notable feats of strength included lifting a world record 309 1/2 pounds with one hand in 1914, lifting 201 pounds with one finger, and lifting 30 Quebec City policemen — each weighing more than 200 pounds — in 1928.

Delamarre was very popular in Quebec. "He was a strongman, and the people believed, they really believed in him," said Legs Langevin.

Before he became a wrestler, Delamarre had worked as a police officer, following in the footsteps of his idol, Louis Cyr, the famed Quebec strongman. Delamarre died in 1955 in Montreal, and is a member of the Canadian Sports Hall of Fame.

PAUL DEMARCO

While working as Paul Demarco, Hamilton's Paul DeMarchi might have been one of the most underrated and hated wrestlers of all time. After graduating from the Factory that was Steeltown, DeMarchi got his break as a colour commentator on a CBC Saturday afternoon wrestling show. After proving he could talk, the next step was proving he belonged.

PAUL DEMARCO.
PHOTO: TERRY DART

Dressed to the nines on TV, with silk suits, diamonds and alligator shoes, Paul Demarco cut quite the figure. He could back up the talk — both his boasts and whatever his manager of the day claimed — in the ring. "He was a hell of a wrestler," said Ed "Moondog" Moretti. "One of the best workers that I ever saw." DeMarchi had great success in California, where he held the U.S. title, and in the southeastern part of the U.S.

In 1973, he walked out of the business, fed up with the crooked promoters, and the racy lifestyle. DeMarchi came back for a run in the AWA as the Russian, Igor Gordienko, in the mid-'80s. He settled in northern California and worked a variety of jobs, including running a wrestling gym for a time.

Hamilton — What's in the Water?

They called it The Factory, and having survived it, wrestlers could go into any territory, say they were from Hamilton, Ontario, and be hired on the spot. The respect for the training in Hamilton was simply that great.

No other place in the world could lay claim to the calibre of names that came out of Hamilton: The Sharpes, The Tolos Brothers, The Flying Scotts, Johnny Powers, Dewey Robertson, Billy Red Lyons; all were born, raised and trained in Hamilton. Others like Ivan Koloff came to Hamilton to hone their skills.

There's a number of reasons that Hamilton, a large industrial city about an hour's drive from Toronto, churned out so many tough guys.

According to Chuck Molnar, who wrestled for five years, Hamilton was a city "where construction and steel plants produced an environment of tough young men who needed an outlet to prove to themselves that they were capable of progressing physically beyond their workplace, and wrestling became their outlet."

WENTWORTH'S GYM. PHOTO: BOB HODGSON

Youth who wanted to be wrestlers found mentors galore in Hamilton, whether it was in one of the many gyms where the pros worked out, or with the family up the street whose son was in the business. Mike Sharpe used to work out in his yard, and that's how Sandy Scott first met him and started to bodybuild.

The gyms and the trainers in Hamilton are easily the biggest part of the legacy.

Al Spittles, whose wrestling name was Al Hamilton, ran a colourful gym where bodybuilders and wrestlers shared space in a two-car garage. The mat would come out at 7 p.m. Spittles helped everyone with the weight training, and Jimmy "Red" Simms handled much of the work on the mats. According to Jack Laskin, the gym left quite a bit to be desired. "It was a horrible place. You had to be dedicated to want to go to Spittles." It wasn't insulated, and had a wood stove to try to keep the entire garage/gym warm. "It should have been condemned a long time ago."

Eventually the garage *was* condemned, and Spittles opened a new location in the Westdale part of Hamilton. The filthy, hard mat went along for the move. "I never realized how hard that mat was until I had been away for a while wrestling professional," Laskin said.

Spittles wasn't the only place in town in the 1940s and '50s. "We had lots of facilities to work out in. There were several gyms, besides having weights and the rest of that, that had good wrestling rooms, mats," said Dano McDonald. "A lot of the guys that were real top wrestlers, they didn't just stay in one gym all the time. They'd go around. I think that way they got exposed to different people. Any of them that looked like they had any sort of promise, they'd take an interest in them."

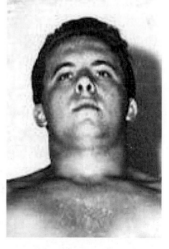

CHUCK MOLNAR

The other big gym in Hamilton, from the mid-'50s onward, was Jack Wentworth's. Over 100 wrestlers came out of the gym, run by Jack Hodgson, who wrestled as an amateur and as a pro, his biggest successes coming in England. "Powerlock" Johnny Powers was one of the grads. "Jack Wentworth, he worked you out. When you left him, you were reasonably tough and you also knew the game." Another noted Hamilton trainer, Benny Lima, worked out of various establishments.

In the '70s, Dewey Robertson's place in Burlington was the scene for training and biweekly cards between students and other local talent. In the '80s, Nick Decarlo ran a gym for a while. Over the years, many different facilities hosted wrestling, from the municipal swimming pool — where the ring would be set up over the pool — to the Forum, Copps Coliseum, and the Kiwanis Boys and Girls club.

Once they were trained, the wrestlers had many choices of places to work, being deep in the heart of the most populated part of Canada. In the '50s, Joe Maich ran the "bullshit" circuit, as it was called, around southern Ontario, but everyone aspired to working the mecca — Maple Leaf Gardens in Toronto. American big towns like Buffalo, Cleveland or Pittsburgh weren't too far away either.

It's important not to discount the impact of seeing the local boys making good. A fan in the stands knew very well that, with hard work, they could be in the ring too. "The faces that I saw at the weekly wrestling events became the same faces that I encountered coming out of these gyms," said Molnar. "I suppose we all shared the same dream, and that was to become one of those stars of the mat that we wanted to emulate. I had seen some of the wannabes cry because they either weren't big enough, tough enough, good enough to get into the pro ranks. I don't remember working at anything so hard as I did at getting to the pros."

PAUL DIAMOND

There are two Paul Diamonds enshrined in our Canadian Roll Call of Greats, and Toronto's Paul Lehman was the first, debuting in England in 1960 and wrestling for 12 years. He isn't happy with sharing the ring name. "Tom Boric used a lot of names, and the only recognition he got was when he used my name. I never thought about it until I got on the Web," Diamond said. "I realized 'I wuz robbed.'"

PAUL DIAMOND NAILS GIL HAYES WITH A DROP KICK IN THE LATE 1960S. PHOTO: BOB LEONARD

The name Paul Diamond was actually based on David Janssen's character on the '60s TV show *Richard Diamond, Private Detective.* Diamond worked New York, Cleveland, Tulsa, Houston, San Francisco, Los Angeles, Vancouver, Oregon and Japan. In 1969, he was scheduled to main-event Maple Leaf Gardens against The Sheik, but didn't show up, having scheduled himself to work in California. It led to many difficulties for Diamond getting work after that, as the promoters also worked together to blackball him.

Diamond's last wrestling run was in 1971–72, for Roy Shire in San Francisco. According to Diamond, Shire said that he was "too confident and cocky" and Diamond quit the business a short time later after a falling-out with booker Pat Patterson. He ran a successful deli in Silicon Valley for a number of years following his retirement.

PAUL DIAMOND

PAUL DIAMOND.
PHOTO: MAY COLLECTION

Born in Croatia and raised as a teen in Winnipeg, Tom Boric fulfilled his lifelong dream of becoming a pro soccer player in the old North American Soccer League in the early '80s. Playing in Tampa Bay when the league folded, he decided to give pro wrestling a kick, and learned from the Malenkos at their Florida training school.

In the ring, Boric was Paul Diamond, and found success primarily as a tag team wrestler. He was a part of an early team, called American Force, with a young Shawn Michaels in Texas. Later, he would work for many years with Pat Tanaka as Badd Company, achieving tag gold in the AWA and in Memphis. Diamond worked in the WWF for three years, mostly under masks as Kato the Orient Express, and as Max Moon.

After being released from the WWF in 1993, Boric bounced around for years, working small independents, ECW and running training schools in Texas and Winnipeg.

MICHEL DUBOIS

If you speak French, and your English is weak, it's only logical that you end up as a Russian in the ring, isn't it? That's what happened in the case of Michel Lamarche, of Saint-Lim, Quebec.

Lamarche trained with Edouard Carpentier and started out in 1970 as Michel "Le Justice" Dubois, a name suggested by Montreal promoter Legs Langevin. The Dubois family in Montreal was always in the news, always in trouble with the law. After six months in Kansas City, Dubois terrorized the

scene in Quebec and the Maritimes. "Things were rolling real well for me," recalled Lamarche. "The fact that I was speaking French, I could get the people really hyped."

After finding only moderate success outside Quebec, as Mike "The Justice" Dubois, in 1977, Lamarche made a monumental decision — he needed a new gimmick. On tour with Ivan Koloff, he realized that "The Russian Bear" got heat from the crowd just because he was billed as being from the U.S.S.R. (he was, of course, another Canadian). Koloff suggested Lamarche consider leaving his judicial gimmick behind. "He told me, 'Why don't you change your gimmick to a Russian? There's not too many Russians in the business,'" Lamarche remembered. "'It's easier to do some interviews' because in those days I could barely speak English. So you go to TV and say we are the greatest minds, blah, blah, blah and that was it. So it was easier for my interviews. I would shave my head and it would look really good."

So in 1977, Lamarche went west to San Francisco and, without doing any research on the Russian way of life, became "The Mad Russian" Alexis Smirnoff. The character was a big hit, and he became a star, particularly in Japan, where he even held the IWE World title in 1979 for a stint.

Lamarche retired in 1988 to the San Francisco area, trained wrestlers for a while and has dabbled in acting.

EMILE DUPRÉ

EMILE DUPRÉ.
PHOTO: TERRY DART

In 1956, Shediac, New Brunswick's Emile Goguen was told he had potential as a pro wrestler. He trained under a couple of Maritime old-timers, Vic Butler and Reggie Richard, and debuted in Boston a short time later as Golden Boy Dupré, with bleached blond hair.

But after a few years on the road, the lure of coming home was too much and Dupré ended up taking over the Atlantic Grand Prix promotion from Cowboy Len Hughes in the mid-'60s. "I got involved bigger and bigger and bigger and finally I end up with a television show that lasted 17 years," recalled Dupré. "Then I had some of the best wrestlers the world ever produced."

A roll call of greats came through the Maritimes for decades, usually for the summer tours — the weather was great, scenery spectacular, travel light and expenses low.

These days, having parlayed his wrestling success into many investments, Dupré is content to help his son, Rene E. Dupré, with his wrestling career. The youngster recently signed a developmental deal with the WWE.

PAT FLANAGAN

The story of how Billy Potts became Whipper Watson has been told many times, but the flipside was that his friend Winnett Watson, whom he filled in for in a match in England, was forced to became Pat Flanagan. The new moniker apparently came from a dockside pub on the Irish Sea.

PAT FLANAGAN.
PHOTO: MICHAEL BURNS

Born in Toronto's Beaches area, the youngster excelled at swimming, lacrosse, football and hockey before getting involved with wrestling at the YMCA in 1936. There he met Potts, and they started together overseas. During World War II, Flanagan was in the Royal Canadian Air Force. After the war, he became a regular in the southern Ontario wrestling scene — as a wrestler, TV commentator and referee.

"Peerless" Patrick, or just "Flan," had a career that lasted 40 years, and his speciality was the mule-kick. In March 1985, he died in Whitby, Ontario, after a lengthy illness.

RON GARVIN

"Hands of Stone" Ronnie Garvin reached the top of the wrestling world in 1987 when he beat Ric Flair for the NWA World title. It was also the beginning of the end for him. "I don't think I would have wanted [the World title] two, three years," said Garvin, whose real name is Roger Barnes. "It's hard. You're never home. It's demanding. You've got to do extra, extra, extra all the time. Usually if you just wrestle, you just wrestle. But you have to go special, an interview for this.

Because you're the world champion, you've got to make an appearance."

Once Garvin dropped the belt back to Flair, it wasn't long until he was in the WWF as "Rugged" Ronnie Garvin. The experience further soured him on wrestling, and he quit for good in 1990 at 45 to devote his life full-time to piloting, which he had done since the mid-'70s.

Garvin grew up in Montreal, and was friends with future grapplers Pat Patterson (Pierre Clermont) and Terry Garvin (Terry Joyal). All three trained at Loisiers St. Jean de Baptiste, which was run by a priest. "They had everything at this place. They had boxing, judo, wrestling, professional wrestling, amateur wrestling," said Garvin. Pat Girard turned him into a pro wrestler, and helped him get started on small shows around Montreal.

NWA World champ Ronnie Garvin.

Garvin won numerous titles during his many years in the ring, including tag titles with Terry Garvin. He was also often paired with Jimmy Garvin, his real-life stepson.

TERRY GARVIN

Terry Joyal broke into pro wrestling in the early 1960s in Montreal with his friends Roger Barnes (Ronnie Garvin) and Pat Patterson (Pierre Clermont). Teaming with Barnes as Terry

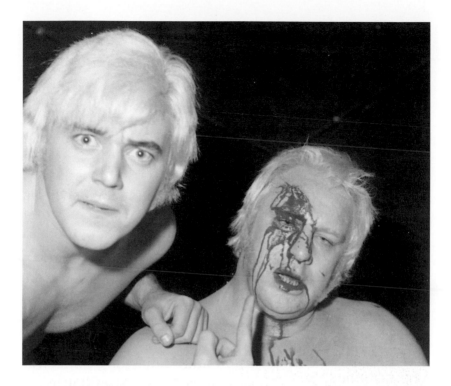

A YOUNG JIMMY GARVIN ISN'T IMPRESSED BY THE BLOOD ON HIS "BROTHER", TERRY GARVIN. PHOTO: L'IL AL COLLECTION

Garvin, the duo were billed as brothers and captured numerous titles together, especially in the southern U.S.

"Terry was a hell of a heel," said Ed "Moondog" Moretti. "Great worker, good reputation in the business. Played a lot of ribs on a lot of guys, but a fun guy to be around."

In 1985, Patterson got Garvin a job in the WWF front office, effectively ending his career in the ring, though he did occasionally referee. In 1992, three former employees came forth with allegations of sexual abuse by WWF personnel, including Garvin, who was subsequently fired. He died in August 1998 from cancer.

GEORGE GORDIENKO

Though considered one of the toughest, most skilled shooters ever in pro wrestling, praised by oldtimers like Lou Thesz and

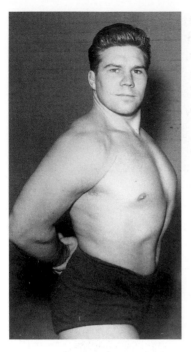

Stu Hart, George Gordienko purposely distanced himself from his previous life after his career ended. Gordienko became a painter and a poet, hiding out on Vancouver Island.

Born in Winnipeg, Gordienko fell under the spell of the great amateur Ole Olsen at 15, which led to his pro training under Joe Pazandak. Debuting after World War II ended, he was dubbed "Wonder Boy" early in his career, but also worked as Flash Gordon. Early stops included San Francisco, Buffalo and Minneapolis.

After taking some time off to try various other jobs, Gordienko was lured back to wrestling by his friend Stu Hart. He would return often to Calgary over the years.

GEORGE GORDIENKO.
PHOTO: AL OLSEN

Knowing that getting work in the U.S. with his heritage would be difficult amidst the Communist hysteria created under Senator Joe McCarthy, Gordienko left North America and never looked back. He started in Australia, but on a whim, headed to Italy instead of Canada. Europe became Gordienko's home, off and on, for the rest of his wrestling career. He was celebrated in England, France and other countries for his wrestling skill and great physique.

Paul Vachon worked with Gordienko in England, and recounted a story he had heard about Gordienko's trip to India. "The Indian wrestlers, they had a big reputation. If you go to India, watch out for them Indian wrestlers, they'll hurt you. He went there, and Gordienko beat them all," the Butcher said. After Vachon had been to India himself, he asked Gordienko what he thought of the Indian wrestlers. "Greatly overrated," was the reply.

It was in Europe that Gordienko became serious about painting, attending St. Martin's School of Art. He even sat down for coffee on one occasion with Pablo Picasso. Turns out the master was also a wrestling fan.

In 1975, Gordienko said goodbye to wrestling for good, settling in Italy. "Europe was very good to me, very rich in cultural experiences that could perhaps be described as unparalleled," he wrote in his autobiographical outline for the Cauliflower Alley Club. In 1990, he returned to Canada to have a hip replaced and to be closer to his brother. Gordienko died in May 2002 of melanoma cancer.

RENÉ GOULET

When his hockey ambitions fizzled, Quebec's Robert Bedard turned to pro wrestling. He started in 1956, wrestling occasionally until 1963, when he got his big break by going to Minneapolis and the AWA. There, he took the name René Goulet, and proceeded to carve out a reputation for himself.

RENÉ GOULET.

Goulet worked as both a babyface and as a heel — Hello Sgt. Jacques Goulet, master of the claw hold! He was a consummate pro, helping new stars like Hulk Hogan develop their skills, and wrestling around the world. He fit in wherever he went. "When you worked in a new territory, everything changed. Most of the time, you would have a different opponent every night, you didn't wrestle the same guys, the same bullshit. That's how you learned the business and became a hell of a worker," Goulet said.

Goulet's biggest successes came in the WWWF, where he was a tag champ with Karl Gotch. Later, as his career ran down, he hosted a segment called Café René on the old *Tuesday Night Titans* TV show. Goulet worked as a road agent for the WWF as well, for 15 years, before being released in 1997. These days, he's retired in Charlotte, NC.

HANGMAN NEIL GUAY

"THE HANGMAN" NEIL GUAY.
PHOTO: BOB LEONARD

There have been many wrestlers to use the moniker of The Hangman over the years, but Quebec's Neil Guay carried around the noose better than most. Whether it was in the WWWF, facing the likes of Bob Backlund or Pedro Morales, or in New Japan, battling Antonio Inoki, Guay was a top-notch grappler.

Guay was a policeman who excelled at judo in his spare time when wrestler Denis Gauthier convinced him to give the mat game a chance. Pat Girard was his trainer. Around Quebec, he would wrestle as Le Bourreau (The Executioner).

In 1986, Guay stopped wrestling because he "wanted to take a break." Five years later he was in a major car accident, and broke his neck. These days, he walks with a cane and his memory is not "too good." He is also an accomplished painter.

OWEN HART

The youngest of the Hart boys, Owen was reluctant to get into wrestling. He wanted to be a phys ed teacher or a fireman, but

MARTHA, ATHENA, OWEN AND OJE HART. PHOTO: MIKE LANO

started wrestling amateur and later went pro to appease his father and brothers. He was great at both, and though he was only 5-foot-11, 220-pounds, Owen soon became a raved-about talent in Stampede Wrestling after his debut in 1986.

Owen took to the road, wrestling in Japan, England, Germany, Mexico, Austria, learning from the different styles and his many opponents. On his initial WWF run, Hart was billed as The Blue Blazer, a masked high flyer. The gimmick didn't take off, so he returned to Japan. In late 1991, he returned to the WWF where he was in various tag teams until his brother Bret got a big singles push. It was natural to play up the sibling rivalry, and a bad guy Owen versus good guy Bret headlined a few pay-per-views. Owen loved being the heel. "[It's the] stress-release of telling people to shut up. You can tell it like it is. Where as a good guy, you have to smile. If a fan mouths off to you, you have to pretend like you didn't hear it," he said in 1998.

As an established WWF superstar, Owen Hart went on to different roles — tag team champion with partners Yokozuna,

Davey Boy Smith and Jeff Jarrett, Intercontinental champion, King of the Ring, and member of the Hart Foundation.

In 1999, Owen returned to the Blue Blazer character, which mocked the good-guy preaching of the 1980s. Hart was pressured by the WWF to take the Blue Blazer further, and an elaborate entrance from the top of the Kemper Arena in Kansas City was set up for the May 23 Over The Edge pay-per-view event. As fans worldwide watched, Hart fell from his perch into the ring, and his death was announced an hour later by the emotional WWF broadcast team of Jim Ross and Jerry Lawler. The accident made headlines and unfortunately will always overshadow his stellar ring career.

GIL HAYES

GIL HAYES.
PHOTO: BOB LEONARD

During his 17-year wrestling career, "Mrs. Hayes's bad boy, Gilbert" travelled the world, and fought the best. He wasn't the biggest of wrestlers — just 5-foot-10 and 247 pounds — but somehow, he managed to keep up with the big boys. "I was a small man in a very big man's business and I had to take my bumps and bruises not just because I was a wrestler, but because I was a small guy in comparison with some of the 300, 340 pounders."

Hayes began his wrestling career in 1966 after meeting Gene Kiniski after a show in Fort Francis, Ontario. Hayes had been a wrestling fan since age 10. After debuting in Winnipeg, Hayes made his way to Calgary, where he carved out a reputation for himself as an egotistical glory-hound. "I always felt that if people came to see me, whether they came to see me get a shit-kicking or come out on top, either way they were coming to see me. And the ones that were coming to see me get a shit-kicking, when I got my hand raised, I let them know what I thought of their attitude. Does that make me egotistical? Or does that make me Gil Hayes?"

Besides his success with Stampede, Hayes had many tours of Japan, and was one of the first outsiders to make it big in Puerto Rico.

Hayes retired from wrestling in 1981 while in Hawaii, with both knees blown. "I quit four times before I finally got out of it," he said. "It's in your blood. You can't manufacture something like this. It's there, and you have no answer for it. You could leave your wife and kids crying at the door but you've got to go do it because it's in your blood."

RON HUTCHISON

"Wonderboy" Ron Hutchison was addicted to wrestling as a child growing up in Toronto, watching legends like The Sheik and Dewey Robertson. So at age 17, while still in high school, he enrolled at Sully's Gym to learn pro wrestling from Sweet Daddy Siki and Johnny Powers.

Though his wrestling career was not that noteworthy, primarily consisting of small Ontario promotions, WWF TV tapings in Toronto and Brantford, and a couple of tours of the Maritimes, Hutchison remains one of the best-known people in the business. Why? It's not because of what he's done, but who he's trained.

RON HUTCHISON WITH MISSY HYATT. PHOTO: MARKO SHARK

In 1983, Hutchison was asked by Siki to train wrestlers with him after Powers left. Hutchison agreed, and continued to train future stars even after Siki left the business in 1994. Graduates of his classes include Edge, Christian, Trish Stratus, Tiger Ali Singh, Johnny Swinger and Joe E. Legend.

DON JARDINE

DON JARDINE IS "THE SPOILER." PHOTO: L'IL AL COLLECTION

For New Brunswick's Don Jardine, wearing a mask, whether it was as The Spoiler or The Super Destroyer, was a liberating experience. "I felt it suited me to be mysterious and intriguing. I like the anonymity of not being harassed by people when I wasn't wearing the mask, because no one knew me," Jardine told the Mid-Atlantic Gateway web site.

Jardine started in wrestling in 1955 with some local wrestlers in New Brunswick. When he moved to Toronto, he found work as "Baby Face" Don Jardine, and Whipper Watson took a liking to him. His career trajectory set, Jardine took his act all over the map. In 1967, Fritz von Erich and Jay Strongbow came up with The Spoiler gimmick for Jardine, and wearing a mask would shape the rest of his career.

The Spoiler was one of the great masked men. Even at 6-foot-4, 250 pounds, Jardine could do remarkable moves — including walking along the ropes while still applying his dreaded claw hold on his opponents. In the early '90s, Jardine promoted shows in Florida before moving to Wetaskin, Alberta. He writes poetry, manages a car wash and is working on a novel about pro wrestling.

ROCKY JOHNSON

As a teenager in 1960s, Wayde Bowles came west to Toronto with his family from Nova Scotia. He was into boxing, but gave wrestling a shot. He would drive a forklift during the day and head to Hamilton to train at Jack Wentworth's gym at night. Soon he was working locally around southern Ontario and developing an excellent physique.

He adopted the name "Soulman" Rocky Johnson and never looked back. Wherever Rocky wrestled, he was a top star, held countless titles, and was always a fan favourite. He also had a memorable stint under a mask as Sweet Ebony Diamond in the Mid-Atlantic territory. Johnson's biggest runs were in California, Florida, Texas, Memphis and the Pacific Northwest. In 1983, Johnson held the WWF tag titles with Tony Atlas.

ROCKY JOHNSON EARLY IN HIS CAREER. PHOTO: OLIVER COLLECTION

Showing the importance of family in his life, after his WWF contract expired, Johnson returned to Hawaii where he was married to Ata Maivia, daughter of High Chief Peter and Leah Maivia, the promoters on the island. He worked out of Hawaii for the duration of his career, often teaming with his brother Jay, a.k.a. Ricky Johnson, who is 10 years younger. When his son, Duane, gave up on football and decided to become a wrestler, Rocky Johnson was there to help him train in Florida. Today, Duane is best known as WWE superstar and actor The Rock. Rocky Johnson still trains wrestlers today, and was involved as promoter and booker for the Urban Wrestling Alliance.

JOHN KATAN

An incredibly successful amateur wrestler, John Katan took to pro wrestling with ease in 1928. He quickly moved up the ranks, and is probably best known for holding the British Empire title on three occasions, starting with his defeat of the great Earl McCready in 1940.

Born in the Ukraine, Katan came to Canada at age four. As a teen, Katan worked in the coal mines near Lethbridge, Alberta, developing strength that would serve him well as a pro.

He travelled widely, and was a star in New Zealand and Australia. On the way to another tour of Oceania, Canada declared war on Japan. "Honest" John found his way home on a Canadian military boat, training the men in hand-to-hand combat during the long trip.

In 1947, Katan bought two wrestling companies in Hamilton and became a promoter. For two years, he wrestled and ran the office, until it became too much for him. In 1949, he retired from the ring but ran the promotion until 1958, when he sold out to Frank Tunney. At that point, Katan bought a golf club in Brantford, Ontario and ran that until his passing in 1968. He was 67 years old.

PAT & MIKE KELLY

The twin tag team Pat and Mike Kelly started out in Hamilton at Jack Wentworth's gym. At 6-foot-2, 240 pounds, with their neatly trimmed red beards and balding heads, they were a memorable duo. When they started out in the mid-'60s, they were known as the Scuffling Hillbillies, complete with a rooster they would place on a corner turnbuckle. "I used to say,

'That rooster works better than you guys.' The rooster would sit there and would never move. They'd carry it in, set in on the turnbuckle, have their match, then take the rooster and go," Ernie Moore recalled. "Apparently, at home, in the morning, it would cock-a-doodle-do, and the neighbours complained. So, eventually, they ended up killing it and eating it. So I always said, 'They killed the best part of that whole tag team.'"

PAT & MIKE KELLY.
PHOTO: TORONTO SUN FILES

As the Kellys, the twins wrestled across North America, but are best known from southern Ontario into Michigan. Like other twin tag-teams, the Kellys would switch in the ring behind the referee's back. They are probably better known for their work in commercials — Oh Henry chocolate bars, Pizza Delight, Coors beer, Canada Trust — and TV appearances on *Seeing Things*.

Pat Kelly, whose real name was Victor Arko, was killed July 5, 1988 in Newfoundland in a van crash with Dave "Wildman" McKigney and Keith "Adorable Adrian Adonis" Franke. Mike Kelly (William Arko) was also in the car, but survived with leg injuries. Mike Kelly was involved in a few Hamilton-based promotions after the accident, but has since left the business.

KLONDIKE BILL

Bill Soloweyko was an accomplished amateur wrestler in Alberta in the '50s when he decided to turn pro. He turned to Stu Hart for training, and impressed everyone with his

KLONDIKE BILL SENDS OKI SHIKIRA FOR A RIDE IN 1970.
PHOTO: L'IL AL COLLECTION

strength. "I wrestled basically as a lumberjack strong man," Soloweyko explained years ago. With his big, barrel-chested physique, beard and bearhug, he went as Klondike Bill. When he was clean-shaven, and feeling like a decent fellow, he would wrestle as Bill "The Brute" Soloweyko, particularly early in his career.

Wrestling took Bill around the world, but he had his greatest successes in Canada and in the Mid-Atlantic territory around Charlotte, NC. After befriending the Crockett family, who owned Mid-Atlantic, Soloweyko was hired as the groundskeeper for the Crockett-owned, Baltimore Orioles-affiliated Charlotte O's baseball team. When the Crocketts sold the team, Bill returned to wrestling, transporting and setting up the ring in each town, a job that he kept when wcw took over the promotion.

In his 40-plus years in wrestling, Soloweyko made many, many friends, as was evident during his last days. Stricken by a neuromuscular disorder similar to Bell's Palsy, he lost the use of his tongue and was speechless for the last months of his life. Friends rallied around him, but Bill lost his fight in October 2000, passing away at 68.

IVAN KOLOFF

The date January 18, 1971 and Ivan Koloff will forever be connected. That was the day "The Russian Bear" did the unthinkable, defeating Bruno Sammartino for the WWF World title. Sure, he only held the belt for three weeks before dropping it to Pedro Morales, but the victory made Koloff into a big-name star.

It was the Rougeaus in Montreal in 1967 that took a young Ontario man working as Red McNulty and turned him into a vicious, Russian heel, with shaved head and beard. Koloff shot to the top, wrestling all the top stars that came into Quebec. "I was wrestling these famous guys that I had heard about — Hans Schmidt and his tag team partner, the Rougeaus, Edouard Carpentier.

IVAN KOLOFF (AS RED McNULTY) TRAPS JERRY CHRISTY WITH A CLAW HOLD. PHOTO: BOB LEONARD

Guys I had heard about, seen on TV, and here now I was wrestling them. That was really a big highlight for me."

Following his loss of the WWWF title, Koloff hit the road, and found much success as a tag-team wrestler, claiming the NWA World tag titles on five occasions, with four different partners — Ray Stevens, Don Kernodle, Nikita Koloff (twice, and, no, they are not related), and Manny Fernandez. Koloff had a great ability to rile up a crowd, spewing Communist rhetoric.

In 1989, he quit wcw rather than move from his Charlotte home to the new Atlanta base. For the next five years, he wrestled on the independent circuit. Today, Koloff is involved in helping people, whether through his ministry or donating his time for autograph sessions for charity.

SANDOR KOVACS

SANDOR KOVACS PUTS THE FLIP ON BIG BILL DROMO WITH A HIP TOSS IN A 1964 MATCH. PHOTO: BOB LEONARD

Having come to Canada at age 10 from Hungary, Sandor Kovacs had to work extra hard at everything to succeed. Wrestling was no different, and he took to it quickly at high school in St. Catharines, Ontario. When World War II broke out, Kovacs enlisted in the navy, but never left Halifax. Instead, he was kept around to wrestle and entertain the troops. Stu Hart and Al "Krusher" Korman were two of the men he would fight against.

When the war ended, Kovacs returned home and quickly became disillusioned by the idea of working on an assembly line. He took Hart up on his invitation to come down to New York, and was quickly thrilling fans in the ring. At 5-foot-11, 220 pounds, Kovacs had to struggle to keep his weight up. Much of his success over the years came in the traditional light-heavyweight territories.

Kovacs found a complementary tag-team partner in his second wife Betty, a ballerina and dancer comfortable with the vagabond life on the road. When their son reached school age, they decided to settle down in Vancouver. "We thought: this is very pretty, a growing city; it was very nice. So we settled here," said Betty Kovacs. "About two years later, the local promotion came up for sale. We borrowed a bunch of money from the bank, and off we went. He bought it with two partners [Gene Kiniski and Don Owen]." The heyday of All-Star Wrestling in B.C. was 1967–73, and Kovacs was the booker for part of that time.

In 1980, the promotion was sold to Al Tomko, and Kovacs moved on to help Betty run a dance school in Vancouver. In the late 1990s, Kovacs suffered from a number of ailments, including Alzheimer's, and he's now confined to a wheelchair in a B.C. nursing home. Betty Kovacs blames the bumps over the years. "His body is riddled with arthritis, because he never got a new knee, which he should have. But he hated operations, so he never got the new knee, and now he's really suffering." Still, she said that her husband of 45 years has no complaints about his career. "No regrets. It took him around the world, every part of it."

DAN KROFFAT

While working as a lifeguard in Vancouver, Dan Kroffat was approached by former Mr. Universe Earl Maynard about considering pro wrestling. He worked out with Maynard before being shipped off to Stu Hart in Calgary. "He liked me right away," said Kroffat of Hart. It wasn't that long until Kroffat was headlining Stampede against the likes of Archie "Stomper" Gouldie ("We set some records that have never been broken" in the old Calgary Corral), Gil Hayes and Tor Kamata.

COWBOY DAN KROFFAT.
PHOTO: BOB LEONARD

Kroffat's biggest run was in Los Angeles. He was dubbed King Crow by the promoter, and held the United National championship. Los Angeles "probably catapulted me into the big time," said Kroffat. His peak was in a title match against Seigi Sagamuchi, that was actually broadcast via satellite back to Japan. A star was born, and on his first — and only — tour of Japan, Kroffat was treated like royalty and headlined across the nation. "I never had the interest to do it again," said Kroffat of Japan. He says the money was good, but it just wasn't for him.

Up until 1976, Kroffat went at the mat game "full-tilt." After that, he cut back on his matches, picking his spots, and started focusing on what he wanted to do after wrestling. Retiring for good in 1985, Kroffat opened Daniel's Auto Wholesale Centre in Calgary.

KILLER KARL KRUPP

KILLER KARL KRUPP.
PHOTO: OLIVER COLLECTION

As Killer Karl Krupp, George Momberg was an imposing German heel, striking terror into fans and opponents alike. But having lived through World War II in Holland before coming to Canada in 1951, it was a gimmick that he was never totally comfortable with. "It really irked him," said his brother Hank Momberg. "He was a First World War-type German, with the monocle and all. He didn't want to get involved with Nazism at all."

When Momberg came to Canada he was 16, and he quickly got involved with many sports. He was into rowing and did amateur wrestling at the Hamilton Jewish Centre and the Hamilton YMCA. Despite never playing high-school football, he picked up the game and played regularly on the Tiger Cats' junior squad, making the CFL for a few games in Hamilton and Ottawa.

Krupp turned to pro wrestling in the late 1960s, working as "The Flying Dutchman" Dutch Momberg, Mad Dog Momberg and later as Krupp. His greatest successes came in the Maritimes, Texas, and in Japan, where he teamed with Fritz von Erich as The Iron Claw Masters. He wrestled into his late 50s, and died in August 1995 in Moncton, N.B. from hepatitis A, which he picked up during a tour of Japan.

COWBOY FRANKIE LANE

Frank Luhovy wanted to be a cowboy. Growing up on a farm in the small Ontario community of Alvinston, Frank saw wrestling as an opportunity to achieve that goal. While working at Ford in Windsor, he enrolled in the wrestling school run by the Detroit promotion and when he felt he had enough experience, Luhovy took the name Frankie Lane, after the popular singer.

COWBOY FRANKIE LANE AND COOL CAT JACKSON.
PHOTO: TERRY DART

His first stint on the road came for the AWA, but ended abruptly when he neglected to renew his work visa. In the late '60s, he headed for Leroy McGuirk's promotion in Oklahoma. "Leroy McGuirk was, of course, blind, but he had a good perceptive image of each individual person just by the way you sound," said Lane. "I told him where I wrestled and all that. I said, 'I'd like to wrestle as a cowboy.' He said 'Got yourself a vest and a cowboy hat?' I said, 'Nope, but I can get them.' He says, 'Okay, if you want, you can wrestle as a cowboy.' It was that easy."

Cowboy Frankie Lane hit just about every territory there was, except, ironically enough, Texas. He held the Stampede North American title for a while, and was a major success near the end of the 1970s in Puerto Rico teamed with "Dirty" Dutch Mantell. Along the way, Lane had a hand in starting the career of Abdullah the Butcher, who he knew in Windsor, and Jimmy "Superfly" Snuka, who he met at a gym in Hawaii. In the early 1980s, Lane's dad asked him to come home and take care of the 800-acre family farm, where the cash crops are soya beans and wheat. Lane agreed and he continues to work the farm to this day. Lane wrestled and promoted in southern Ontario and Michigan until a car accident in 1989 ended his wrestling pursuits.

BUDDY LANE

The son of Wild Bill Kochen, Lane trained under the watchful eye of Verne Gagne in Minneapolis, with an all-star class that included Ric Flair, Rick Steamboat, the Iron Sheik, Ken Patera and Buddy Rose.

Lane picked up lots of experience getting pounded around the ring by the likes of Angelo Mosca, Stan Hansen and Blackjack Mulligan, and studied the techniques of technicians like Nick Bockwinkel and Billy Robinson. Lane knew that he had to stick with it to persevere. "If you want to be a wrestler, whether you're smaller or not, if you know your craft inside out, you work out, you show the fellows that you're there to stay, eventually you're going to pound out a spot for yourself."

Lane was a regular in the AWA for years, chasing the light-heavyweight belt. Besides stints in Vancouver and Calgary, Lane is best known on the East Coast, where he worked in Emile Dupré's Grand Prix Wrestling office while wrestling each summer.

LEGS LANGEVIN

Bob "Legs" Langevin has had an amazing life, even if one were to ignore his contributions to the squared circle. He's received the Order of Canada, has been decorated by the Queen, and received a papal blessing from Pope John Paul II.

His story starts in Magog, Quebec, where he was orphaned at the age of four. At seven, he was working on a farm. As a teen, he got a job at the Dow Brewery, carrying cases of beer. "I built my legs by squatting. Taking the case of beer down and up." Having experimented with amateur wrestling, Langevin signed up to learn the pro game with Yvon Robert at Camp Maupas, the famed training school in the Laurentians.

Bob Langevin (left) with Dino Bravo, Guy Soucy and Paul Leduc. Photo: Leduc Collection

Langevin took to his new profession quickly, working as a babyface overseas and usually as a heel in Quebec. His massive legs were his gimmick, and he used a type of leg scissors as a finisher. At 19 in St. Jerome, Quebec, he was attacked by a fan with a piece of wire. The attack left him impotent. Still, he insists, he received many marriage proposals over the years, despite his injury.

During World War II, Langevin worked part time as a policeman on the murder squad with the Quebec Provincial Police. Following the War, he owned a nightclub for a time, worked with the Quebec Liberals, and served as a bodyguard for former Prime Minister of Canada, Louis St. Laurent, as well as for Elizabeth Taylor, Richard Burton and others. All the while he wrestled, helping newcomers like Edouard Carpentier get their break in Quebec.

In 1966 at 51, Langevin's life changed drastically. He was diagnosed with cancer, and had an urgent colostomy, which removed part of his intestines and colon, and left his powerful legs paralyzed. It took seven months of physiotherapy to be able to walk again. During that time, he tried to commit suicide twice.

Langevin's old friend Johnny Rougeau came to his aid, and offered him a position as the figurehead promoter for Rougeau's operation in Quebec. It kept him involved in wrestling, even if he wasn't physically able to do the things he once did. With the rest of his time, Langevin helped others, speaking to groups about his battles with cancer and suicide, and working with the Ileostomy-Colostomy Association, the Canadian Cancer Society, and a hospital in Montreal. Now almost 90, Langevin isn't as involved as he used to be with his various projects, but he still enjoys talking wrestling.

Langevin's many, many honours and awards are well-deserved. The wrestling world honoured him during a WWF show in Montreal in 1995, when Jacques and Rayond Rougeau presented him with a plaque in mid-ring celebrating his many decades of dedication to the mat game.

Camp Maupas

Pro wrestling in Canada owes a great debt of gratitude to Emil Maupas and his esteemed Camp Maupas. Without him, Quebec would likely not have developed great wrestling talents like Yvon Robert, Tony Lanza, Legs Langevin, Sammy Berg, Harry Madison, Leo Lefebvre and Larry Moquin.

Maupas was a Greco-Roman grappler and boxer in his native France and came to Canada in 1894 to wrestle. He had to adapt his style to combat bigger men in the catch-as-catch-can style that was prevalent in North America. He was the top star around Montreal, but couldn't crack the elite of the wrestling world, losing to the likes of the great Frank Gotch twice in 1905. Newspapers described Maupas as rough, fast on his feet, and clever.

TONY LANZA (LEFT) AND YVON ROBERT TRAIN AT CAMP MAUPAS IN 1955. PHOTO: TONY LANZA

In 1923, Maupas bought the property on Raymond Lake in the Laurentian mountains near Val Morin, Quebec, that was to become Camp Maupas. He had already been training athletes at gyms around Montreal, including the Palais Nationale, but Maupas wanted a place he could call his own to promote his unique thoughts on physical fitness.

Campers would be expected to work hard all day — running 16 km, swimming two miles, using a medicine ball — on top of whatever it was they were studying with the specialists. Besides wrestlers,

FRANK GAGLIARDI ENDURES
THE STRANGE TRAINING OF
EMIL MAUPAS. PHOTO: TONY
LANZA

Maupas took in the Montreal Canadiens on one occasion, plus other hockey players, cyclists, runners, boxers, skiers and fencers. Everyone was expected to be in bed by 8 P.M. and rise at 7 A.M. Yvon Robert came to the camp in 1931, stayed 10 months, and became the prize pupil.

"Every morning, there was a physical culture in the place, in the centre. That was regular," said Bob "Legs" Langevin. "Then we used to take walks and ski. We used to ski in bathing suits. That was the nature of the old man. We had to do what he said, otherwise, we didn't count."

Tony Lanza called it an "old-country camp" that offered "plain exercise and a place to rest." Lanza learned a lot from the bodybuilding coach on hand as well.

In September 1948, Maupas was working at his camp, setting dynamite off on rocks to prevent flooding in the spring. When a charge didn't go off as expected, he went up to look at it. The dynamite exploded and Maupas was thrown 15 feet onto rocks and killed. In a tribute published three days after his death, *Le Devoir* columnist X.E. Narbonne called Maupas "the most brilliant athlete that Canada had ever known."

═══════

TONY LANZA

Whether it was competing in the ring, training wrestlers, or taking photos at ringside or in the dressing room, Montreal's Tony Lanza has had a sterling career. It all began in 1936, when he joined the pro ranks after dabbling in boxing and amateur wrestling. His first alias was Young Sandor, and he would go on to countless other masked names — The Black Devil, The Hooded Terror, The Strangler — all in an effort to hide his identity as the Montreal Forum's official photographer. His most memorable gimmick was as The Gorilla, in the early 1960s, for which he donned a monkey suit.

Lanza wrestled until he was 52, and then shared his knowledge as a trainer for another 15 years. But if you ask anyone associated with the Quebec wrestling scene, it's for his photography that Lanza is best known. In 1943, he started

REFEREE EDDY CREATCHMAN RAISES THE ARM OF TONY LANZA PHOTO: CREATCHMAN FAMILY

TONY LANZA SHOWING OFF HIS PHYSIQUE. PHOTO: TONY LANZA

shooting for Joe Weider, taking shots of bodybuilders for Weider's many magazine titles. That led to more work as a wrestling photographer. Having all the photos led to being the editor of various programs and magazines dedicated to wrestling in Quebec. "That was a hobby for me. My real life was as a wrestler," Lanza said.

Now 83, Montreal continues to be home to Lanza, who dabbles in sculpture as well as photography. His photographs are still sought by publishers worldwide.

JACK LASKIN

JACK LASKIN (RIGHT), IS HONORED AT THE CAULIFLOWER ALLEY CLUB. PHOTO: MIKE LANO

The Hamilton-born Laskin turned to pro wrestling to improve his health. "I said I was going to join the YMCA and make a man of myself," Laskin said. He debuted in 1952 with fellow rookies John Foti, Skull Murphy, Tiger Joe Tomasso and Billy Red Lyons.

Having travelled from territory to territory, wrestling served Laskin's "insatiable yearn to travel." His stay in Vienna was a career highlight. The wrestlers would get up and have breakfast, then take a trolley to a park on the Danube where they'd work out with weights, swim, and play games. They'd bring along picnic lunches, drink beer and gorge themselves. At 5 in the afternoon, they would head back to the hotel, then to the arena where'd they wrestle, then go out for dinner after the matches.

Laskin retired in 1962, settling near San Francisco and working at a variety of businesses. He has written both a play and an autobiography about his life, titled *One of The Boys*.

JOS LEDUC

Jos LeDuc is easily one of the wildest and strongest characters ever to enter a wrestling ring. Whether it was cutting his own arm with an axe, being hit over the head with a sledgehammer, dragging a bus, or bleeding all over his opponent, The Canadian Freight Train made his mark.

In 1965, Michel Pigeon gave up a job as a Quebec police officer and started wrestling at the encouragement of Paul Leduc. He trained under Montreal promoter Jack Britton. The "brother" tag team took off. In the early '70s, Jos hit the road as a singles competitor and established a reputation as one of the craziest strongmen in wrestling.

Jos Leduc.
Photo: Terry Dart

THE LEDUCS AND ROUGEAUS COME TOGETHER FOR RAYMOND'S
(LEFT) 1971 DEBUT. PHOTO: LEDUC COLLECTION

Pigeon had epic feuds with the likes of Jerry Lawler, Dusty Rhodes, Archie "The Stomper" Gouldie and Jack Brisco. In 1989, a brief, forgettable stint in the WWF, as The Head Banger, signalled the end of his career, except for occasional spot shows. Pigeon died May 1, 1999 in Atlanta from a lung infection.

PAUL LEDUC

ANDRÉ THE GIANT AND PAUL LEDUC PEDDLE AROUND THE NEIGHBORHOOD. PHOTO: PAUL LEDUC

At only 5-foot-10, 195-pounds, Paul Leduc faced an uphill battle when, in 1957, he decided to become a pro wrestler. He trained hard at a Montreal gym, and got his first big break by heading to Mexico for two years.

In 1965, he met and befriended Michel Pigeon. Encouraged by Leduc, Pigeon made his debut in Portland as Paul's "brother" Jos, and a legendary lumberjack tag team was born. Together they stormed rings around the world, with especially memorable matches against the Vachon brothers. When Pigeon died in 1999, the fact that the Leducs were not really brothers was still a big deal to the Quebec media.

Other than teaming with Jos, Paul Leduc may be best known for getting married in the ring at the Montreal Forum in 1971. He retired in 1978, and went to work for Quebecor. He has since retired and runs a wrestling school and promotion in Quebec in conjunction with his son Carl Leduc, who is following in his father's footsteps.

SKY HI LEE

Hailing from farm country just outside Toronto, Sky Hi Lee (Robert Leedy) burst onto the wrestling scene in the mid-'40s. Usually a villain, the towering cowpoke was an expert at eye-gouging, hair-pulling and strangle holds. Sky Hi Lee had many legendary matches against other big men, especially Killer Kowalski.

But it was outside the ring that the mystique of Sky Hi Lee was formed. George Scott recalled Lee ordering a shot in a bar. "He bit the glass, chewed the glass open and ate it!" Others tell of him eating lightbulbs. Both Ed Whalen and Don Leo Jonathon recounted how Lee would down at least a 40-oz. bottle of whisky a day.

SKY HI LEE AND LITTLE PANTHER. PHOTO: TERRY DART

During his wrestling career, he ran a dude ranch and restaurant outside Toronto, and was married to country performer Billy Allen. Lee died a number of years ago.

PIERRE LEFEBVRE

Growing up, Pierre Lefebvre was an extra member of the Rougeau family. When his best friend Raymond followed his famous father and uncle into the ring, it was only natural for Rougeau to train Lefebvre as well, and he made his debut at 17 in 1972.

Lefebvre's career was made in the mid-'70s, when he teamed with Michel "Le Justice" Dubois, and feuded with Mad Dog Vachon. His skills improved noticeably, and he excelled

A YOUNG, CLEAN-CUT PIERRE LEFEBVRE. PHOTO: TONY LANZA

in the heel role. From 1981 to 1984, Lefebvre held the International Wrestling tag-team belts on three occasions, with three different partners — Pat Patterson, Billy Robinson and Frenchy Martin. He feuded with the likes of the Rougeaus, Gino Brito, Tony Parisi, Dino Bravo and others. Everything seemed to be going great.

But at Christmas 1985, tragedy struck. Lefebvre, manager Tarzan Tyler, and referee Adrien Desbois were on their way home from the matches in Chicoutimi on the evening of December 20 when all three were killed in a terrible car accident.

LOVE BROTHERS — JOHNNY EVANS and WES HUTCHINGS

The Love Brothers are proof that the right gimmick at the right time can transform two journeymen wrestlers into stars. Hamilton's Johnny Evans and the Newfoundland-born, Hamilton-raised Wes Hutchings both trained at Al Spittles' gym. They became friends and occasional tag-team partners.

In 1968, the Buffalo-based NWF promotion was looking to create a new tag team with a really "out there" look. The promoter wanted "a couple of men that didn't look like the humdrum wrestler, the big cauliflower ears and all that stuff," said Evans. The hippie movement was in full swing, and wrestling was introduced to Hartford (Hutchings) and

Reginald (Evans) Love — the Love Brothers. Decked out in the style of the time — bandannas, long, flowing hair, flowered pants, bell-bottoms, and beads — the Love Brothers would preach peace but create war in the ring.

"Jesus, the people hated us. You've either got to be well-liked in wrestling or well-hated, and we were well-hated, so we were making good money," said Hutchings. "People wanted to come see us, these two Love Brothers that were causing all the trouble." Evans was a wizard on the microphone, and Hutchings could bump with the best of them in the ring. Besides the NWF, the Love Brothers were big in the IWA and Toronto,

REGGIE (STANDING) AND HARTFORD LOVE. PHOTO: OLIVER COLLECTION

and also worked Georgia, the Carolinas, and Florida. Al Costello and Bruce Swayze both served as managers for the team at different times.

The Love Brothers were together for almost a decade. Evans had to give up wrestling when his back deteriorated badly. Since retiring, he has worked in various businesses around Hamilton, and spends winters in Florida. Hutchings returned to Newfoundland in 1980, and owned a night club while continuing to wrestle. He was working against "Adorable" Adrian Adonis on Bearman McKigney's tour in 1988 when Adonis, McKigney and Pat Kelly were killed in a car accident. That was the last time he put on the tights. These days, Hutchings buys and sells furniture and runs a taxi service.

BILLY RED LYONS

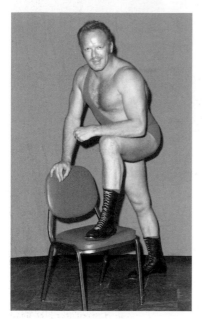

BILLY RED LYONS.
PHOTO: L'IL AL COLLECTION

With his shock of red hair, it wasn't long until Hamilton's Billy Lyons became Billy Red. He started out in Hamilton at the YMCA and later in Spittles' Gym. Jimmy "Red" Simms was his instructor at the Y. "We'd go down to the Y for an hour, two hours with Jimmy Red when he had time at lunch," Lyons said. The 6-foot-2, 240-pound Lyons was soon working around southern Ontario.

Lyons is best known for two tag teams — one with fellow redhead Red Bastien, and another, under masks, with Hamiltonian Dewey Robertson. In the AWA, Lyons made a memorable debut, unmasking his brother-in-law Dick Beyer, who was working as Dr. X. He worked quite a bit in Texas and Oklahoma.

Lyons stopped competing in 1985 and stepped into a role as an announcer for Maple Leaf Wrestling. When the program was cancelled, he retired but continued to work out regularly until he suffered a stroke in 1996. Lyons now lives in Dundas, Ontario.

DANO McDONALD

As World War II was starting, Jim "Dano" McDonald was just beginning his wrestling career in Hamilton under Herb Larsen. His job at Stelco, however, kept him close to home and the steel company wouldn't release him to enlist. As a result, McDonald's initial wrestling jaunts were close by. "You couldn't go very far. The furthest I'd go would be Detroit or Chicago once in a while, but I'd have to go on the train because you didn't have enough gas to go around."

After the war ended, McDonald quit his job at Stelco and hit the road. Because he was barely 200 pounds, he decided to try Mexico first, where a lightweight fit in, no problem. By the time he got to Chicago and promoter Fred Kohler a few years later, Dano had matured, which meant bigger paydays. "I got a little bigger and they could start booking me with the bigger guys."

Dano McDonald's biggest successes came in the American Southwest and Northwest. He settled near Portland, Oregon for the later part of his career. In 1962, he became a part-time mortician while still wrestling. In 1970, he quit the mat game, except for a brief comeback in 1974.

DANO McDONALD

DAVE McKIGNEY

Dave "Wildman"' McKigney gave his life to wrestling. Starting out in Toronto gyms in the early '50s, he began wrestling as Gene Dubois, but soon found his calling as the Bearman.

McKigney wasn't the only wrestler who travelled with a bear from town to town, but he is perhaps the best known. With a long, mangy beard and hair to match, he took the appearance of a bear to heart as well. The bear brought a crowd to the matches. Down in the southern U.S., it was a new spectacle, while in northern Ontario, fans just wanted to see for themselves who would be crazy enough to wrestle a bear.

A CLEAN-SHAVEN DAVE McKIGNEY LEADS TERRIBLE TED
FROM THE RING IN CALGARY. PHOTO: BOB LEONARD

Terrible Ted was his first bear, picked up after a carnival show went bankrupt. But his best-known bear, for tragic reasons, was Smokey. In July 1978, McKigney left the bear's cage door open as he went to answer the phone. Smokey entered the house, went upstairs, and mauled McKigney's girlfriend, Lynn Orser, to death. The incident made headlines, and McKigney's animals were taken away by the Ontario Humane Society.

The Bearman was also a small-time wrestling promoter, scratching out a living in Ontario, with occasional summer tours of Newfoundland. Many a young talent — like the Wildman Sabu — got their start on his tours. It was on one of these tours in 1988 that he met his death, when the van he was driving crashed on the Trans-Canada Highway as he tried to avoid a moose. Keith "Adrian Adonis" Franke, and Victor Arko (Pat Kelly of the Kelly twins) were also killed.

His daughter later wrestled as Rachel Dubois.

ROY McCLARTY

"The Winnipeg Bomber," Roy McClarty, is definitely someone to be celebrated. A successful amateur and a top-notch athlete, he got into pro wrestling in the late 1940s, learning from Joe Pazandak and George Gordienko. "He was just an all-around great athlete. Phenomenal," said Moose Morowski. "He had such a sense of balance and co-ordination, and was an excellent wrestler. And tough."

McClarty headed to England first, and quickly moved up the cards. Tours around Europe followed before he decided to return to North America in the early 1950s.

ROY McCLARTY.
PHOTO: MELBY COLLECTION

The well-muscled blond found success wherever he went, headlining from Boston to Chicago, and Calgary to Toronto. McClarty used a variation of the sleeper hold as a finishing move, one in which his opponent's arm was tied up as well.

During the later part of his career, McClarty settled on the West Coast, working Oregon, Washington and B.C. In the 1970s, he refereed and drove the ring truck for the Vancouver promotion. The veteran was sought out by youngsters like Ed "Moondog" Moretti for advice. "I had heard from guys before I went there. 'When you get up to Vancouver, hook up with Roy McClarty, because he's a guy that will take care of you, show you around and everything.' If he likes you, he'll help you out," Moretti said.

After a long fight with Alzheimer's disease and a year-long stay in a nursing home, McClarty died in April 1998 from heart failure.

VELVET McINTYRE

VELVET McINTYRE.
PHOTO: VELVET McINTYRE

Vancouver's Velvet McIntyre, a top women's star in the 1980s, was known for her good looks, high-flying moves and for wrestling barefoot. Trained by Sandy Barr in Oregon alongside Princess Victoria, McIntyre debuted in 1980, and soon began to travel the world. She would seek out new places to wrestle, just to experience new things. Her biggest claim to fame was wrestling The Fabulous Moolah at WrestleMania II, but that wasn't her choice. "There was a trip for the girls to Kuwait, and I always liked to go where I hadn't been. But I was told, 'Nope, you get to stay here and do WrestleMania,' so I was pretty bummed out about that," she said.

McIntyre wore boots for the first four years of her career, then one day as a joke, someone stole one of them. She wrestled barefoot and never looked back. "My footing was better, my leverage, everything was better."

In 1998, Velvet wrestled her last match while unknowingly carrying twin boys. Raising the twins has kept her out of action since their birth. "If I didn't have the kids, I'd probably still be doing it. But your priorities change. Now it matters if I break my neck!"

HARRY MADISON

The barefoot boy from Verdun, Harry Madison, was an accomplished amateur before he trained at Camp Maupas. He worked in the 1930s and 1950s, and was renowned for his toughness, despite being a light heavyweight at about 195 pounds.

Tony Lanza recalled taking on Madison many times. "He was a streetfighter . . . and I was also a streetfighter, so we didn't get along very good in the ring!" Lanza said. Madison stayed around Quebec for most of his career, working for a railway company.

HARRY MADISON. PHOTO: TONY LANZA

"He's definitely a legend," said Paul "Butcher" Vachon, who recalled Madison's toughness even in his old age. "I read in the newspaper, the *Journal de Montréal*, where he'd been arrested for disturbing the peace. Two guys — he was having a beer up north in the tavern in the little town — he's 80 years old and they started pushing him around. He beat the shit out of both of them. Knocked them out." Madison died a few years ago.

OMER MARCHESSAULT

After failing to make the 1936 Canadian Olympic wrestling team for the Berlin Games, Montreal's Omer Marchessault turned to pro wrestling. He wrestled for 14 years, mostly part time, while working as a firefighter. The downtime at the fire hall allowed him the chance to sculpt his body. He was in such great shape that he was named Mr. Canada in 1950.

For a while, the fire department was uncomfortable with Marchessault's other profession and they asked him to wear a

REFEREE OMER MARCHESSEAULT RAISES THE HAND OF ANDRÉ THE GIANT ALONG WITH EDOUARD CARPENTIER. PHOTO: TONY LANZA

mask. And so the Masked Marvel was born, a heel to counter Marchessault's old babyface gimmick.

After his ring career ended, he worked as a referee for another 24 years. He thought that he had retired in 1975, but was brought back in 1983, hired by the provincial athletic commission to be a timekeeper at wrestling, boxing and kickboxing shows.

In September 1995, Omer was honoured by the WWF at the final Montreal Forum show along with Bob "Legs" Langevin for their 60 years of service to pro wrestling in Montreal. Marchessault died on Boxing Day 1996 after a long illness.

MICHEL "MAD DOG" MARTEL

From his debut in 1968 to his untimely death following a match in Puerto Rico in 1978, Michel "Mad Dog" Martel was a top export. Martel often teamed with his "brother" Pierre (later known as Frenchy Martin) as the Mercenaries. They were a successful team in the Maritimes, Quebec, and especially in Puerto Rico.

Martel also did numerous trips to Japan and Mexico. He later helped his younger brother, Rick, break into wrestling in 1973. "He paved the way for me. We went to Japan together when I started and all that. He helped me a great deal," said Rick Martel.

On June 30, 1978, Martel collapsed following a match against Invader 1 (Jose Gonzales) in Puerto

MICHEL MARTEL.
PHOTO: BOB LEONARD

Rico and died on the way to the hospital. This being wrestling, a feud between Invader 1 and Pierre Martel was a big draw after Martel's death.

FRENCHY MARTIN

Frenchy Martin is proof that the name one wrestles under doesn't necessarily matter. Whether he worked as Pierre Martel in Puerto Rico, Don Gagne in the Maritimes or at Stampede, or under a hood as The Destroyer for a short while in Montreal, he had the ability to rile the crowds up.

After breaking into wrestling in 1971, Martin became great friends with Michel Martel. Together they would team as the Mercanaries. "Frenchy and my brother were together all the time," explained Rick Martel. "He's like a big brother to me." Mad

FRENCHY MARTIN
PHOTO: BOB LEONARD

Dog Martel's death made Martin an even bigger draw, cata-pulting him into stardom on the island of Puerto Rico. He had numerous runs, with various titles, and was booker for different promotions as well.

In the Maritimes, he had epic feuds with the Cormiers, primarily Leo Burke. In the late 1980s, he was brought into the WWF as a manager for Dino Bravo. He proudly waved the Quebec flag there until the summer of 1990, when he retired for health reasons.

AL & TINY MILLS

THE PRIDE OF CAMROSE, ALBERTA — TINY (LEFT) AND AL MILLS. PHOTO: BOB LEONARD

Camrose, Alberta's Al and Tiny Mills were among the top brother tag teams of the post-war period. First into the mat game was Albert, who met Jack Taylor in Calgary and was training soon thereafter. He was often called Lord Albert Mills, took numerous titles as a singles competitor, and was one of the first big stars of Stampede Wrestling.

When Tiny Mills followed his brother into wrestling in 1949, they achieved great success, particularly in Alberta, Manitoba and Ontario. The notorious duo were dubbed "Murder Inc." and the *Toronto Star* called them "the most hated men in all of grappledom." With neither brother known for their good looks, one of Tiny's gimmicks was to pull his long, black hair over his face when he was mad.

Because of their age difference, Tiny's career was taking off as his brother's was ending. Tiny went to Minneapolis and teamed up with Stan "Krusher" Kowalski. The new duo, also known as Murder Inc., travelled the world, wreaking mayhem.

Both Al and Tiny Mills have passed on.

GUY MITCHELL

Trying to get the history of Hamilton's John Hill straight is pretty tough. He worked under so many different names, masks and identities that it's almost mystifying. He's best known as "Gentleman" Jerry Valiant in the Valiant Brothers three-some, and as Guy "Stomper" Mitchell. Some of the other names he used included Guy Heenan ("brother" to Bobby Heenan), The Masked Stranger, The Strangler, Mr. X (a big star in Vancouver), Spoiler #3, The Destroyer in Australia, Dr. A, The Bounty Hunter, Red Devil and Assassin #2. On occasion, he even went under variations of his real name.

Hill was doing an apprenticeship at the *Hamilton Spectator* newspaper with Ernie Moore when both fell into pro wrestling, in the mid '50s, under the encouragement of Hurricane Smith. He trained with Moore at Spittles' gym and soon made his way out onto the road.

A YOUNG GUY MITCHELL.
PHOTO: OLIVER COLLECTION

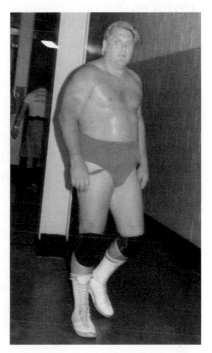

JERRY VALIANT.
PHOTO: TERRY DART

According to manager Percival A. Friend, Hill was a "good wrestler in the ring. He knew his stuff." Jimmy Valiant said that Hill fit in very quickly with the Valiant Brothers when he joined the team in 1979. "Johnny always said there's no difference in the Valiant brothers. The only difference in the Valiant Brothers was that Johnny was Luscious, I was only Handsome and Jerry was only the Gentleman of the three of us." Waldo von Erich remembered him for something else. "He had the longest toes of any wrestler I ever saw. They were almost as long as your fingers!"

After getting out of wrestling in the early 1980s, Hill settled down in Indianapolis and worked for the WWF on a part-time basis in the area, driving the ring truck and refereeing occasionally. Hill now runs a landscaping company.

GETO MONGOL

Newton Tattrie created one of the greatest gimmick tag teams ever when he took a young Josip Peruzovic (later Nikolai Volkoff) under his wing in Calgary. They shaved their heads, leaving only a spot of hair on the back of their skulls, and grew moustaches. The Mongols — Geto (Tattrie) and Bepo (Peruzovic) — were born, and were a top team from the late '60s until the early '70s. Tattrie also had his student Bill Eadie (Masked Superstar, Demolition Axe) team with him as a Mongol.

Tattrie was born in Springhill, Nova Scotia, but grew up on the streets of Toronto. He found a gym where he thought he could learn boxing, but instead found Gene Dubois ("Wildman" Dave McKigney) training wrestlers. He had a rough start, not finding enough work, so he turned for a time to the oil fields of Alberta. The Mongols gimmick led to full-time ring work for the first time.

In Pittsburgh, Tattrie ran the hot Spectator Sports promotion in the early '70s, with hometown headliner Bruno Sammartino, and helped to break in Larry Zbyszko. Tattrie quit wrestling in 1982, and ran a gym for a while before retiring to a quiet life in Virginia Beach, VA.

BEPO (LEFT) AND GETO MONGOL.
PHOTO: L'IL AL COLLECTION

ERNIE MOORE

Ernie Moore was just another gym rat down at Spittles' in Hamilton in the mid-'50s. He debuted as a pro at 16, tagging up with John Hill, who later gained fame as Guy Mitchell. His was a pretty average career until Moore was asked by promoter Harry Light to wear a

ERNIE MOORE.
PHOTO: ERNIE MOORE

mask as one of The Hangmen. "I near caused a riot," recalled Moore, who also learned that he liked being the bad guy.

Moore created The Executioner character, and terrorized wrestling crowds across North America with his dark mask.

It all came to an end for Moore after a car accident in 1979. Throughout his wrestling career, Moore had worked at the *Hamilton Spectator* newspaper in production, so he had a job to fall back on. Since retiring from the paper, Moore has helped to train young wrestlers in and around Hamilton.

LARRY MOQUIN

LARRY MOQUIN.
PHOTO: TONY LANZA

Larry Moquin was Robin to Yvon Robert's Batman in the Montreal territory from 1942 to 1967. Trained at Camp Maupas north of Montreal under the guidance of Robert, Moquin was athletically gifted. He had everything it took to be on top — except desire.

"The guy had natural talent, a natural athlete. He played golf good, any kind of sport, but he just didn't seem to take anything to heart," said Gino Brito Sr., who wrestled during the later years of Moquin's career. "Some days he would make moves that would amaze me. He wasn't in good shape, even at the end, but he could move like hell in the ring. But he didn't care apparently in his prime neither, and that's why Yvon Robert always remained on top. He was like second banana all the time."

Instead, Moquin found satisfaction helping out in the office of Montreal promoter Eddie Quinn, and running Hotel Larry Moquin in Ste. Anne de Bellevue until it was destroyed by fire in 1964. After getting out of wrestling, he became a salesman for Victoriaville Hockey Sticks. Moquin died December 12, 1988 from cancer. He was 65.

MOOSE MOROWSKI

After beginning to wrestle at 17 in Winnipeg, Stan "The Moose" Mykietowich was more than happy to take his act around the globe for the next 30 years. "They were always looking for talent all over the world. Once you got yourself established, then promoters are willing to use you if you have that name."

Mykietowich was best known as Moose Morowski, during stints in Stampede Wrestling, Vancouver's All Star and the AWA. But his resume reads more like an atlas — Puerto Rico, Trinidad & Tobago, Antigua, Australia, New Zealand, 20 trips to Japan, South Africa, Rhodesia, and Germany. "Millionaires couldn't afford to do what we did at that time. We always enjoyed ourselves. The nightlife was fantastic."

MOOSE MOROWSKI.
PHOTO: MOOSE MOROWSKI

Moore knew it was time to retire in 1983 when his body "started to give out." Since leaving wrestling, Mykietowich has volunteered his time with a variety of organizations.

SKULL MURPHY

Two things come up again and again in the life of Hamilton's John Joseph "Skull" Murphy — his hairlessness and his ability to draw heat. The hairlessness was a result of a childhood disease, and according to those who knew him, a source of anguish at

SKULL MURPHY (LEFT) AND
BRUTE BERNARD GO WILD.
PHOTO: MIKE LANO

times. "That really bothered him," said Moose Cholak. "He used to have one or two hairs grow on his face that you couldn't see, and he'd buy a razor blade and soap and shave. Every day, every morning he'd shave — and you couldn't see it!"

Murphy broke into the wrestling business along with other Hamiltonians like Billy Red Lyons, Chuck Molnar and Paddy Ryan in the 1950s. "He was a natural and he was a great guy," said Lyons. After working around Hamilton, and on a successful tour in northern Ontario for Larry Kasaboski, Murphy was ready for the big time.

His biggest successes came as a tag-team partner with Montreal's Brute Bernard. They were champions in many locations, including the WWWF and Australia. "They really knew how to get heat," said long-time Australian promoter Jim Barnett. "He took terrific bumps." One of Murphy's favourite heat-generating moves was to rip up a young fan's autograph book.

On March 23, 1970, Murphy was found dead in his Charlotte, North Carolina apartment, having apparently overdosed on sleeping pills; most considered it suicide. A magazine report of Murphy's death said that he had died of a heart attack, and gave a fitting tribute to the heel: "His hairless head, leering face and superbly developed body would never again menace an opponent or drive fans to such states of frenzy that they would try to storm the ring."

BRONKO NAGURSKI

In Bronislau "Bronko" Nagurski, Canada can lay claim to a legend in both football and pro wrestling. Born in 1908 in the small border town of Rainy River, Ontario, Nagurski became a gridiron star at the University of Minnesota from 1927 to 1929, and was the only player in U.S. college history to make all-star at two positions — fullback and tackle. In 1930, he was signed by George Halas to the Chicago Bears, and helped them to championships in 1932 and 1933.

"The Bronk" first tried wrestling in 1933 after the football season ended. As a grappler, Nagurski hit his peak during the late '30s and early '40s, when he held the NWA World title twice, beating Lou Thesz June 23, 1939 for his first win.

BRONKO NAGURSKI. PHOTO: MELBY COLLECTION

Nagurski would lose the title to Ray Steele March 7, 1940, and regain it from Steele a year later on March 11, 1941. Sandor Szabo finally took the gold from Nagurksi on June 5, 1941.

Stu Hart remembered Nagurski. "He was a pretty big draw. He was pretty tough to bring down in wrestling. He wasn't that fancy a wrestler, either. But he was good enough to be recognized as world's champion."

Nagurski retired from wrestling in 1960 a physical wreck, and for the last years of his life, he ran a gas station in International Falls, Minnesota. He died January 8, 1990.

LOU NEWMAN

Lou "Shoulders" Newman (Reino Nyman) followed his uncle Vaino Ketonen into pro wrestling in the early 1930s, wrestling in vacant lots in British Columbia. In 1937, his career took off, and Newman performed across Canada, the U.S., Australia, New Zealand, South Africa and Japan.

During his career, Newman went under a variety of identities — The Masked Marvel in Toronto, Masked Medico in Japan, Mr. X in Hawaii, and as Lou Schnabel in The Iron Russians, with Hands Schnabel. Wearing a mask to conceal one's identity could be dangerous, he explained to the *Whatever Happened To . . . ?* newsletter. "When you're working with a mask, you're kind of blind. I'd leave the ring and people would run up and jab lit cigars into my calf muscles."

LOU "SHOULDERS" NEWMAN.
PHOTO: SHIRLEY NEWMAN

Newman retired from the ring in 1967, and became an auto and truck salesman in Honolulu and, later, in Bellingham, WA. He died from a stroke in March 2001.

OLE OLSEN

While his job in the Winnipeg fire department kept him close to home for most of his wrestling career, Albert "Ole" Olsen had a significant impact on the scene. He debuted in 1950, after his pro football aspirations fizzled and his amateur wrestling career took him just short of qualifying for the 1948 Olympics.

Trained in Minneapolis by Wally Karbo and Tony Stetcher, Olsen was a big name in Winnipeg, taking on all the top stars who would come through town. He made trips to territories like Stampede, Toledo or Minnesota during holidays from the fire department. When he had a falling out with Winnipeg promoter Alex Turk, Olsen became a promoter himself, giving young local talent another place to work.

OLE OLSEN.
PHOTO: MAY COLLECTION

In the mid-'60s, Olsen gave up wrestling. He is currently retired in Winnipeg.

DANNO O'SHOCKER

Born in Scotland and raised in Hamilton, Ontario, Jack Lloyd was one of the top wrestlers in the world in the 1950s and 1960s. Coming out of the Royal Canadian Navy, Lloyd learned the mat game through Jimmy "Red" Simms at Al Spittles' gym in Steeltown.

He hit the road in 1951, heading to the U.S., where he was fortunate to make a name for himself by appearing on an early TV show out of Chicago. The name Danno O'Shocker was pinned on him by an American promoter who wanted to attract Irish fans. For a time, he also wrestled as Danno Geohagen, "brother" to Tim Geohagen.

As his career progressed, promoters relied on Lloyd to teach newcomers — Wahoo McDaniel, Reggie Parks, and Bruno Sammartino were among his charges. Lloyd died in California in August 1997 of pneumonia.

TONY PARISI

Tony Parisi.
Photo: Terry Dart

Coming to Canada from Italy as a youth, there is no way that Tony Parisi could have known the impact he was going to have on people's lives. After competing as an amateur for a number of years around Niagara Falls, ON., at 19 Parisi turned pro, and learned the sport from Detroit promoters Bert Ruby and Harry Light.

Alongside best friend Gino Brito, "Cannonball" Parisi would rise to the top, usually as a tag-team wrestler, inspiring legions of Italian-Canadians along the way. In Pittsburgh, he was even billed as a cousin to the great, home-town champion Bruno Sammartino. Parisi and Brito (as Louis Cerdan) were WWWF tag champs in 1975, and Tony formed other tag teams with the likes of Dominic Denucci, Dino

Bravo, Bruno Sammartino Jr. (David Sammartino), and even Gino Brito Jr.

Parisi promoted some shows in southern Ontario, especially the yearly CHIN Picnic, and continued to wrestle on those shows well into his 50s. In the 1970s, Parisi bought a motel in Niagara Falls and later opened a restaurant called Big Anthony's, complete with hundreds of pictures, memorabilia and other mementoes of his career. Parisi died in August 2000 of a heart attack. He was 58.

REGGIE PARKS

Edmonton-born Reggie Parks may be the wrestler who held the greatest number of championship belts — not many others can claim to have held hundreds. Of course, it helps that he designs and makes them.

Almost 40 years ago, Parks was wrestling in Omaha, Nebraska. The promoter there, Joe Dusek, had a great big tag-team trophy instead of a belt. "The trophy was about six feet tall, and when anybody touched it, it would fall apart," Parks laughed. His tag-team partner Doug Gilbert (who was Mr. Low to Parks' Mr. High) suggested they make up some title belts, and Dusek agreed. "From there, word got out," Parks said. "I made belts for the WWF for 10 years, wcw, independent groups. Just about everybody you could think of."

AN INCREDIBLY FIT REGGIE PARKS.
PHOTO: BOB LEONARD

As a youngster in Edmonton, Parks fell under the tutelage of Stu Hart, then hit the road to further improve his skills. Parks's reputation was based in large part on his physique, strength, and his "cast iron stomach." One time, a Volkswagen Bug was driven over his stomach to prove his toughness. Some called Parks the "Quiet Superman."

PAT PATTERSON

PAT PATTERSON (LEFT) AND RAY STEVENS. PHOTO: MIKE LANO

Forget what you might have seen recently on WWE TV, Pat Patterson as one of Vince McMahon's "stooges." Fans should know about Patterson, the headliner — the man who was half of one of the greatest tag teams ever with Crippler Ray Stevens, who was the top star in Roy Shire's Northern California promotion, and who moved to the WWF at the end of his career to reign as its first Intercontinental champion.

Patterson was born Pierre Clermont in Montreal, and in his late teens trained under Pat Girard with his friends Roger Barnes and Terry Joyal, who would later become Ronnie and Terry Garvin. After his debut in 1960, Patterson puttered around, developing a "pretty boy" effeminate character.

Patterson's first big break outside of Montreal came in the Pacific Northwest, where he was tag champion. He duplicated the tag team success in the San Francisco area, taking the NWA World belts with Rocky Johnson on three occasions, then with Ray Stevens. He also had five runs as the U.S. champion in San Francisco as well. In the late 1970s, he travelled to Florida, the AWA and Los Angeles before settling into the WWF.

Pat's years in New York are marked by a memorable face turn, and his run with the newly created Intercontinental belt — "won" in a fictional tournament said to have taken place in

Lou Thesz (left) and Patterson share a laugh as Kurt Angle looks on. Photo: Mike Lano

Brazil — and his bloody Boot Camp match at Madison Square Gardens against Sgt. Slaughter, considered one of the top matches of the '80s.

Patterson had a last run through Montreal in 1982–83 before settling into a behind-the-scenes role with the wwf. He served as an on-air announcer for both the French and English wwf broadcasts at one time or another, and hosted a segment on the French shows where he would mock his guests in French then ask questions politely in English.

Often referred to as Vince McMahon's right-hand man, Patterson was the principal booker for the group during its glory years from 1986 into the '90s. He left the company for a while in the middle of the decade, but was quickly lured back. Today, Patterson serves a number of roles with the wwe, including talent-scouting and match-making, and is particularly sought out for his ability to create finishes for matches.

STEPHEN PETITPAS

Growing up as a neighbour in Shediac, nb, to Maritime wrestling legend Emile Dupré had its advantages, especially

if, like Stephen Petitpas, you grew to be 6-foot-3, 220 pounds by the age of 15. Dupré was quick to take the young charge under his wing, initially having him help out setting up the ring, and later as a wrestler.

Like Dupré, most of Petitpas' success came close to home. In the Maritimes, he stood tall for the people, proud of his Acadian heritage. "I know a lot of people looked up to me, being the babyface," he said. Born in Germany, where his father was stationed with the Canadian Forces, Petitpas went to Europe to much hype and a mega-push because he could be promoted as a hometown hero. In Montreal, he was Sheik Ali, and was one of the top heels in the last days of Lutte International.

STEPHEN PETITPAS WITH THE ATLANTIC HEAVYWEIGHT CHAMPIONSHIP. PHOTO: BOB LEONARD

Numerous knee operations forced Petitpas to retire from wrestling in 1995, but it couldn't keep him from his real love — playing hockey. When he's not driving a truck for a living, Petitpas can be found lacing up the skates to play for numerous senior teams in New Brunswick.

GILLES "THE FISH" POISSON

Blessed with one of the truly great pro-wrestling names, Charles Berger rose to fame quickly as the heel Gilles "The Fish" Poisson when he first got into wrestling in the early 1970s. He had been a notable amateur wrestler before turning pro.

His first promotion was the Vachons' Grand Prix in Montreal, and Poisson moved through the ranks, portrayed as another in the long line of Quebec strongmen like Louis Cyr and Victor Delamarre. Poisson used a bear hug as a finishing move. Bruno Sammartino got him into the WWWF, where he actually worked as Louis Cyr for a short while, with Freddie Blassie as his manager. In the AWA, he was also known as Pierre Poisson for a time.

GILLES POISSON CRUSHES PAUL LEDUC'S FACE.
PHOTO: LEDUC COLLECTION

Poisson held Stampede's North American title briefly in 1976, and held tag titles in Montreal with both Killer Kowalski (1973) and Sailor White (1982). When International Wrestling faded from the Quebec wrestling scene, so did Poisson.

BIG JOHN QUINN

Big John Quinn was always a little leery of pro wrestling. He wanted to wrestle amateur and prove his skills, but workouts with Edouard Carpentier and Whipper Billy Watson proved to him that one could be both — a pro with a solid amateur foundation.

The Hamilton-born Quinn — cousin to NHL player and coach Pat Quinn — started in northern Ontario

BIG JOHN QUINN.
PHOTO: L'IL AL COLLECTION

for Larry Kasaboski, then hooked up with Watson. He was a headliner in Vancouver and Calgary for years. Quinn's wrestling odyssey took him to Europe for 14 years, where he was one of England's biggest stars. He also wrestled in Austria and Germany. "I loved it. Made good money. I was making $100,000 a year without tax," Quinn said.

A falling-out with a promoter signalled the end of his European vacation in 1987, and the end of Quinn's wrestling career. He didn't have any interest in changing his style to fit with the gimmick-mad WWF of the late '80s. These days, Quinn lives in B.C. and drives a one-ton truck.

RON RITCHIE

Trained under Tony Condello in his hometown of Winnipeg, Ron Ritchie debuted in 1978. At 5-foot-11, 235 pounds, Ritchie wasn't a big man by any means, but he was a solid grappler. After working locally, including in a championship tag team with Dave Kochen (Buddy Lane), Ritchie moved on to the AWA, where he never cracked the top of the roster.

His first success away from home came in Kansas City, where he held the tag belts in 1983 with ex-CFLer George Wells. Ritchie also competed in the Pacific Northwest, the Maritimes and did a few trips abroad. In 1986, he held Stampede's North American title, beating Kerry Brown and losing to Strangler Steve DiSalvo two months later. Ritchie also held the Stampede tag titles with Leo Burke in 1986.

In the late '80s, and early '90s, Ritchie was a regular with the CNWA in Calgary, the promotion that followed Stampede. He held their heavyweight title during 1990 and 1991. When the action dried up, so did Ritchie's career, and he is no longer involved in the business.

YVON ROBERT JR.

Having earned his MBA from UCLA, Yvon Robert Jr. knew there was still a part of himself that needed to follow in his legendary father's footsteps and try pro wrestling. Initially,

Robert Jr. worked as Bob Brunnell in the United States to avoid comparisons. But when he was told by his dad that he was ready to wrestle in Montreal, he reclaimed his name.

The Roberts were a part of the Vachon-led Grand Prix Wrestling promotion that started up in opposition to the Rougeaus in 1971. Robert Jr.'s business experience came in handy. "My career was more administration than trying to win a belt. Because if you're the son of somebody, you know you're going to be criticized all your life. And you get that, 'Hey, you're not as good as your father!'" he said. "You'd better believe it. Nobody was as good as my father, so nobody could do it."

Robert Jr. got out of wrestling when he sold off his interest in Grand Prix. In 1977, he started selling real estate, which he continues to do to this day, despite recent health scares, including having part of his foot amputated.

BUDDY ROBERTS

THE HOLLYWOOD BLONDS (FROM LEFT) DALE ROBERTS, SIR OLIVER HUMPERDINK, AND JERRY BROWN.

Dale Hey was a successful bodybuilder and weight lifter in Vancouver, B.C. when he met a wrestler known as Red McNulty. The two became fast friends, and Hey decided to join the pro wrestling ranks as well.

In 1967, he headed out to Stampede for three weeks, lived in the Hart basement, and found bookings hard to come by. Hey changed his mind about becoming a wrestler and returned to Vancouver. McNulty called again, and invited him to Montreal, where he had just become a mad Russian named Ivan Koloff. Dubbed Dale Roberts, Hey quickly fell in with the stars of the Rougeau promotion.

It was as half of the Hollywood Blond tag team with Jerry Brown that Roberts first hit the heights of stardom. Mid-South promoter Leroy McGuirk came up with the idea to pair the two, and to dye their hair. "We really did click. We were together seven years," Hey said. Later, they added Sir Oliver Humperdink as their manager, and had successful championship runs in Montreal, Florida, Georgia, California and the Mid-Atlantic.

In 1980, Hey became Buddy Roberts and teamed with Michael Hayes and Terry Gordy in the unique Fabulous Freebirds team. The wild trio complemented each other perfectly — Hayes was the cocky talker, Gordy the brawn and Roberts the skilled veteran. The Freebirds had an incredible run, peaking in World Class Championship Wrestling in Texas, when they battled the von Erichs in front of sellout crowds. According to Hey, the rebellious nature of the Freebirds suited him perfectly. "I was kind of a rebel all my career. I didn't put up with any crap from the office people, but they liked my work, so they put up with my not agreeing with all their garbage."

By 1989, the wrestling business had shrunk, and Roberts faded out of the spotlight. He worked construction in Chicago until he got throat cancer in 1996. He is cancer-free now, and enjoying a quiet life in the Windy City, showing up to sign autographs at occasional small shows.

DEWEY ROBERTSON

A weight-training fanatic, Hamilton's Dewey Robertson got into pro wrestling under the guidance of Al Spittles in the 1960s. After moderate success around southern Ontario, Robertson met Whipper Watson and became a protegé of sorts. A handsome, well-built babyface, Robertson quickly shot to the top and stayed there.

As a single, Robertson was the Canadian champ in Toronto in 1980, and fought throughout the southern U.S. Teamed with Dennis Stamp in Oklahoma, he fought epic battles against the Hollywood Blonds, Jerry Brown and Dale Roberts. Back in Canada, Billy Red Lyons was his tag team partner in The Crusaders, first under white masks, and later without the hoods.

DEWEY ROBERTSON
PHOTO: L'IL AL
COLLECTION

But Robertson is perhaps best known for his abrupt change in the early 1980s, dumping his clean-cut babyface

role to paint his face green and blue, cut his hair into a single tuft at the top and bang chairs against his head as the wild Missing Link. The move rejuvenated his career, even if it confused and confounded friends. Colleagues couldn't believe it was the same man, and Robertson played the role away from the arena as well, often with his "handler" Sheena — his then-wife Gail.

As the Link, Robertson made it to the WWF in the mid-1980s. The run was cut short when drugs took control of his life. His career essentially over, Robertson puttered around trying to make ends meet, settling in once again in Hamilton where he worked for a while as a court officer, and lectured to Ontario schools and businesses on drug and alcohol dependency. In July 1993, he had a kidney removed — in his opinion, the organ failed because of his prolonged use of marijuana.

Robertson's two sons both wrestled for a short while. Mark Robertson never made it much out of southern Ontario, while Jason, usually working as Jason Sterling, had a short run in the southern U.S. These days, Robertson works odd jobs and is working on his life story.

DAVE RUHL

During the 1960s and 1970s, Watts, Alberta's Dave Ruhl was one of the fiercest competitors on the Stampede Wrestling circuit. He's best remembered for his epic battles with Sweet Daddy Siki and Archie "The Stomper" Gouldie for the North American title.

"Dave was a very solid wrestler. He wasn't as spectacular as some of the boys we had," Stu Hart explained in 1997. "They believed in him. He had a full nelson that was pretty hard, not too many people broke it on him. Once he got it, he did a pretty good job on you."

Ruhl started wrestling in 1946 and worked until 1974, when an injury forced him to retire. Besides being well-known in the Prairies and the West Coast, Ruhl also travelled on many occasions to Japan and the Far East. He died in 1988.

DAVE RUHL CLAMPS A HANG-MAN BACKBREAKER ON ERIC FROELICH. PHOTO: BOB LEONARD

PADDY RYAN

Earl Patrick Freeman had numerous aliases during his wrestling career, which spanned from the 1950s to the 1980s, but it was as Paddy Ryan that he was best known. He also went as The Zebra Kid in Japan and as Bud or Ace Freeman.

At 305 pounds, and only 5-foot-10, he was a big man with an even bigger heart. He always had time for the fans, and handicapped children were the ones that really touched him. When they were brought to the matches in their wheelchairs, Ryan would often come out before the

PADDY RYAN BRANDISHING HIS TRUSTY IRISH SHILLE-LAGH AFTER A BLOODY BATTLE. PHOTO: BOB LEONARD

event to make sure they got the autographs and pictures they wanted.

Ryan retired from the ring in 1982, and passed away in December 1989 in his home in Port Moody, BC from an apparent stroke which lead to a massive heart attack.

HANS SCHMIDT

HANS SCHMIDT.
PHOTO: L'IL AL COLLECTION

"The Teuton Terror," Hans Schmidt was easily one of the most hated pro wrestlers ever. At 6-foot-4, 250 pounds, he towered over most of his opponents. Besides the German gimmick, he didn't need weapons or props — he was just plain evil in the ring, happily destroying the most beloved of fan favourites.

After World War II ended, Joliette, Quebec's Guy Larose decided to give pro wrestling a try. Training was tough, but not as tough as the crowds that mocked his real name when he started wrestling outside Quebec. A change was needed. "I met a promoter in Boston, Paul Bowser. He was German and he told me I looked like a German. That's when he gave me that name, Hans Schmidt."

Under his new ring name, he faced every big star going at the time — Lou Thesz, Argentina Rocca, Verne Gagne, Edouard Carpentier. Near riots followed in his wake. Schmidt had legendary feuds with both Whipper Billy Watson and Johnny Powers, and formed tough teams with Dick "The Bulldog" Brower, Hans Hermann and Fritz von Erich. In the mid-'70s, Schmidt stopped wrestling but continued to help out with the Montreal promotion for a while. He retired to the Laurentian mountains north of Montreal.

GEORGE & SANDY SCOTT

Hamilton's George and Sandy Scott had a storied run as a tag team, especially out in Stampede, where they headlined consistently for years. Taking advantage of the early boom in televisions across Canada, the Scotts knew TV could make them fresh, and give them new opponents. "In the summertime, we'd come on down and work some shots in Toronto and get on TV," explained Sandy Scott. "At that time, it was going across Canada. That would re-invent you a little bit. It just kept you up there all the time.

SANDY (LEFT) AND GEORGE SCOTT. PHOTO: GEORGE SCOTT

"Toronto would have guys like the Millers, the Kalmikoffs, Kiniski — all those type of guys. All those guys would be on that TV and they would come out to Calgary. Of course, we were the top team, so we would meet these guys and automatically be selling out all over." Legend has it that bouts against the Millers turned away thousands of people all across the territory.

It was a simple system of promoting incoming stars, and both Scotts learned it well and applied it later when they worked behind the scenes in various promotions. In fact, one could argue that as booker for the WWF during its national expansion and first two WrestleManias, George Scott was one of the most important Canadians ever in pro wrestling.

Growing up in Hamilton, George was an athletic youngster and fell in with the crowd that worked out at the YMCA. He debuted at 17 in 1956 and took to the southern Ontario "bull-shit" circuit. He headed out on his own to Toledo, North Carolina and Texas. When his brother Angus, five years his junior, decided to follow him into wrestling, a fabulous sibling act was born. All that was needed was a name change. "I'd get out in the sun in the summertime, and my hair got lighter," recalled the younger Scott. "[George] said, 'Geez, it looks like sand. Why don't you use Sandy?' I said 'Okay.'"

Outside of Calgary, the Scotts were exceedingly popular in the Carolinas, and both settled there for much of their lives. They also had significant runs in Australia. George and Sandy were certainly not a grounded tag team. "We did a lot of flying head-scissors, drop kicks and moves in the ring, which they called the Scott Aerial Attack," said Sandy. "We were known for our speed and for the aerial attacks."

After breaking his neck in 1972, George reconsidered his career, and was offered a chance to be the booker for Jim Crockett's Mid-Atlantic promotion. He had helped Stu Hart book a little in Calgary, and had hoped all along to get a chance to write the scripts. "That was my dream," he said. As the booker for Mid-Atlantic from 1972 to 1983, George was responsible for developing some of the greatest talent ever — Ric Flair, Ricky Steamboat, Roddy Piper and Jimmy Snuka all had their careers take off in the Mid-Atlantic territory. On occasion, George would don the tights, often teaming with Sandy, to help someone get over. He also owned a piece of the Toronto promotion with Crockett and Jack Tunney.

After quitting Crockett's promotion in 1983, George looked at different opportunities before getting a call from Vince McMahon Jr., who needed help with the wwf, when his father was very ill. Scott agreed and quickly moved up the ranks to become lead booker. There were some heady times. According to him, the wwf was pulling in between $3 million and $4 million on weekends. "Things just started popping," he said. Scott was instrumental in the first two WrestleManias, and for NBC's *Saturday Night's Main Event*. In 1986, after the second WrestleMania, Scott quit, believing that the workload was too heavy. He worked with a few other promotions after that, but his passion was gone and the industry totally changed. These days, George Scott can be found in Florida, where he works with condo developments and hits the golf course whenever possible.

Sandy's career floundered without his brother, and when he was offered the opportunity to join the Mid-Atlantic office — booking towns, and setting up TV and print ads — he jumped at the chance. When Jim Crockett Jr. sold his promotion to Ted Turner, Sandy stayed around for a while, until the constant interference and ineptitude of the suits running the promotion became too much for him. Shortly thereafter, Scott found himself in one of the last true territories, Jim Cornette's Smokey Mountain Wrestling, where he served in a variety of roles. Sandy now lives in Roanoke, Virginia, dabbles in investing and real estate, and takes care of his grandson.

IRON MIKE SHARPE

Iron Mike Sharpe. The name alone brings up an image of a black forearm band and a lot of yelling. Proclaiming himself "Canada's Greatest Athlete," Sharpe was a regular on the WWF broadcasts of the mid-'80s — often staring up at the lights after losing to WWF faces like Tito Santana or Junkyard Dog.

Sharpe is the son of wrestler Mike Sharpe, who together with his brother Ben formed one of the top tag teams of the '50s. Born in Hamilton, Sharpe Jr. grew up in California, then went to high school and university in Hamilton. Dewey Robertson trained Sharpe Jr. after he had tried boxing and weight-lifting.

IRON MIKE SHARPE.
PHOTO: TERRY DART

During his career, Sharpe Jr. met success in Vancouver, Louisiana and Stampede before entering the WWF. Initially he was a challenger for champion Bob Backlund, but within a couple of years, he was a pretty easy roadblock for babyfaces on their way up the card. For the last number of years, Sharpe Jr. has been running a wrestling school in New Jersey. Some of his best known grads are Crowbar Chris Ford and Nova.

RHONDA SINGH

RHONDA SINGH IN ACTION.
PHOTO: TERRANCE MACHALEK

Growing up in Calgary and going to the Stampede matches, Rhonda Singh dreamed of becoming a pro wrestler. Spurned by the Harts, she sought out women's wrestling legend Mildred Burke for training, and was scooped up by All-Japan almost immediately.

Singh blazed new ground on the Japanese women's scene as the fearsome Monster Ripper, and met initial resistance. "The Japanese girls resented it because they never had to lose. If they lost, they lost to each other. They never lost to a foreigner." Trips to Japan and Mexico over the years made Singh a star internationally. Domestically, she did numerous shows in Stampede Wrestling as Rhonda Singh, a part of the Karachi Vice, and had a lame run in the WWF as trailer-park trash Bertha Faye, and a brief appearance in WCW during its last days.

In July 2001, Singh died suddenly in Calgary at 40, leaving behind a real legacy as Canada's most successful woman wrestler ever.

CYCLONE & HURRICANE SMITH

Hurricane & Cyclone Smith were a rough-and-tumble twin tag team in the 1950s and 1960s. The pair used to caddy for Whipper Billy Watson and Pat Flanagan at a golf course in Toronto's east end and, encouraged by The Whip, they learned to wrestle in Hamilton under Jimmy "Red" Simms and Al Spittles.

CYCLONE AND HURRICANE SMITH. PHOTO: BOB GRIMBLY

Initially, the twins split up. Bob Grimbly, a.k.a. Cyclone, debuted first in California as Suicide Schmidt. Maurice, or "Mo," started in Calgary for Stu Hart. When they teamed, the duo were said to hail from Red Deer, Alberta, because of their red hair.

In 1962, the 6-foot-2, 270-pound Smiths were in San Francisco working on a new gimmick when it all came crashing down. "We were going to resurrect George Wagner, Gorgeous George, and I've got pictures of us with our blond hair. We were going to wrestle with Gorgeous George as the Georgy Twins," said Bob Grimbly. "We had a tour lined up in Japan and the doctors came in and pulled my brother's license because he had a heart murmur."

Forced into retirement, Cyclone worked at Dofasco for 25 years. He's now retired and living in Florida. Hurricane joined the Hamilton police force, and wrestled part-time until 1966. Today, he does a lot of work with his church.

Australia —
A Canadian's Home Away From Home

When you look at a list of the greatest stars ever down under in Australia, you'll find an inordinate number of Canadians. Killer Kowalski, Dominic Denucci, Skull Murphy, The Destroyer (Guy Mitchell), Baron Mikel Sciculna, The Spoiler (Don Jardine) and Stan Stasiak were all recognized as IWA World champions during the heyday of Australian wrestling, from 1964 to 1971.

According to Jim Barnett, who promoted for 10 years during that period, there's a good reason for that — taxes. As members of the British Commonwealth, Canadian citizens didn't have to pay Australian taxes. It was a major incentive for Canadians to go on the long journey.

"Americans, after about six weeks, had to start having so much money withheld from their salaries, whereas the Canadians didn't," Barnett explained.

The schedule in Australia was hectic, with much more flying than was usual in North America. Generally, the

wrestlers lived in Sydney; there'd be TV in Sydney on Saturday morning and a card in Melbourne the same night, with Melbourne TV tapings on Sunday mornings. Next up was a flight to Perth for a show on Monday, Adelaide on Tuesday, Brisbane on Wednesday, Brisbane TV on Thursday, then back to Sydney for a match Friday night.

Barnett ran a strict company, too. "They had to wear coats and ties on airplanes. They couldn't drink, they had to be gentlemen, they had to pay their bills. There were a lot of rules and I wanted to be sure I had a promotion I could be proud of and the people could be proud of." The wrestlers enjoyed the trips, and went back.

"My first trip to Australia, I was there one whole year," said Killer Kowalski. "That was when I was world's champion. Then I left, and every six months, I came back, stayed six months. My first time there was in '65, and my last show there was about in '73."

The big secret for promoting in Australia was to cater to the ethnic populations that poured into the country following World War II. Time and time again, Barnett found himself looking to multi-cultural cities like Toronto for talent, whether it was Italian or Hungarian. "As long as they spoke the language, that was okay. If they just were Canadian-Hungarians, that was no good. They had to be able to speak Hungarian."

George and Sandy Scott held the IWA tag belts on three occasions. Sandy called the fans "tremendous." George agreed. "The people were friendly and it was kind of a different attitude. We just had a great time out there."

STAN STASIAK

On the advice of a coach, Arvida, Quebec's George Stipich gave up a promising hockey career in the early 1950s to enter pro wrestling. His first match was in 1958. A promoter told him

STAN STASIAK DELIVERS HIS TRADE-
MARK HEART PUNCH TO JOHNNY
FOTI. PHOTO: BOB LEONARD

that he resembled a wrestler from the 1920s named Stan Stasiak, so Stipich changed his name and success followed.

As Stan "The Crusher" Stasiak, he succeeded as a babyface for years in the Portland, Oregon area, claiming the territory's top title six times. As Stan "The Man" Stasiak, he was an evildoer who won belts in Stampede, Texas and Australia. His finisher was a taped-fist heart punch.

But it's for his nine-day reign as WWF World champion in late 1973 that Stasiak's best remembered, defeating Pedro Morales and losing to Bruno Sammartino. "My dad was the fifth wrestler in the history of that company to become the WWF champion," his son and current wrestler, Shawn Stasiak said. "Even though it's a worked business, it's entertainment, but to me that's pride."

In the early 1980s, Stasiak was a commentator for the Portland territory and a car salesman. In 1984, he moved to Toronto and worked as a security guard, returning to Oregon 10 years later. He died in 1997 at 60 from heart failure.

BRUCE SWAYZE

For the first five years of his career, Hamilton's Bruce Swayze was a weekend warrior, working in the steel mill Monday through Friday and wrestling wherever he was needed on weekends. He started training with Jack Wentworth, and debuted on the weekly shows at the gym in 1961. Swayze would head out with other Hamilton grads like Ivan Koloff and Terry Yorkston to Detroit, Pittsburgh or Buffalo to job to better-known talent.

When Buffalo's Pedro Martinez hooked him up with the Love Brothers in the late '60s, his career was set. Swayze was often in three-man tags with Hartford and Reginald Love, and sometimes served as their manager. "We were hot too. We got a lot of heat, the three of us. If I think about it now, wow, unbelievable," he said. "We could hardly get to the ring, let alone out of it." Swayze would also work Florida, California, Oklahoma, the Carolinas and the IWA during his 15-year career. Some of his biggest moments came in Puerto Rico.

Swayze stopped wrestling full-time in the early '80s, to settle into his wife's family's packaging business, but still wrestled on occasional spot shows until 1988. He also promoted charity shows around Kentucky. Swayze has found that being a salesman and a pro wrestler go hand in hand. "The wrestling background is a tremendous help to me because so many people were closet wrestling fans. They knew who I was, and I have some great stories. That's basically what really got me over in the sales department."

BRUCE SWAYZE

TIGER TASKER

Sent to England in 1936 along with Bill Potts, Al Korman and Tommy Nelson, Kenneth Tasker was a man in search of an identity. He used the name "Thor" Tasker for a while until a British promoter dubbed him Tiger Tasker. The name stuck, but his Toronto heritage was rarely acknowledged.

In Britain, he was "the Alaska gunman of a thousand thrills," the "Canadian star from Montreal," and: "The most sensational and dynamic personality the Ring has ever known. Roughest HE-MAN ever seen in the Ring." Back in North America, he was a more pedestrian, mid-card wrestler who used Boston as a base for much of his 20-plus years of fighting.

In 1964, the former rule-breaker took a strange turn, and became a wrestling referee around southern Ontario, until finally stepping out of the squared circle in 1978. Until his retirement, he worked as a security guard at a Toronto racetrack.

JOHN TENTA

The career of British Columbia's John Tenta is one of abrupt changes of direction — and a few bad gimmicks. He started out as a successful amateur wrestler and football player at Louisiana State University before surprising everyone in January 1986 by picking up and moving to Japan to become a sumo wrestler.

In Japan, Tenta was an oddity. Known as Kototenzan (Heavenly Mountain Harp), he was only the second non-Japanese to try to become a sumo, and had difficulty creating the proper sumo hairstyle because of his thinning hair. Tenta quit after a little more than a year, tired of the servitude expected from someone on the lower echelon of the sumo ranks.

For a "normal" life, Tenta took up pro wrestling under the tutelage of Giant Baba in Japan and Al Tomko in Vancouver. He debuted as a pro in 1987 in Japan, and worked a few shows with the faltering All-Star Wrestling promotion in B.C.

In November 1989, Tenta entered the WWF as Earthquake, attacking the Ultimate Warrior after a push-up challenge along with Dino Bravo. He fought all the top names in the WWF, including Hulk Hogan, Jake "The Snake" Roberts, and André the Giant. As a part of the tag team Natural Disasters, with Typhoon, Tenta even claimed WWF gold.

JOHN TENTA AS THE SHARK IN WCW.
PHOTO: MIKE LANO

Then one day, he up and quit the WWF, resurfacing in WCW under a variety of poor gimmicks including Avalanche and The Shark. Tenta eventually found his way back to the WWF under a mask as Golga, but that didn't last.

Looking back, Tenta says Earthquake was his favourite character. "It was probably the best time of my career, anywhere, including Japan."

Tenta has opened up a wrestling school in Florida, and works occasional dates on the independent circuit.

FRANK THOMPSON

Hamilton's Frank Thompson isn't reluctant to admit that he spent most of his wrestling career as a jobber. "I was a carpenter's carpenter," he said, using the wrestling lingo. "I spent about 15 years in the business and put over some of the best."

Thompson broke into wrestling in the late 1940s with Joe Maich in Brantford, Ontario. He worked around Ontario, but realized that at 225 pounds, he was too small for an area dominated by heavyweights. After quitting his job with Stelco, Thompson got a break in Buffalo for Ed Don George, before heading out to territories like Detroit, Charlotte, Toledo, Kansas City, Texas, Nashville and North Bay.

Outside the ring, Thompson was an officer for the Ontario Provincial Police for a while in the 1950s, and was forbidden to wrestle. He also ran a barber shop, and sold freezers and organs during his life. These days, the 81-year-old Thompson is a motivational speaker and a trained hypnotherapist.

CHIEF THUNDERBIRD

CHIEF THUNDERBIRD

From his debut in 1932 until his retirement a couple of decades later, Saanich, B.C.'s Chief Thunderbird was the first big-name Native wrestler. "He was one of the originals when it came to the Indians wrestling," said Don Leo Jonathon.

Entering the ring in full Native regalia, including a feather headdress with drums pounding, Chief Thunderbird (Jean Baptiste Paul) was a noted attraction across North America, but even moreso in England. "He preceded me to England," said Billy Two Rivers. "When I got there, the people I met spoke of Chief Thunderbird and assumed I knew him! I said, 'No, this is a big country.' I never met the man."

Chief Thunderbird was actually the elected chief of the Saanich people on Vancouver Island. From his west coast home, he made many trips to Australia, New Zealand and Hawaii.

OSSIE TIMMINS

O.J. "Ossie" Timmins always had a real job to fall back on during his wrestling career, but it didn't limit his contributions to the Maritime mat scene. Timmins joined the Halifax

Police Department of the National Harbours Board in 1959, then joined the water services before retiring in 1984 as the Chief Fire and Safety Officer.

Timmins began wrestling as a pro after World War II, and hung around until the 1960s. He was almost always a heel during his career, especially during his stint as The Red Secret. After he stopped wrestling, he refereed occasionally, until the early 1980s.

When Timmins got out of wrestling, he did a two-year stint as commissioner of boxing and wrestling for the Halifax Athletic Commission, and was a commissioner for a New Brunswick promotion in the early '90s. Timmins died in March 2001.

TIGER TOMASSO

Tiger Tomasso was one of the all-time great villains of Stampede Wrestling. He was too small to be a main-eventer, but he could entertain a crowd within the ring, and more importantly, with the microphone. Tomasso had a running battle with Stampede announcer Ed Whalen, and on one occasion the two even wrestled. During his interviews, he would make reference to his (imaginary) birds, earning him the memorable nickname of "Tweet Tweet" Tomasso.

A SERIOUS TIGER JOE TOMASSO. PHOTO: BOB LEONARD

TOMASSO AS THE BAT. PHOTO: BOB LEONARD

Born in Montreal, but raised and trained to be a wrestler in Hamilton, Joseph DiTommaso headed out to Calgary in 1952 and never looked back. "He was an indestructible little bastard," said Stampede promoter Stu Hart.

Tomasso retired in 1976 and did some promoting, sold real estate and used cars until his death after a heart attack in April 1988.

AL TOMKO

A BLOODY CRAZY LEGS HIRSCH, LATER KNOWN AS AL TOMKO. PHOTO: BOB LEONARD

All things considered, Al Tomko had a great impact on the Canadian wrestling scene from the early 1950s — when he ran the Olympia Wrestling Club in Winnipeg — to the demise of his All-Star Wrestling promotion in Vancouver in 1989. Add his long ring career to his promoting accomplishments and you have one of the most important people in western Canada's wrestling legacy.

Tomko's Olympia Club trained wrestlers and promoted occasional shows. After taking some time off in the mid-'50s, he returned to wrestling as a top villain at Winnipeg's Madison Club. A decade later, he got the opportunity to be the local promoter for Verne Gagne's AWA. Tomko would run shows in Winnipeg for years, working on cards himself as "Crazy Legs" Leroy Hirsch. At the encouragement of Gagne, Tomko bought out and shut down the competing Madison Club, setting the stage for the myriad of promoters who would run Winnipeg over the next decades.

In the late 1970s, Tomko bought Sandor Kovacs' share of the Vancouver All-Star promotion and worked with Gene Kiniski until Kiniski had had enough. "His idea of promoting wrestling was different," was all Kiniski would say. The Tomko-run All-Star promotion is best remembered for its cheesy TV production values in front of a small studio audience; goofy angles; and blatant self-promotion of Sgt. Al Tomko and his two sons Terry, a.k.a. The Frog, and Todd, a.k.a. Rick Davis.

Still, Tomko's influence on a new generation of workers in the 1980s cannot be denied. "He was a funny guy," said Mark Vellious, better known as the character Michelle Starr. "He had all these old stories that he'd tell you about a hundred times about his old days working for the AWA and stuff. You'd hear each story about 10 times a week." At a time when promotions were giving in to the WWF's expansion, Tomko hung around until 1989, giving wrestlers a place to work on a regular basis. He even tried an all-female promotion during the '80s that went nowhere.

For the last few years, Tomko has lived in Washington State, out of wrestling altogether. "He's in a different business now," said Moose Morowski, often a foe of Tomko's in the ring. "He sort of felt they pushed him out — that Vince kind of pushed him out."

BILLY TWO RIVERS

Before Jesse "The Body" Ventura became better known for his politics than his wrestling antics, there was Canada's wrestler-turned-public-servant Billy Two Rivers. After 24 years in the ring, Two Rivers was approached by friends about running for council on the Kahnawake reserve, outside Montreal. He declined initially, but ran in 1978 and served the Mohawks as Chief in Council for 20 years.

His wrestling experience helped when Two Rivers found himself in the public eye, including during the controversial blockade of Montreal's Mercier Bridge in 1990, usually referred to as the Oka Crisis. Since he stopped serving on council, Two Rivers has helped as an advisor to the Assembly of First Nations.

BILLY TWO RIVERS.
PHOTO: BILLY TWO
RIVERS

In 1950, wrestling superstar Don Eagle came home to Kahnawake to recuperate from the trials of the road. He befriended a young Two Rivers, and when he went back to wrestling, Eagle took the 15-year-old Two Rivers with him to Columbus, Ohio. "He saw some potential in me becoming a wrestler. He invited me to go back with him when he went back to his training process after his back had healed properly," said Two Rivers. After two years of training, Two Rivers got up to 205 pounds and made his debut in February 1953.

In 1959, Two Rivers broke away from his mentor, hitting Florida and the Carolinas. But it was a decision to go to England to wrestle — made on a coin flip, which Stampede lost — that changed his life and made him a star overseas. Entering the ring wearing a full-feathered headdress, which he'd remove to reveal a Mohawk haircut, Billy was a natural for English television. In the ring, he would go into a war dance when he lost his temper. But Two Rivers is not one to brag about himself. "I was more or less a journeyman. I travelled and was more of an attraction. People went to see the Indian."

After six years in England, he came home to Kahnawake and worked for the Montreal-based Grand Prix promotion run by the Vachons. It allowed Two Rivers to stay close to home and start some businesses on the reserve. His high profile got him involved in various film and TV projects, including a substantial role in the movie *Black Robe*.

TARZAN TYLER

After starting in pro wrestling in the 1950s, Quebec's Camille Tourville evolved into "Tarzan" Tourville and then into Tarzan "The Boot" Tyler. His gimmick was the "loaded" boot — knocking the boot three times on the mat made it "lethal," and he would then clobber an opponent.

TARZAN TYLER.
PHOTO: L'IL AL COLLECTION

Tyler made it big in the southern U.S., particularly Texas and Florida, where he held a number of titles. As a tag-team wrestler, he also had great successes, including a run as WWWF World tag-team champ with Crazy Luke Graham in 1971. Tyler also held titles with Bill Watts, Tim Tyler, Alaskan Jay York and Louie Tillet.

Besides his ring skills, Tyler also served as the booker for a few territories. In Montreal, in the '80s, he became a manager during the last days of the International Wrestling promotion. Just before Christmas 1985, Tyler was killed, along with his protege Pierre "Mad Dog" Lefebvre and referee Adrien Desbois, in a car accident.

FRANK VALOIS

From the age of 18 until he was 56, Frank Valois was a pro wrestler — an amazing 38 years in the ring. Yet he's probably best known for his out of ring actions. It was Valois who brought André Roussimoff, better known as André the Giant, to Canada to learn wrestling in the early '70s, and it was Valois who brought the necessary parties together to create the TV program *Les Etoiles de la Lutte* after the demise of Grand Prix Wrestling in the late '70s.

As a pro, the Montreal-born Valois wrestled as both a heel and a face, and was particularly successful in France, where he even appeared in a few films.

FRANK VALOIS.
PHOTO: L'IL AL COLLECTION

After he met André, Valois became his friend and mentor, taking the Giant from place to place, often wrestling on the undercard. When the WWWF took over the booking of André, Valois was pushed out.

Promotions Varoussac started in 1980 and was initially a partnership between Valois, Roussimoff and Gino Brito Sr. It filled a void in the Quebec wrestling scene at the time, allowing local talent like Dino Bravo, Rick Martel and the Rougeaus to shine against imported heels. Valois died on New Year's Eve 1998 in Ste-Adele, Quebec.

KURT VON HESS

KURT VON HESS.
PHOTO: BOB LEONARD

Hamilton's Big Bill Terry got involved in pro wrestling under the guidance of Benny Lima, and debuted in 1969. After limited success under his real name, he became Kurt von Hess, a dreaded German heel with a goatee, shaved head, and black boots. It was a career that took him around the world.

The greatest success for von Hess came alongside fellow Canadian-turned-German heel John Anson, a.k.a. Karl von Shotz. Together, they won the world tag titles, based out of Detroit. Von Hess also won tag gold with John Quinn in Japan. As a single, he was Stampede Wrestling North American champion in 1971.

He retired from the ring game in 1986 after being diagnosed with a kidney disease. Terry was on a dialysis machine for more than six years, but eventually in 1996, a donor was found. He died of a heart attack in March 1999 at age 56.

KARL & KURT VON STEIGER

Lorne Corlett and Arnold Pastrick were a couple of decent hands around the Winnipeg territory in the 1960s when they teamed up and hit the road as the German heels Karl and Kurt von Steiger. They excelled during the 1970s, employing quick tags and double-team moves. Together, the von Steigers worked Portland, Tennessee, San Francisco, Stampede, Australia, the AWA, and the Carolinas.

KURT AND KARL VON STEIGER. PHOTO: MELBY COLLECTION

"Kurt and Karl were both great, great hands. They were ring generals, both of them. A pleasure to work with," said Dutch Savage, who also co-owned the Portland promotion. In February-March 1971, they took the AWA tag belts from the Vachons, though the change was never recognized by the promotion.

Kurt von Steiger (Pastrick) also promoted in Phoenix for a bit, and helped train Afa the Samoan, Big Bill Anderson, and Bobby Jaggers. He worked around Portland for a number of years until retiring to run a business in Oregon. Karl von Steiger (Corlett) had a wanderlust that his partner didn't, and continued to travel. He formed a championship tag team with Killer Karl Krupp in Japan.

SAILOR WHITE

The story of St. John's, Newfoundland's Edward John "Sailor" White is one of triumph and destruction. Wrestling fans will remember the tattooed White as a terrible rule-breaker, a madman able to enrage fans and bleed profusely on both

SAILOR WHITE IN SOUTH AFRICA. PHOTO: LEDUC COLLECTION

opponents and the crowd. After breaking into wrestling in 1972, White became a huge star from Montreal to the Maritimes, headlined South Africa as Big John Strongbo, and was WWF tag team champ in 1981 as Moondog King (along with Moondog Rex Randy Colley).

Sadly, Sailor White was a man bent on self-destruction. Addicted to booze, drugs and sex, his wrestling success only fed his desires. His marriage destroyed, family in tatters, White spent time in prison for drugs, pimping, uttering death threats, assault and break-and-enter. He cleaned up with the help of a treatment clinic in Montreal and returned to Newfoundland. White has had numerous heart attacks, is a diabetic and has lost three toes off his right foot. He also suffers from Bell's Palsy.

White has trained a number of wrestlers in his home province, and has also tried his hand at promoting. In the summer of 2000, he ran in a federal by-election, and came fifth. It gave him a chance to talk about some issues that are close to his heart. "I've been trying to get a youth centre going and I got tired of getting the runaround. So I thought maybe if I get into the election, I thought I'd have a chance to speak my piece, get the word out that I'm trying to get a youth centre and also something to help the senior citizens," he said.

ABE ZVONKIN

Abe Zvonkin was known under many aliases, surprising considering that he was a successful tackle for the Hamilton Ti-Cats before he embarked on a wrestling career under the guidance of Whipper Watson in the 1940s.

At various times, Zvonkin was Mr. X, Mr. E, one of the Masked Purple Heart Brothers (with Jack Dillon), and the Masked Phantom. In New Zealand, he was Abe Zhukov, playing off his legitimate Russian heritage. Born in New York City, Zvonkin came to Hamilton with his parents when he was just two years old. He attended Queen's University in Kingston, Ontario, studying education and teaching.

ABE ZVONKIN.
PHOTO: JEAN ZVONKIN

In the mid-'50s, Zvonkin's attention shifted to his love for dogs. He ran a grooming business, and competed and judged at dog shows. His family travelled with him all through the United States. "I remember going down Broadway in New York in the trailer, with the three kids and seven dogs. It was a little odd. Our life has always been a little different," said Jean Zvonkin, Abe's wife of over 70 years. He died in August 2002 after a long battle with cancer. He was 91.

HOCKEY AND WRESTLING CAME TOGETHER IN THE '60S WITH THE
'SUR LE MATELAS' HOCKEY TEAM OF QUEBEC WRESTLERS.
PHOTO: LEDUC COLLECTION

Adopted Canadians

FRED ATKINS

Aussie wrestler Fred Atkinson arrived in Canada shortly after World War II, and bought a house in Crystal Beach, Ontario, where he lived until his death in May 1988 at 77. In an 1983 interview with the Toronto *Sun*, Atkinson — best known as Fred Atkins — called his home "a perfect

FRED ATKINS IN 1949.
PHOTO: TUROFSKY BROTHERS

location. In the country, but easy to get to the Buffalo airport, then Los Angeles, then Japan. Or, the other way to Toronto and Europe."

It was Atkins who stripped Whipper Billy Watson of the British Empire title when nobody thought it could be done. The Whip considered Atkins among the 10 best in the world at the time. "You'd never see Fred do a drop kick, never a flying tackle. That was not his style. His was Greco-Roman style, closer to Olympic-type wrestling than anybody else," Watson said in the same *Sun* article.

Atkins retired from active wrestling in the 1960s, but worked as a referee into his early '70s. A complete fitness nut, Atkins trained wrestlers in the basement of his house. Tiger Jeet Singh is his best known grad. Recognizing his talent for improving overall health and flexibility, the Buffalo Sabres and Toronto Maple Leafs employed him at various times to whip their players into shape.

HERCULES AYALA

HERCULES AYALA LIFTS
KERRY BROWN OVERHEAD.
PHOTO: BOB LEONARD

Puerto Rico's Hercules Ayala was wrestling in Germany in 1977 when he met Bret Hart and Dynamite Kid. "They talked to me, they say my dad is a promoter in Canada, blah, blah, blah. And I say I'd like to go and they called Stu Hart and that's when they booked me," Ayala said.

"In the beginning, I thought that Canada was a big place. I said that that was going to be good for me," Ayala laughed. "I was supposed to come only for six months, and I stayed eight years! A long time!"

Ayala met his wife Susan in Edmonton, and now has landed-immigrant status in Canada.

Besides his time in Stampede, Ayala had a good run in Montreal, where he was champion, beating Dr. D. David Shults for the promotion's top title in January 1987, and losing the belt to Abdullah the Butcher a month later. In the Maritimes, Ayala did a number of tours as Hercules Cortez.

He's probably best known for his heel turn on Puerto Rican legend/promoter Carlos Colon, and their subsequent bloody feud.

EDOUARD CARPENTIER

In 1956, a man of Polish descent named Edouard Weicz came to Montreal from France. He was a gymnast, and veteran of the French resistance during World War II. Within months, as

Edouard Carpentier, he would revolutionize Canadian wrestling with his acrobatic moves and his impressive physique, shooting to the top of the wrestling world.

"When I come in 1956, I come because I'm the European champion and I have no more competition," Carpentier explained. Montreal promoter Eddie Quinn seized Carpentier and was soon promoting him across North America. Carpentier's biggest successes came early in his career. He defeated NWA champ Lou Thesz in June 1957 by DQ when Thesz couldn't fight in the third fall. Some promoters began recognizing Carpentier was the world champ and that led to the formation of the AWA in the American Midwest. Carpentier was to win many more titles, both in singles and tag teams.

The Flying Frenchman's drop kicks, somersaults and cart-

EDOUARD CARPENTIER COMES IN FOR A WELL-CONTROLLED CRASH LANDING ON ARCHIE "THE STOMPER" GOULDIE IN THE COURSE OF THEIR 1967 WAR. PHOTO: BOB LEONARD

wheels were the showy part of his solid repertoire, which included training in judo, boxing and savate. Killer Kowalski was a regular opponent. "I did all the work in the ring. I carried him," bragged Kowalski. "He was a jumping bean. I'm not being mean here, but a lot of the things he did were not my ideas. But he was all right. He was another Pollack." Besides the Killer, Carpentier had major feuds with Don Leo Jonathon, Hans Schmidt, Ivan Koloff, and John Tolos.

Throughout his career, which lasted into the mid-'70s, the 5-foot-10, 225-pound Carpentier was a good guy. "He was just loved in Canada, and anywhere in the States where he wrestled," said Gene Kiniski. "Carpentier was great."

Carpentier is also well known as a trainer of wrestlers. Some of his protegés include Michel "Le Justice" Dubois and Yvon Robert Jr., and he helped to polish stars like André the Giant and Rick Martel. He has also done work as a stunt man. Carpentier's nephew Jacky Weicz wrestled in the 1970s as André and Roland Carpentier.

After retiring from wrestling, Carpentier served as a colour commentator for the WWF French broadcasts.

BAD NEWS ALLEN COAGE

Bad News Allen Coage has always meant good news for the box office of Stampede Wrestling. In between his tours of Japan, Coage always seemed to find himself battling the likes of Bret Hart and Dynamite Kid in Calgary.

On one occasion, he missed both the heel and the face buses in Edmonton, but ended up meeting his future wife, Helen, instead. Now a landed immigrant in Canada, Coage has had a storied career.

Bad News Brown drags Randy Savage during his WWF stint. Photo: Terry Dart

He took bronze for the United States as a heavyweight in judo at the 1976 Montreal Olympics before heading to Japan to learn pro wrestling. In the Orient, he was a big hit, fighting top stars like Antonio Inoki.

The year 1988 saw Coage head to the WWF, where he stayed for two years as Bad News Brown. It isn't an experience he cherishes. "It wasn't a fun time for me," Coage said. "You see, when I left there I was really happy. I was brought there under false pretenses. They never kept their word to me. I was just sick of the lying all the time and fighting for my money. That was two and a half years of my life that I really didn't enjoy."

After 22 years of bumps, knee surgery stopped Coage's career. He has been involved with various wrestling ventures since, including as a colour commentator on the briefly resurgent Stampede Wrestling.

CUBAN ASSASSIN

Professional wrestling has taken Angel Acevedo, a.k.a. The Cuban Assassin, around the world, including 17 trips to Japan and eight trips to Germany. But it's Canada that won his heart.

He settled outside Calgary in 1976, marrying his second wife in 1978, and the short, stocky Puerto Rican-born, Cuban-raised commando with the wild hair has been here ever since.

THE CUBAN ASSASSIN CLAMPS ON A CHINLOCK. PHOTO: BOB LEONARD

Acevedo actually trained as a boxer in Cuba, but turned to wrestling because the money was better. He debuted in Florida under the guidance of Eddie Graham.

Beyond a shadow of a doubt, "Cubie" calls the Maritimes his favourite place in the world to wrestle. "The money is steady, it's summer, and I like the place. That was the first place, I came from Cuba to the United States, and the United States to Canada. And the first border that I crossed, I was driving from Boston to St. Stephen, New Brunswick. It was summer, and I never spent a winter there. I love the summer there."

In Calgary, The Cuban Assassin was one of the senior wrestlers on the Stampede circuit. That meant Acevedo had to help bring along the youngsters. "Bret Hart's first match was against me in Saskatoon in 1977, I think," he said. "Chris Benoit, he was like a kid when he started in the business."

DOMINIC DENUCCI

DOMINIC DENUCCI.
PHOTO: TERRY DART

Dominic Denucci came to Canada from Italy in 1955 at the age of 20. He settled in Montreal, where his great-uncle lived. Denucci quickly found friends at the Palais Nationale, where all the amateur wrestlers trained and the pros would come by to work out. There Denucci worked out with the likes of Maurice Vachon. He was approached by Yvon Robert and Tony Lanza about entering pro wrestling, and despite the fact that Denucci really didn't know anything about it, he trained under Lanza.

Denucci started around Montreal in the early 1960s, but moved on to Detroit where he was teamed with the original Dino Bravo as Dominic Bravo. Stints in Calgary, San Francisco, Los Angeles, Japan and Australia followed. The Roy Shire San Francisco territory was an early highlight. "I think the best thing for me was when I was in San Francisco. That was the first one, when I beat Ray Stevens for the championship, United States champion. That, at that time, was very exciting, because I was still young."

In the WWWF, Denucci rose to prominence as a tag-team wrestler, holding the tag belts with partners Pat Barrett, Victor Riviera and the younger Dino Bravo from Montreal. His favourite partner? "I'm not knocking Victor because Victor was a really good worker too, but Dino Bravo, I think was my best."

Vince McMahon Jr. and Denucci had a falling out in 1983, and Denucci left the WWF just before its big expansion. He wrestled around the world until 1988, organizing tours of locations like Saudi Arabia and the Philippines before retiring for good. Denucci got involved in running a wrestling school in Pittsburgh, and trained world champs Mick Foley and Shane Douglas. These days, he runs the school on weekends, and works as a driver for the *New York Times* during the week.

ERIK THE RED

Ibe "Eric" Hanson came to Canada from Denmark to seek a new life, settling in Grimsby, Ontario. He was an engineer by trade and had dabbled in boxing. But being a big man — 6-foot-1, 300 plus pounds — he found the wrestling business fascinating and got his break out in Vancouver for All-Star in the late '60s when he survived a televised bout against Karl Gotch.

For most of his brief career, Hanson was billed as Erik the Red, complete with all the accessories one would expect from a Viking. He befriended Bruce Swayze, who got Hanson booked in Buffalo, Oklahoma and Florida. He also worked Toronto and was managed by George Cannon in the IWA. "I thought he was one of the best big men in the business," said

ERIK THE RED. PHOTO: L'IL AL COLLECTION

Swayze. "He was a guy that could walk on his hands. He could take a soccer ball and bounce it for five minutes, either foot."

As the bone-carrying Eric the Animal, Hanson took the NWF North American title off Johnny Powers in 1973. Powers called him "a really good wrestler, really good in the ring." In November 1978, Hanson was hit by a car and killed in Florida, cutting short a promising career.

ERICH FROELICH

One of the most respected wrestlers in the Vancouver All-Star Wrestling promotion was Erich Froelich, the acrobatic, barefooted German. He was the one to test out the newcomers to the territory. "Through my ability, I could wrestle anybody. Any new guy came in to Vancouver, I was over here on TV, and I was the first one to wrestle them, and to find out . . . if he's capable of wrestling anybody," Froelich said.

He came to Canada from West Germany in 1956 to seek

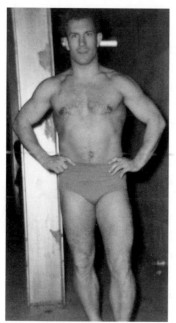

ERICH FROELICH.
PHOTO: TERRY DART

adventure, and to avoid being drafted into the army. Froelich loved gymnastics, and was spotted by wrestling promoter Rod Fenton one day during a public performance. Eventually, Froelich accepted an invitation to work out with some of the local pro wrestlers. "I decided to give it a try because I couldn't eat my medals," he said with a laugh.

Froelich's career lasted 20 years. He's best known in B.C., California and Texas. He also did tours of Japan, Hawaii, Fiji, Puerto Rico and England. After retiring in 1981, Froelich's health deteriorated, and he had open heart, open lung surgery and a hip replaced. He's been on disability allowance ever since, living in B.C. Though he knows some of the health problems were brought on by his choice of professions, Erich has no regrets. "My whole life was a highlight when I was wrestling. I loved wrestling and I enjoyed travelling."

DON LEO JONATHON

Don Heaton first came to visit Canada in the mid-1930s with his father, Brother Jonathon, who was a pro wrestler from Utah. Little did he know he was to fall in love with the country, and become one of its legends of wrestling.

When Heaton got out of the U.S. Navy in 1949, where he had done specialized diving jobs, he decided to follow his father into the mat game, adopting the name Don Leo Jonathon. At 6-foot-6, and working at anywhere from 250 to 340 pounds, he was a force to be reckoned with — indeed, a true Mormon giant.

Don Leo Jonathon quickly became one of the top stars in the sport, and was particularly in demand across Canada during the 1950s. "I was moving around. I'd go to Montreal, and I'd be there maybe six months, then I'd live in Toronto for six months, then I'd go down to Winnipeg or the Maritimes, spend five, six months in the Maritimes," Jonathon explained. The odyssey continued for Jonathon until he decided to settle down outside Vancouver in 1963 and raise his family. He still lives there today.

"I've been in Canada so long people think that I am Canadian!" he said with a laugh. "I'm a landed immigrant, but I wasn't born here."

Regardless of his origins, there is no denying Jonathon's legacy. For 32 years, he was an awesome physical specimen, always in top shape and able to wrestle for long periods of time. In the ring, Jonathon would astound fans and opponents alike with his cartwheels, backflips, sommersaults, drop kicks, nip-ups. "He was just such a phenomenal athlete. The things he could do — sometimes I was just so amazed. He was really, really something," said Gene Kiniski. Killer Kowalski agreed: "He was a very good man, very athletic. Big, big guy

DON LEO JONATHON. PHOTO: HEATON FAMILY

like him, he'd put his hands all over you, flip over the top rope, land on his feet."

Part of the reason for Jonathon's incredible strength and physique came from his outside interests. While wrestling in Colorado early in his career, he also worked as a lumberjack. He returned to diving often, working on oil rigs and doing commercial diving. The work built his body. "I was working out real heavy there, pulling that heavy gear off the sea floor, pulling four-inch hoses in 300 feet of water, and 100 feet of interface. And I went up to 340 [pounds]," Jonathon said. "I used to leave the oil rigs occasionally, and come back and wrestle."

Jonathon would often choose what territories to work based on the hunting and fishing available nearby. "I must have hit every bloody lake in Quebec just because someone told me the trout fishing was good!" he laughed. "Going out into the townships in Montreal . . . I loved making those trips, and I'd do them myself because I would shoot all the way up there. I'd shoot crows and foxes."

Due to his constant desire to keep moving, Jonathon never really had his name established with one particular territory until the end of his career, when he worked regularly for All-Star Wrestling in British Columbia. For that reason, he doesn't have a long list of titles; being loyal and kissing up to promoters wasn't his cup of tea.

Jonathon had two go-rounds with the AWA World title, based out of Omaha in 1961. He defended that belt in the States, Canada, Africa, Austria. "Everybody you wrestled for those title matches, they all wanted it. And some of them, that's their life's dream."

DON LEO JONATHON TOSSES KLONDIKE BILL. PHOTO: BOB LEONARD

Given his size, it's understandable that some of his most memorable bouts came against other giants like André the Giant, Killer Kowalski and even a young Big John Studd in the Maritimes. Yet, he could take on anybody and had great matches with much smaller legends like Edouard Carpentier, Lou Thesz, and Verne Gagne. When a decision didn't go his way, Jonathon let his frustrations out with temper tantrums that left fans terrified by his sheer power.

Since getting out of wrestling, Jonathon has kept a low profile. In the late '80s, he fought off a bladder cancer, but it recently returned. As if facing another opponent, he has a simple plan. "It popped up again, so we're going to have to stomp it."

ATHOL LAYTON

ATHOL LAYTON. PHOTO: TERRY DART

Lord Athol Layton arrived in Toronto in 1950, invited to join the grappling stable of Frank Tunney. He started out as a good guy, before opposing the great Whipper Watson. Seeing how The Whip was number one in town, Layton quickly became a heel. For five years, the native of Australia was one of the most hated men around.

With his extensive vocabulary and prissy manners, Layton was able to enrage crowds wherever he worked. "They hated an Englishman passionately if he got out of line. I played on that. They used to do interviews in the dressing room before the bouts and I would take my time drinking my tea and working up the crowd," Layton told the Toronto *Sun* in 1981.

Layton was running a pub in Australia with his wife when a troupe of wrestlers came through town in the late 1940s. A successful boxer who'd also considered acting, the 6-foot-5 Layton was intrigued. He learned a bit in Singapore and England, but it wasn't until his trip to Canada that his career really took off.

Following his fights with The Whip, it was only natural that at some point he should become a babyface. Layton had made the right decision, and with wrestling starting to appear on TV screens everywhere, he became a well-known announcer as well, for shows in Toronto, Cleveland and Detroit. In

Toronto, Layton was quite involved with the Shriners, had a go at local politics, and became a Canadian citizen in 1958.

After suffering a detached retina during a match with The Sheik in 1976, Layton retired at age 56. He died in January 1984 of a heart attack.

GERRY MORROW

Morrow grew up in Martinique, but learned to wrestle in Paris and Tokyo and became a star around the world. He speaks many languages and has settled in Calgary. Sounds like the type of publicity Cowtown would want, but it's the true life story of Gerard Etifier, better known to wrestling fans as Gerry Morrow.

Having followed his much older brother Eddie into pro wrestling, Gerry became known as a quick wrestler who could

A YOUNG BRET HART IS CAUGHT IN A GERRY MORROW'S TWISTING HEAD SCISSORS.
PHOTO: BOB LEONARD

wrestle technically or overpower an opponent. In 1975, Gerry and Eddie teamed in Montreal, Stampede Wrestling and Vancouver. Gerry decided to stay in Calgary, becoming a Canadian citizen in 1983. "I used to like Calgary because you used to work almost every night, and I met lots of good people there," he said. From Calgary, he went back and forth to Japan, and worked South Africa, Germany, New Zealand and Puerto Rico.

Besides teaming with his brother, Gerry Morrow is best known as a part of the Cuban Commandos tag team with the Cuban Assassin, and for his tag team with former CFL player George Wells. Now out of wrestling, Morrow takes it easy, with his second wife and two dogs.

ANGELO MOSCA

GET OUT OF THE WAY, HERE COMES KING KONG MOSCA! PHOTO: BOB LEONARD

Angelo Mosca was a brilliant self-promoter and no stranger to controversy. He knew the value of seeing one's name in print, giving a good quote, being talked about around the water cooler. Mosca made the right choice becoming a professional wrestler, a profession where that kind of thing was encouraged.

The Mosca most Canadians know is the man who shot to fame in the 1963 Grey Cup game in Vancouver, when he flattened Lions star Willie Fleming just before half-time, sealing his reputation and helping the Ti-Cats hoist the Cup. He was the dirtiest player in the CFL, according to the headlines, and he did nothing to downplay the accusation. In all, Mosca played 15 years in the CFL for Hamilton, Ottawa and Montreal, and was elected to the Canadian Football Hall of Fame in 1987.

Born in Waltham, Massachusetts, Mosca grew into a 6-foot-5, 265-pound behemoth, sought after by colleges. He went to Notre Dame, but was kicked out for bookmaking, something he said he had learned from his father. Next, Mosca went to Wyoming, but was booted out again, this time for theft. His reputation didn't scare off the pro scouts. He was drafted by the Philadelphia Eagles and the Ti-Cats, and went to Hamilton for more money after he graduated from Notre Dame with a degree in business administration.

At the encouragement of many wrestlers, Mosca took up grappling during the off-season in 1969, and quickly realized he could make more money there than in football. His first match was in Ottawa, teaming with Tom "The Emperor" Jones against Hurricane & Cyclone Smith. When he ended his playing career in 1972 (with four Grey Cup rings), Mosca hit the road and dominated territory after territory.

He was King Kong Mosca, and he could brawl and growl with the best of them. Mosca claimed gold in San Francisco, the Bahamas, the Mid-South, Florida and the Mid-Atlantic region. He won the Canadian championship on five different occasions around Toronto, one of the few territories where he was a good guy. For a time, Mosca even teamed with his son Angelo Mosca Jr., but the youngster didn't have his father's size or drive.

When he stopped wrestling actively in the 1980s, Mosca worked briefly for the WWF as a commentator for Maple Leaf Wrestling. When that gig ended, he turned to promoting, bringing in the stars of the NWA to Hamilton for two MoscaMania shows and small tours under the Pro Wrestling Canada banner. Mosca is also well known for his many TV appearances, including commercials for snowmobiles, razors, beer, and cars. Today, he's involved in real estate, and continues to promote the CFL from his Niagara home.

The Canadian Football League —
Wrestling Breeding Ground

GENE KINISKI. PHOTO: OLIVER COLLECTION

Besides the best-known Canadian gridiron stars to make the jump from the CFL to pro wrestling — Angelo 'King Kong' Mosca, Gene Kiniski, Stu Hart — a number of Americans got playing time in the Great White North before putting on their wrestling boots.

Tito Santana got into action for 13 games with the B.C. Lions as a tight end in 1976. "I was young and single and I thought it was a beautiful city, beautiful people, beautiful women," Santana said about Vancouver. "I had a great time. I lived there for a year and a half. It was a very good experience for somebody who came from way down south, a little town with a population of 14,000. That was the beginning of my world tour, I guess."

Before attaining heights as WCW World champion, and later as Faarooq in the WWF, Ron Simmons was a standout at Florida State University. He played six games in 1981 with the CFL's Ottawa Rough Riders.

Another WCW World champ, Lex Luger, took to the field with the Montreal Alouettes under his real name, Larry Pfohl. In total, 'The Total Package' played 14 games for the Als, from 1979 to 1981.

Playing for the Calgary Stampeders or Edmonton Eskimos seemed to be a great way to get recognized by Stu Hart's Stampede Wrestling promotion. Superstar Billy Graham (Wayne Coleman), Bob Lueck, Wilbur Snyder and

Brian Pillman all started in pro wrestling this way. Hart would often use players only in the off-season.

Hacksaw Duggan was a Toronto Argonaut briefly. "I remember doing training camp in Guelph, the university. Had a good time out there. Met a lot of pretty Canadian girls," Duggan said. "You have to pay a lot more attention to Canadian football. With the three downs, you can't be over there flirting with the women and all of a sudden, the punt team's supposed to be out there. So, you really had to have your head in the ballgame."

CFL ALUMNI ANGELO MOSCA (RIGHT) AND WAYNE COLEMAN (LATER SUPERSTAR GRAHAM). PHOTO: BOB LEONARD

As for The Rock, Rocky Maivia, he never actually got into a game for the Calgary Stampeders, spending some time on their practice roster. In his book, *The Rock Says . . .* , he credits his release from the Stamps for turning his attention to the possibilities of pro wrestling.

Some others who played in the CFL before turning to the ring include Joe Blanchard, George Wells, King Curtis Iaukea and Woody Strode.

JIM "THE ANVIL" NEIDHART

An All-American shot-putter and football star, Jim Neidhart's career in the NFL came to an end when the Dallas Cowboys released him in the late '70s. He bounced around for a bit in

Jim Neidhart in Stampede Wrestling, 1979. Photo: Bob Leonard

San Diego before L.A. promoter Mike LeBell suggested pro wrestling. At 6-foot-1, 305 pounds, Jim "The Anvil" Neidhart was sent to Stu Hart to train as a pro wrestler in the early '80s.

Neidhart toughed out the training in the Dungeon, and fell for Stu's daughter Ellie, who he later married. He debuted in 1979 for Stampede Wrestling and worked the territory for years, with occasional side trips, until he made it to the wwf in the mid-'80s. Paired with brother-in-law Bret "Hitman" Hart and manager Jimmy Hart, Neidhart sported a goatee and did a maniacal laugh in the Hart Foundation. "The Pink and Black Attack" dominated the wwf tag ranks and had epic feuds with the British Bulldogs and the Killer Bees.

When Bret graduated into a singles action, Neidhart floundered, teaming for a while with the late Owen Hart. He was a part of the rejuvenated, larger Hart Foundation in 1997 but jumped to wcw after the Hitman's falling out with Vince McMahon. In wcw, Neidhart was basically a well-known jobber. Since he left the company, he has been working the independent circuit both in North America and abroad, based out of his Calgary home.

BARON MIKEL SCICLUNA

After coming to Canada from Malta in 1950, Mike Scicluna fell in with a bunch of workout nuts at a gym near Maple Leaf Gardens in Toronto. He trained to become a pro wrestler with other Torontonians like Waldo von Erich and Dave McKigney. Scicluna debuted as Mike Valentino for Frank Tunney's Ontario promotion in 1954.

At an imposing 6-foot-4, 265 pounds, Valentino was hardly the proper name for him. Vince McMahon Sr. believed in his potential as a monster heel, and brought him to the WWWF, where he became Baron Mikel Scicluna, entering the ring clad in a long, red cape with a Maltese cross on the back. "Vince McMahon thought I should do pretty good, so he pushed me. I wrestled Bruno Sammartino three times in Madison Square Gardens," Scicluna said.

BARON MIKEL SCICLUNA.
PHOTO: MIKE SCICLUNA

Besides being on top in New York, Scicluna was the world champion in Australia in 1968. He retired from pro wrestling in 1983 and worked for the *New York Times* for a number of years as a driver. Scicluna is now retired and, with his wife of over 44 years, living in Pittsburgh to be close to their two grandsons.

SWEET DADDY SIKI

"Mr. Irresistible," Sweet Daddy Siki, is a Texan by birth, but a Canadian by choice. After getting involved in wrestling in 1955 in Artisa, New Mexico, he moved to Toronto in 1961 because it provided a good central location for travel across North America. "When I came to Toronto, I said, 'My God, this is God's country,'" Siki explained. "I fell in love with it." He still lives in Toronto today, and uses it as a base for his country-and-western band and his work as a DJ.

Siki is well known right across Canada, memorable for his bleached blond hair and egotistical style — "A lot of people try to copy me, but there's only one Niagara Falls and only one

Mona Lisa. And there's only one Mr. Irresistible — Sweet Daddy Siki." He fought in Stampede Wrestling for years, travelled with Bearman McKigney's circuit and was a mainstay of the eastern scene. "I always did like Newfoundland. That's about the best province there is. The people there are really nice."

Besides Canada, Siki wrestled across the United States, in Australia, New Zealand, Japan, Puerto Rico, the Bahamas and Trinidad.

GAMA SINGH

The Great Gama Singh (Gadowar Singh Sahota) used the Calgary Stampede promotion as a home base during his long, successful wrestling career. "Whenever I was home, doors were always open for me from Stu Hart," he said. "Stu Hart was good to me."

Born in India, Singh's family immigrated to Canada in the early '60s and he went to school in Merrick, B.C. He wrestled amateur a bit, and met Bill Persack, an old-time wrestler, who trained Singh for six months and suggested that it was then time to move to Calgary and begin his career. Singh's brother Akim would also get into wrestling.

Though most wrestling fans remember Singh best as being the leader of The Karachi Vice in Stampede, his biggest paydays came in other countries, like Barbados, Puerto Rico and Trinidad. South Africa was also particularly good to Singh. "[It has] always been a big market for me," he explained. His first trip was in 1983. "They were looking for an Indian — there's a big market for Indian wrestlers there. My very first trip we set attendance records in several different places . . . it just took off like crazy. I made enormous amounts of money."

Singh does have a big "What if?" in his life,

"Dr. D" David Shultz is trapped tight a chinlock by The Great Gama. Photo: Bob Leonard

though. In the early '80s, Vince McMahon Jr. was just starting to expand the WWF and was looking for an Indian to take to the Middle East. Gama Singh had just started working for Jack Tunney in Toronto, and agreed to the tour. "Their schedule was so hectic, I said 'I'll do the overseas trip for you, but to wrestle here. . . .' I had just gotten married. My wife wasn't too happy with me being on the road with a newborn baby and all that," he said. Singh worked Kuwait, Dubai, Oman, Australia and Hawaii for the WWF from 1980–86. "The only regret that I have is that I didn't stay with the WWF, especially nowadays, financially speaking, with the money that they're making now, the exposure they're getting. At the time when I was there with them, they were just kind of starting out. I didn't have any idea they were going to be as big as they are now."

TIGER JEET SINGH

As the story goes, Jagit Singh Hans arrived in Toronto in the mid-'60s with $8 in his pocket and a dream. The truth may have been stretched a bit, but there's no doubt Tiger Jeet

TIGER JEET SINGH.
PHOTO: OLIVER COLLECTION

Singh's accession to the top of the wrestling world is nothing short of remarkable.

An amateur scrapper in India, the 6-foot-3, 265-pound Tiger fell into pro wrestling with Fred Atkins in Toronto, and started around southern Ontario. In May 1968, his career took off when he captured a version of the U.S. title in Maple Leaf Gardens. "I remember when I wrestled right here in Toronto, Johnny Valentine for the U.S. title. I was a nervous wreck, and didn't know if I was coming or going. I just went wild. And after that I never looked back," Singh said. He would defend the title for four years around Toronto, including a memorable sold-out bout against The Sheik.

In 1973, Singh's life changed forever when he attacked Antonio Inoki outside a department store in Japan. The feud captivated the Japanese audience and Singh's wildness scared fans silly as he ran through the crowds screaming and swinging his sword. From that point forward, Tiger concentrated his career on international tours. A sporting legend in Japan, India, the Middle East and South Africa, Singh even held a Mexican world title. Through the '70s and '80s, Singh wrestled only occasionally in North America, and his part-time schedule allowed him to pursue many other business interests both in Canada and abroad.

Singh invested his earnings well, and is now worth several million dollars, and owns a palatial home just outside of Toronto. He is a prominent member of Toronto's Sikh community, and tried his hand at promoting wrestling in the '80s. In Japan in the mid-'90s, Singh teamed with his son Mick, better known now as Tiger Ali Singh.

DAVEY BOY SMITH

It has been said that Davey Boy Smith's life would make a decent script for a Hollywood movie. There have been triumphs and tragedies, accidents and recoveries, charges and acquittals. Unfortunately, there was no happy ending.

A few years removed from his last aborted attempt at a comeback with the WWF, Smith died in May 2002 in British Columbia of an apparent heart attack. No one who knew Smith could deny that years of drug abuse — steroids, morphine, painkillers, muscle relaxants, sleeping pills — had played a part in his death.

Even after his death, Smith, best known as "The British Bulldog," remains a fascinating character, a working class kid from outside Manchester, England, who rose to the top and had it all crash down around him on more than one occasion.

Smith started training to be a pro wrestler at 12, and debuted in England at 15. He was following in the footsteps of his older cousin, "The Dynamite Kid" Tom Billington, who had gone off to Calgary to wrestle for Stampede. Billington soon had the Harts invite Davey. "Stampede Wrestling was probably some of the happiest days of my life," Smith said. "I was just really happy. It was a really good territory to be in. It was really booming at that time."

Part of the reason for Smith's happiness was the love he found with Diana Hart, youngest of four Hart daughters. Their marriage brought him officially into the family.

When Stu Hart initially sold the Stampede territory to the WWF, he

DAVEY BOY SHORTLY AFTER ARRIVING IN CANADA. PHOTO: BOB LEONARD

The British Bulldog. Photo: Mike Lano

arranged for some of the talent to go to the bigger promotion. The British Bulldogs — Billington and Smith — were among them. They declined to enter the WWF at first, however, enjoying major success in Japan. Eventually, they did, and quickly captured the hearts of fans everywhere.

Billington was an innovative high-flyer and Smith was slightly more grounded, with a more impressive physique. He also attracted a lot more female attention than his cousin. After a long chase, the Bulldogs won WWF gold in April 1986. The constant pounding on his body and a car accident combined to stop Billington's career, and Smith was forced out on his own, both in WCW and the WWF as the now singular British Bulldog.

The pinnacle of Smith's career was a battle with his brother-in-law Bret in London's Wembley Stadium in August 1992 for the Intercontinental title. It's a match both call the best of their careers. WWF tag gold followed with Owen Hart, as did a reign with the newly created European title.

Following Bret's falling out with WWF owner Vince McMahon, Smith returned to WCW. He went nowhere in the politically charged atmosphere, and was seriously injured on a trap door hidden under the mat, set up for a mysterious entrance by the Ultimate Warrior. His career in jeopardy, Smith vowed to return, which he did, briefly, in the WWF.

In Calgary, Smith was a celebrity, and when he went to court in 1996 on a charge of aggravated assault, it was a media event. The Bulldog was cleared of that charge, but found himself in court in subsequent years on similar charges, often against family members. Smith divorced from Diana and took up with Andrea Hart, Bruce Hart's estranged wife. A stint in a drug treatment centre seemed to be an indication Davey Boy wanted to get his act together. He had big hopes for his teenage son Harry Smith, who had begun wrestling, and teamed with him on a show in Winnipeg weeks before his death.

WOLFMAN WILLIE FARKUS

THE WOLFMAN.
PHOTO: TERRY DART

Led to the ring by a chain, clad in animal skins, with an unkempt beard and wild hair, the Wolfman Willie Farkus was one memorable wrestler. Usually billed "from the wilds of Canada," Farkus would gnaw on his opponents in the ring, often forcing the wrestling shows to censor his lunacy. Promoters sometimes even said he had been raised by wolves.

In 1956, Farkus fled Hungary for Canada to escape the Communist regime. He settled in Toronto, and began training in a gym with Mike Scicluna. According to Farkus, Scicluna beat him up pretty bad the first day, but he came back the next to earn his teacher's respect.

Whether it was as The Wolfman, The Hungarian Wolfman or The Caveman, Farkus was never a huge star, but was a valuable mid-card gimmick who riled the people and was a wild, unpredictable heel. He stopped wrestling in the late 1980s, following the death of his long-time friend and tag-team partner Dave "Wildman" McKigney.

Today's
Great Canadians

ANDY ANDERSON

In a little more than six years in pro wrestling, Winnipeg's Andy Anderson has managed to create an impressive resume at a time when places to wrestle are becoming further and further apart. To improve his craft, Anderson was willing to hit the road, working for six months in Tennessee, a few weeks in Japan and Mexico, and almost two years in Puerto Rico.

Anderson has had his proverbial cups of coffee with the big boys too. He had a tryouts with WCW back in 1997, attended the WWF dojo in early 1999, and had another tryout for the WWF in mid-2001. On another occasion, he worked a RAW taping as a security guard who Steve Austin laid out and drank beer over.

ANDY ANDERSON IN PUERTO RICO. PHOTO: IWA

Being on the road all the time has been tough for Anderson. He misses everything: his house, his parents, his friends, his dog, his cats, his car, even the Canadian air. It's never cool in Puerto Rico. "The heat, while I love it, kills me. I sweat very easily and with the humidity here, there's some days — especially with some of the buildings not air-conditioned, there's not a lot of air circulation — it just kills me."

CHRIS BENOIT

CHRIS BENOIT TOSSES THE CUBAN ASSASSIN DURING HIS SOPHOMORE YEAR. PHOTO: BOB LEONARD

Incredibly intense and ferocious in the ring, with the rare ability to make everything he or his opponent does look good, Chris Benoit has probably been the best worker in North America over the past 10 years. Benoit can compete in any style and makes everything look convincing in the ring. But he's shy around praise. "I'm not one for titles or accolades. I really love what I do," Benoit said. "My biggest thing is going into the ring and having a good match, no matter who it's with or what it's about. That's basically where I get my satisfaction."

Growing up in Edmonton in the '70s, Benoit followed Stampede Wrestling from a young age, and dreamed of getting into the ring. He started attending the matches and bugging the wrestlers for advice. After finishing high school, Benoit got his chance to train when he was 17, and would take a bus to Calgary on weekends to work out with the Harts in the Dungeon. Benoit made his debut for Stampede in 1986 when he was 18, teaming with Rick Patterson to defeated Karl Moffat and Mike Hammer.

Modelling himself after his hero, Dynamite Kid (Tom Billington), Benoit quickly found success in Stampede, winning the tag titles twice during his first five months in the business. His Calgary connections got him hooked up with Japan, and he spent a year there training and wrestling. When he returned to Stampede, Benoit was a much more polished wrestler and had filled out considerably. He was thrust back into the championship picture quickly, winning the tag belts on two more occasions, and the British Commonwealth Mid-Heavyweight belt four times.

Despite his success in Stampede, the 5-foot-10, 220-pound Benoit wasn't attracting any of the big American promotions, so he hit the road again, returning to Japan in early 1990 under a mask as The Pegasus Kid. Mexico

Benoit as Pegasus Kid in Japan in 1990. Photo: Mike Lano

followed, where he also worked under a mask. There, Benoit had a storied feud with Owen Hart, the Blue Blazer. New contacts in Mexico helped him get booked in Europe.

"I enjoy going to each country and getting into each style because it's a real challenge. When I go over to Japan, it takes me about three or four days to change my mindset and get into that style. It's almost as if you have to shift gears. It's the same if you go down to Mexico, or even when you go over to Europe, because the wrestling in Europe is so different also. It's run by rounds, so you have five, three-minute rounds and you'll be in the middle of something and the bell will ring and you'll have to go back to your corner. It's really challenging," he said.

In North America, Benoit had a 1993 stint in wcw that went nowhere. In late 1994, he hooked up with the growing ecw promotion, and hit his stride. Almost immediately after he started, Benoit injured Sabu's neck in a match and was dubbed The Crippler. It gave him a new focus both in the ring and, more importantly for success stateside, a chance to do interviews. Yet Benoit was worried about his reputation with his peers. "I felt bad about it," he said. "Thank God it wasn't a career-ending injury. Accidents do happen. I think the people that I work with know me, and the people that know me personally know I'd never take advantage of a situation or someone in the ring like that. They know that it was a mistake. It's a physical, contact sport and injuries are going to happen."

Teamed in ECW with fellow veteran world travellers Eddie Guerrero and Dean Malenko, The Triple Threat took off, and it wasn't long until WCW scooped up the three players.

Benoit started in a rejuvenated Four Horsemen unit, feuding with Kevin Sullivan and his Dungeon of Doom for months. It was during this time that he hooked up with Nancy "Woman" Sullivan, with whom he now lives. When the Four Horsemen disbanded, Benoit was lost in the shuffle at first, until feuding with Raven's Flock and Diamond Dallas Page. WCW gold soon followed, with the TV title, U.S. belt and WCW tag titles all ending up around his waist.

A falling out with WCW led to Benoit leaving the company the day after he finally won the World title. The Radicals — Benoit, Guerrero, Malenko and Perry Saturn — debuted in the WWF in early 2000 and quickly made their presence felt.

Benoit revelled in the team atmosphere of the WWF, content to play his part and step up to the plate when called upon. He's held the WWF Intercontinental title and the WWF tag belts with Chris Jericho, and seemed destined for a world title run when he hurt his neck and was sidelined.

Getting hurt and being off for a year meant that Benoit got to spend more time with his family, and think about what he might do after his ring career is over. "You always think about what you're going to do after wrestling," he said. "I definitely know I always want to have my hands involved in the business, because I miss it so much. I never thought I'd miss it this much."

CHRISTIAN

Though Christian (Jay Reso) and Edge (Adam Copeland) aren't really brothers, they did grow up together in

THOUGH THEY WOULD WIN THE WWF TAG TITLES TOGETHER,
CHRISTIAN (REAR) AND EDGE HAD MANY BOUTS OVER THE YEARS
BEFORE MAKING IT BIG. PHOTO: TERRY DART

Orangeville, Ontario and their lives are so intertwined that
they might as well be. They would wrestle in their backyards,
dreaming of one day holding the WWF tag titles. Copeland
won a newspaper contest and got a chance to learn to wrestle
for free. It put his wannabe tag-team partner in an awkward
position.

"I was finishing high school, I was broke, I didn't have any
money," Reso recalled. "I always knew that it was what I wanted to do, and he was saying, 'C'mon, we said we were going to
train together.' That kind of thing. When I went to college, I
used my money from my student loan to pay for my wrestling
school." Both grapplers trained under Ron Hutchison in
Toronto, Copeland starting in 1992, Reso in 1994. Reso made

CHRISTIAN TAKES GREAT PLEASURE IN HURTING TAJIRI.
PHOTO: MIKE LANO

his debut within nine months. "I did feel like I had a bit of catching up to do, and maybe worked a little harder."

The duo hit the road together, often fighting as the Suicide Blondes. They worked quite a bit in southern Ontario and Michigan, and went on one trip to Tennessee that didn't work out. In the Maritimes for Grand Prix Wrestling, they hit their stride, working every night of the week against veterans like Rick Martel and Bad News Allen Coage. Frank Parker was a referee on that tour, and thought that Reso and Copeland were almost mirrors of each other talent-wise. "I think that people that know ability, and know these guys, instantly know that there's not a big deal of a difference there," Parker said.

As with their training, Copeland was the first to crack the WWF roster. Reso finally got there in September 1998 at the Breakdown pay-per-view in Hamilton, standing at ringside while Edge fought Owen Hart. From there, the duo joined The Brood with Gangrel, and later The Undertaker's Ministry of Darkness. Reso was the first to win a title, claiming the light-heavyweight belt.

But it was as a tag team that Edge and Christian climbed to new heights, both literally and figuratively. "We work really good as a team, we grew up together, we click well, but we don't have to look identical. We can have our own personalities, our own identities," Reso said. They claimed the WWF tag belts that they had dreamed about as kids on many occasions, and had awe-inspiring matches with the Hardy Boyz and Dudley Boys, complete with monster ladders, tables, and chairs.

In late 2001, Christian's jealousy over Edge's King of the Ring win proved to be too much for the old friends, and the team was split up during a RAW taping in Toronto. Since the split, both have held the Intercontinental title, the tag belts and wrestled a variety of opponents.

STEVE CORINO

Former ECW and NWA champion Steve Corino is a true "Old School Hero" despite still being under 30. He believes in the power of good wrestling, telling compelling stories and surprising fans. "Wrestling is positive, fun, good versus evil, and good wins in the end," he said. "Wrestling should be like a magic show. If you see the guy with the mask reveal the secret, then where's the fun in watching the trick?"

He was born in Winnipeg, and lived there until he was five, when his family moved to Philadelphia. Corino trained with Tom Brandi and debuted in 1994. He hit many American indie promotions before catching on with ECW, gaining new fans with his work on the microphone and his dedication to the business. Besides his run as ECW champ, Corino had a great feud with Dusty Rhodes that saw both men spill buckets of blood.

When ECW closed down, Corino became NWA World champion and travelled the continent, defending the belt in the affiliated promotions, including a memorable return to Winnipeg for the Canadian Wrestling Federation.

CYRUS

It's been an interesting ride for Don Callis in the pro wrestling business. Starting out in Winnipeg on a bit of a whim after

CYRUS THE VIRUS IN ECW.
PHOTO: MIKE LANO

getting a degree in political studies from the University of Manitoba, he soon found himself appreciated more for his brain than his brawn. Never a huge, muscle-bound wrestler, the 6-foot-2, 210-pound Callis became the cocky heel The Natural in front of the crowd, and was matchmaker and the coordinator of the TV show behind the scenes for Winnipeg's IWA promotion, run by Tony Condello.

He did tours of South Africa and Japan, and had successful runs with "The Model" Rick Martel as a partner in both Winnipeg and the Maritimes before catching the WWF's eye. In September 1997, Callis debuted as The Jackyl, manager for the Truth Commission. His motor mouth garnered him TV time, but the team he managed did not inspire anyone. The WWF regrouped, and attempted again with Jackyl leading the Human Oddities, another gimmick that went nowhere.

Released from the WWF, Callis hooked up with ECW in early 1999 and became Cyrus. In his new role, Callis became the spokesman for "The Network," protesting ECW's content as an alleged mole for TNN. The new character worked, and Callis enjoyed an unprecedented run as a character until ECW went into bankruptcy.

The switch from wrestler to commentator/character was a welcome one for Callis. "Vince McMahon really did me a favour, in that he evolved me into more of a manager. As a wrestler, you have that pride where you want to go out and take the bumps — 'I want to wrestle, I don't want to be a manager' — that sort of thing. But, Vince had it right. My talking was something that got me over. Vince focussed on that strength, and Paul [Heyman] continued that when I went to ECW."

Back in Winnipeg, Callis is still very involved with wrestling. He promotes occasional shows, both on his own and in conjunction with Tony Condello and Joe Aiello. Callis also writes a weekly column for the Winnipeg *Sun* and co-hosts a radio show with Aiello.

DR. LUTHER

His speciality may be extreme hardcore matches with barbed wire and base-ball bats, but Dr. Luther has a solid grounding as a techni-cal wrestler. Schooled at the Hart Family Dungeon, he broke into wrestling as Lenny St. Clair in Stampede Wrestling, just as the promo-tion was about to go under. Forced to find work, he did, and has probably worked for just about every western indie promotion over the past 12 years. Under the name Atomic Punk, he worked Japan's FMW promotion as well.

DR. LUTHER.
PHOTO: MIKE LANO

In 1994, he took the name Dr. Luther for a trip to Japan, based partly on the movie *The Silence of the Lambs.* The new character stuck, and fit in well with the new emphasis on hardcore wrestling in FMW and the IWA. Teamed with Freddy Krueger (Doug Gilbert), he captured the IWA barbed wire tag belts.

When he's back in North America, Dr. Luther works out of

his Washington State home for indies around the Pacific Northwest. He's been especially successful and influential in the Michelle Starr-run Extreme Canadian Championship Wrestling promotion, based in Vancouver.

EDGE

By now, Adam Copeland's story has been told many times. He won a "Why I want to be a wrestler" contest in the *Toronto Star* at 17, and got the chance to train with Ron Hutchison and Sweet Daddy Siki in Toronto. He trained for over a year before he had his first match. Within five years, he debuted in the WWF as the mysterious Edge, complete with cool vignettes on the TV shows.

ADAM COPELAND (EDGE) AND JAY RESO (CHRISTIAN) LISTEN TO REFEREE HARRY DEE EARLY IN THEIR CAREERS IN HAMILTON. PHOTO: KEVIN HOBBS

Growing up in Orangeville, about an hour from Toronto, Copeland always dreamed of becoming a wrestler with his best friend Jay Reso, who would become his tag-team partner and "brother" Christian in the WWF. "Jay and I would wrestle in his backyard, and would always be WWF tag-team champs. That's honestly what we dreamed about, talked about and aspired for," Copeland said.

At 6-foot-4, 235 pounds, Edge is a solid competitor in the WWF, and with his long blond hair and great physique, he's a hit with the ladies as well.

But make no mistake, Copeland paid his dues to get where he is today. His usual names on the indie circuit were Sexton Hardcastle and Adam Impact. He had a successful tag team called Sex & Violence in a small Detroit promotion with Joe E. Legend, and later teamed with Reso as the Suicide Blondes. He's done the northern Manitoba hell tours for Winnipeg promoter Tony Condello, starved during attempted tours in the U.S., and worked a couple of summers on the Grand Prix circuit in the Maritimes.

Copeland was discovered by WWE Canadian president Carl DeMarco on a small Toronto show, and asked to work on a show in Hamilton. Eventually, he was invited down to a training camp and signed a contract shortly thereafter. Before he

EDGE IS READY TO DEFEND HIS BELT. PHOTO: MIKE LANO

even debuted, WWF writer Vince Russo was hyping him, comparing Copeland to Ric Flair and Shawn Michaels. "I take it as a compliment but I don't feel I have to live up to anything. If that's what people perceive and think is going to happen then that's great. But, I am not going to lose sleep if I don't feel I am not on that path," he said.

After his debut, the Edge character joined with Christian and Gangrel as a gothic, vampire-like trio known as The Brood. From there, he was a part of The Undertaker's Ministry of Darkness before setting out with Christian as a tag team.

In late 2001, the Edge and Christian tag team was split up, stemming from the jealously Christian had for his brother winning the King of the Ring tournament. Edge has been given a chance to shine as a singles competitor, and even had a run as a champion tag-team partner with Hulk Hogan.

CHRIS JERICHO

It's hard to believe Chris Jericho has only been wrestling since 1990. The first-ever WWF-WCW unified World champion is so polished in the ring, and confident in his abilities and on the microphone, you'd think he had been around the wrestling business all his life.

Born Chris Irvine in New York City in 1970, he grew up travelling from city to city with his father Ted Irvine, who played in the NHL from '67 to '77 with the New York Rangers, Los Angeles Kings and St. Louis Blues. Winnipeg was always their home. According to his dad, Jericho has always been an entertainer: "His creativity mentally doesn't surprise me. As a little guy, from the comic books, to the Dungeons & Dragons, to his music, to his rock groups, to his plays in high school, he's always had an entertainment-type mind. He has a great view of life and how to entertain people."

At 16, Chris decided that he wanted to be a wrestler, having grown up watching Stampede Wrestling and the WWF. After finishing high school in Winnipeg, Jericho enrolled in the journalism program at Red River College. Then it was off to Calgary to train with the Harts for two solid months at age 19.

CHRIS JERICHO SALUTES HIS FANS IN JAPAN ALONG WITH CHRIS
BENOIT IN 1993. PHOTO: MIKE LANO

"You went there every day for three hours and got beat up and
thrown around and stretched out. After that I was a wrestler,"
said Jericho. Keith Hart was his primary trainer.

Stampede Wrestling wasn't promoting when Jericho graduated, so he debuted on a few Alberta independents. He
struggled to come up with a name, not wanting to play on his
father's reputation. One day, he found himself flipping
through the Bible and his record collection, where he came
across *Walls of Jericho* by Helloween. "I just thought Jericho
would be a cool name to use. Chris Jericho. I had never heard
the name before, and that's basically why I chose it. It was an
original one."

Jericho went to Japan in October 1991 for Frontier Martial
Arts. "It wasn't really my thing. It was more like a 'blow-up-
everything' kind of company," he said. After more Canadian
indies, including a tag team called Sudden Impact with fellow
Dungeon grad Lance Storm, Jericho got a chance at the end of
1992 to go to Mexico for a small promotion. His talent shone,
and he was soon working for EMLL, the top company in that
country.

Through EMLL, Jericho got booked in WAR in Japan. "My dream was always to work in Japan. It's all I ever wanted to do, because I used to watch a lot of tapes from Japan. Before I went to Mexico, I knew that I needed a name because they couldn't pronounce Jericho. You know, 'Yericho,' or whatever. So I came up with the name Lion Heart, because all the guys I used to watch in Japan, they all had the name of an animal. Eddie Guerrero was Black Tiger. Chris Benoit was Wild Pegasus. Too Cold Scorpio, Jushin Liger, Ultimo Dragon, Tiger Mask. So I thought if I was a junior heavyweight, I had to have the name of an animal. So I came up with Lion Heart for Mexico and Japan. Of course, Mexico changed it to Corazón de Léon, which is Spanish for Lion Heart."

Jericho was one of the top stars in both Mexico and Japan over the next couple of years. He also did a few other tours, including Germany. Jericho teamed again with Storm in the Jim Cornette Smokey Mountain Wrestling promotion as the Thrillseekers. According to Sandy Scott, who was involved in the SMW promotion, it was the right place at the right time for two developing stars. "Jericho, he was a go-go-go kind of guy. The other guy was laid back a little bit, Storm. Both nice guys, they were just starting out at that time . . . they got a real education there," Scott said.

In Japan, Jericho befriended Chris Benoit, who hooked him up with ECW for his first big-league North American exposure. "There's no denying the fact that Paul E. Dangerously [ECW boss] is a very smart guy and he gave a lot of chances to guys who had never had chances before," Jericho said. "For Dean [Malenko] and Eddie and myself, and Rey Mysterio, and even Chris Benoit, he saw something in us that no one else did."

His stint in ECW, where he held the TV title, got him noticed by the much bigger WCW, and Jericho was soon duking it out on the hot *Nitro* programs. Initially, he was a successful cruiserweight babyface, but a heel turn allowed his microphone skills to shine for the first time. He whined, complained, stole masks, and mocked "Stinko" Malenko. Oftentimes, his rants, egomania ("Monday Night Jericho") and skits (Ralphus as his

WWE SUPERSTAR RETURNS HOME TO WINNIPEG TO VISIT LOCAL
TRAINER TONY CONDELLO. PHOTO: TONY CONDELLO

security guard in Goldberg-like entrances) were the highlight
of wcw's programs. Jericho was a star on the way up, but
unfortunately he was in wcw, where the "big boys" like Hulk
Hogan and Kevin Nash conspired to keep the smaller talent
down.

Jericho debuted in the wwf in August 1999, and quickly
became a main attraction, verbally duelling with The Rock
from day one. As "Y2J," complete with a major exploding
entrance, Jericho went up and down the card, winning the
Intercontinental title a few times, and the tag titles with fellow
Stampede grad Chris Benoit. He's had memorable feuds with
the likes of The Rock, Kane, Chris Benoit, Kurt Angle, and even
Chyna.

In mid-2001, Jericho started the transition back to a heel.
Put into the main-event mix, he traded the wcw title with The
Rock before fighting off both him and Stone Cold Steve Austin

to claim the unified WWF and WCW titles at Vengeance in December 2001.

Away from the ring, the "Ayatollah of Rock 'n' Rolla" was able to pursue his musical interests as well. He got together with members of Stuck Mojo to form a group called Fozzy Osborne, a power-metal band that performs cover material and released an album in 2001. "It's a fun, pastime hobby that I kind of like to do, and surprisingly we're really good at it. So we're having a good time, and want to just keep it on the side, as a project," he said.

KURRGAN

Robert Maillet is the nicest, most pleasant, scary-looking monster you could ever meet. Dwarfing everyone around him, the 7-foot, 350-pound New Brunswick native gained fame in 1997 as Kurrgan in the WWF. He debuted as a part of the Truth Commission, with fellow Canuck Don Callis as The Jackyl, the team's manager. Maillet later morphed into more of a good-guy character, waving his hands in the air as a part of the Human Oddities. "I've always been a nice guy," he said. "I've always gotten along with everybody. I'm always quiet, not complaining about everything. That's the way I was brought up."

Maillet broke into wrestling after convincing Maritime mainstay Stephen Petitpas to train him. A very short time later, he was wrestling around Grand Prix Wrestling on Canada's East Coast as The Acadian Giant. He befriended Leo Burke, who trained talent for the WWF and was on the same tour, and was soon signed up. His WWF stint only lasted until 1999.

Since his departure from the big league, Maillet has kept busy working shows around the world, including stints in Mexico, Korea, and across Canada. He often uses other aliases, like Goliath, because WWE still own the rights to the Kurrgan name.

PHIL LAFON

Phil Lafon was just another gym rat in Calgary when Davey Boy Smith and Dynamite Kid came in to work out. They liked what they saw in Lafon, and invited him to the Hart House to learn to be a pro wrestler. More than 20 years later, Lafon is still making a full-time living wrestling. "I never knew I was going to be a pro wrestler until I became one," said the man also known as Dan Kroffat, Phil Lafleur, and Rocky Ventura.

PHIL LAFON. PHOTO: PHIL LAFON

Born in northern Ontario, and raised in Montreal, Lafon was always into sports. He followed a girl west to Calgary at 19. Mr. Hito was his primary trainer in the Dungeon, and Lafon was well schooled in the tighter Japanese style. After two years with Stampede Wrestling, Lafon headed to the Maritimes, where he was René Rougeau. He befriended The Cuban Assassin, who hooked him up in Japan. Lafon's best guess is that he's been back more than 50 times.

"First time I went to Japan, I was hooked. I liked the style better," he said. "It's more serious, more solid. It's not so much Hollywood. They're a little more serious with their sport. I really liked that. They showed more discipline." Giant Baba hooked Lafon up with American Doug Furnas, a tag team that lasted eight years, through thick and thin in ECW and the WWF.

He figures that the teaming with Furnas succeeded because they were both young, hungry and strong. "I was the worker, Doug was the manager. That's how basically it worked." When the team disbanded after a car accident and their WWF release months later, Lafon was left without all the contacts Furnas had. He worked in a salvage yard in Calgary for a while before getting back into pro wrestling full time. "I'm not ready for the real world yet. You have to do that eight hours. It's so hard. Being a wrestler for 20 years, then going to a real job is very hard for me."

LEATHERFACE

Fans in North American can be forgiven if they do not know the name Rick Taras. The fact is, he has had very little exposure here; but in Japan, he has done more than 70 tours as Leatherface, based on the character from the cult film *The Texas Chainsaw Massacre*. Complete with mask and costume, Taras makes his way to the ring each night wielding a spark-flying chainsaw, parting the sea of fans who crowd the aisle as he makes his entrance, sending them scurrying for safer ground.

It's an odd development for the 6-foot-3, 320-pound grappler from Winnipeg, who debuted in 1982 alongside his brother Barry as the Bruno Brothers. He worked various territories like Vancouver, Stampede, Grand Prix and Central States, usually as Rick Patterson.

In 1993, Patterson was referred by Eddie Watts to Japanese promoters to fill the Leatherface character while Mike Kirchner (a.k.a. Corporal Kirchner) was in jail. "When I walked out the first night the character was so over I couldn't believe it. I knew it was all what Kirchner had done. It was all his doing in getting the character over. I just sort of fell into it and tried to get the momentum up that he had," Taras said.

During his time in the hardcore Japanese IWA promotion, Leatherface has teamed with the equally bizarre character, Jason the Terrible, and fought hardcore legends like Cactus Jack Mick Foley. Leatherface is best remembered for his battle with Terry Funk in August of 1995 during the IWA's King of the Death Match tournament at Kawasaki Baseball Stadium. "It was terribly hot and humid that day," recalled Taras. "Terry just about broke my neck. We climbed up on the baseball [backstop] fence 30 feet in the air and he tried hanging me with a chain."

Taras' international success has hardly been limited to Japan. In Mexico, Taras has wrestled as la Policia Canadiaense

RICK PATTERSON IN 1983. PHOTO: TERRANCE MACHALEK

(The Canadian Mountie) and as a part of the trio The American Gringos (with fellow Canadian Mike Stone and Ken Timbs). He's done numerous tours of Korea and Puerto Rico, and had his life threatened during the matches in South Africa. "I hit the ring and attacked everybody and attacked the promoter and knocked everybody down and next thing you

LEATHERFACE THREATENS TERRY FUNK IN
JAPAN. PHOTO: MAY COLLECTION

know . . . some gun shots went off in this outdoor arena. They
were just mad that I beat the crap out of all them. They didn't
like me. They were at the top of the building. The police said
later it was a guy with a 9mm."

When he needs a break from his hectic international
schedule, Leatherface can be found on the occasional
Canadian indie show, usually in Manitoba or in B.C., before
heading out to another tour of the Orient.

JOE E. LEGEND

Just Joe was a WWF character that didn't really take off. The
mouthy, tattletale in multiple backstage vignettes didn't do
justice to the talented Joe Hitchen, best known to fans as Joe
E. Legend.

After training with Ron Hutchison in Toronto for two
years, the 6-foot-2, 250-pound Hitchen took to the road and is

JOE E. LEGEND (CENTRE) WITH GOTHIC KNIGHT AND A FAN.
PHOTO: TERRY DART

a veteran of worldwide rings now. He's a regular in Germany and England, and has been to places like Japan and South Africa as well. In Canada, he was a hit in the Maritimes on the summer circuit, and has done many tours for Tony Condello's Manitoba promotion.

While working for a Detroit promotion, Hitchen teamed with Adam Copeland (Edge) as Sex & Violence.

PIERRE CARL OUELLET

Carl Ouellet was mired in the mid-card mix in Puerto Rico in 1993 when Jacques Rougeau Jr. came to his rescue. Rougeau was returning to the WWF, and wanted his new friend to come with him. Ouellet agreed, added Pierre to his name, and they entered the WWF as The Quebecers. With Johnny Polo (later known as Raven) as their manager, Ouellet and Rougeau won tag gold three times. The first win, beating the Steiners with the help of a hockey stick, ranks among Ouellet's favourite moments. "We didn't sleep all night. We were just talking about the match."

PIERRE CARL OUELLET WORKING AS KILLER KARL WALLACE IN PUERTO RICO AGAINST JOSE GONZALES.
PHOTO: CARL OUELLET

At that point, Ouellet had been wrestling for six years, but was a virtual unknown in Canada. He trained in Montreal under Pat Girard in 1984, polished his skills with Edouard Carpentier, and did a few spot shows for International Wrestling. As half of the Super Bees with Eddie Watts, he did a tour of the Maritimes and quickly had to grow up. Ouellet was homesick, couldn't speak English and was only learning the business. The Bees were in the main events many nights, battling Masa Chono and Bulldog Bob Brown, who was also booker for the territory.

But Ouellet's big break came overseas. He got hooked up in England, then Germany, Austria, South Africa, Puerto Rico, and Japan, often teaming with his friend Nelson Vellieux. In Japan for the w*ngs promotion, he worked alongside Bill DeMott, a.k.a. Hugh Morrus, as Crash & Bash.

When Rougeau initially told him he was going to try to get him into the wwf, he was sceptical, thinking that Jacques was only trying to encourage him. Then after two tryout matches, Ouellet realized it was possible. When they signed their deals, Jacques was reluctant to return quickly. "I remember that Jacques didn't want to start until November 5th, because it was J.J.'s [Jacques's oldest son] birthday and he wanted to be home. Me, I was dying for six, seven years on the road and I knew I could start in June and he was pushing back the date! I couldn't believe it! It was funny. We finally started in July." The Quebecers went on to numerous wwf tag title runs, and later had a less-than-memorable run in wcw.

As a singles wrestler, Ouellet was Jean-Pierre Lafitte, a pirate, and had a decent feud with Bret Hart. It was an exciting but frustrating time for Ouellet, and he can now recognize that he grew too big for his britches, refusing to do what was asked of him on occasion. "I know what it is to have a great push, and how you feel and how you want to react," he explained. "Most of the time, you think that it's you that is over, but in a way, that's Vince [McMahon] that gave you the push, so it's kind of a confusing thing."

For the last few years, Ouellet has been working occasional international tours, including a run with All Japan, and was on a WWF developmental deal in Memphis as Kris Kannonball. He is the centrepiece of Rougeau's Montreal-based Lutte International 2000 promotion and well-known across Quebec. He's hopeful for a return to the WWE one day, but is going back to university to have something to fall back on.

SHANE SEWELL

Hidden away down in Puerto Rico is Shane "The Glamour Boy" Sewell. Though he is one of the biggest draws for the World Wrestling Council due to his charisma and athletic ability, Sewell is virtually unknown in Canada or the U.S.

SHANE SEWELL.
PHOTO: PRWRESTLING.COM

Sewell started wrestling in 1989 after hanging around a wrestling gym in Toronto. Local wrestler Steve Ocean got him booked in England, and Sewell was hooked. He befriended Sean Morley (a.k.a. Val Venis) and the two formed a championship tag team in both Ozarks Mountain Wrestling and Puerto Rico, where they held the WWC tag titles seven times. Besides the tag belts, Sewell has held all of the top singles titles in WWC.

He's had his opportunities with the big companies, including a number of TV tryouts for the WWF and time in WCW's Power Plant. "I'm in good shape. I'm ready to move up," said Sewell. "Sometimes a window opens up and you've got to be ready."

TIGER ALI SINGH

D'Lo Brown and Tiger Ali Singh. Photo: Mike Lano

Tiger Ali Singh (Gurdip "Mick" Hans) is living proof that it can be extra tough to follow a famous father into pro wrestling. As the son of the legendary Tiger Jeet Singh, Tiger Ali has put up with the comparisons since he began his pro career in the mid-'90s. "In the start, I did feel pressure but I no longer look at it as pressure. I look at it as an asset because every time I come back I have the great opportunity of seeking advice," said Tiger Ali, whose name is a tribute to his father and Muhammad Ali.

When Tiger Ali signed with the WWF in January 1997, the comparisons increased. Up until then, he was a relative unknown in North America, content to wrestle on tours of the Orient with his father. Tiger Ali's WWF stint has been rocky, at best. He won the WWF's Kuwaiti Cup in April 1997 and seemed destined for a babyface push, but never caught on with the fans. The WWF retooled his character, and he became a rich braggart, "Asian royalty," and was able to flaunt his family's real-life wealth.

Though the new gimmick did better, Singh wasn't able to stay on the active WWF roster. An attempt to have him manage D'Lo Brown and Chaz as Lo-Down didn't go over either. While working in Puerto Rico for the WWE-affiliated IWA promotion he was injured and a return to the ring again is in doubt.

LANCE STORM

Lance Storm is an anachronism in today's wrestling game. He's a serious wrestler and person, grounded in his fundamentals and family life and lacking a grandstanding, showboating style. There's no doubt he would have had the same success in any era, but the fact that Storm has succeeded so well over the past decade is a testament to hard work, dedication to the business, and the fact that sometimes, being old-school is a good thing.

Storm was born Lance Evers in Sarnia, Ontario, but grew up in North Bay. He became a fan a little late in life, with the whole "rock-n-wrestling" boom of the mid-'80s. When he

STORM AND TAMMY SYTCH, A.K.A. SUNNY. PHOTO: MIKE LANO

LANCE STORM STRETCHES RANDY ORTON. PHOTO: MIKE LANO

became frustrated at Wilfrid Laurier University in Waterloo, Ontario, both with the Business Administration program and his varsity volleyball coach, Evers took a pass and headed out to Calgary to learn pro wrestling from the famed Hart family. Not one to brag, he says he tried wrestling because he thought he "would be halfway decent at it."

Upon his graduation from the Hart Dungeon, where he trained primarily with Keith Hart (one of the other students at the time was Chris Jericho), prospects for work in Canada were slim. So Storm hit the road, catching on in Europe and in Japan. Back home, he would appear occasionally for promotions in Winnipeg and Calgary.

Jericho was a frequent tag-team partner. They were known as Sudden Impact in Calgary, and later as The Thrillseekers in Smokey Mountain Wrestling in Tennessee.

When Jericho hooked him up with Paul Heyman and ECW, Storm got his first big exposure in North America. Always trumpeting that he was from "Calgary . . . Alberta . . . Canada," Storm had memorable tag teams with both Chris Candido and Justin Credible, and was able to develop his character, his mic skills and as a ring technician. He aspires to more behind-the-scenes work down the road.

Storm's increased confidence and TV time attracted WCW, and he became one of the last bright spots in a company on the way down. WCW created a Team Canada around Storm, and his now-signature line, "If I could be serious for a minute," emerged during this period. Storm excelled in the new environment. "I think if you try to make people do things that aren't them, it doesn't work," said Storm. "The Ric Flair promo is a great promo but not everybody can do Ric Flair. So, I think you have to find what you're good at and what you're comfortable with and just go with that."

When WCW was sold to the WWF, Storm fought his way onto the roster and has been a regular mid-carder ever since. Despite his success, he still believes that he's the most "unlikely guy to be in the business," because of his commitment to family and lack of a real wild side.

TRISH STRATUS

Toronto fitness model Trish Stratus had her wrestling career come together quickly. While at York University, studying biology and kinesiology with thoughts of medical school, Stratus

TRISH STRATUS GETS IN SHAPE BEFORE HER WWF DEBUT.
PHOTO: TODD GILLIS, TORONTO SUN

caught the attention of WWF talent scouts. She had been appearing regularly around town, hyping her love of wrestling on Toronto-radio show *The Law* and TSN's *Off The Record*. The WWF liked what they saw, and she began training with Ron Hutchison at Sully's Gym, the same school of hard knocks that graduated Edge, Christian and Tiger Ali Singh.

Once her visa came through, Stratus debuted in the WWF in early 2000, acting as the manager for Test and Albert, better known as T&A. Her first appearance on the microphone was memorable in its awkwardness. "Yeah, I was a bit stunned, to say the least," she said with a laugh.

Stratus is as well known for her clothing — colourful cowboy hat, revealing top, short shorts, thigh-high boots and full-length leather coat — as she is for her wrestling. During her WWF run, she has been both a heel and a babyface — and she has been happy with the way it has been changing. "I think it's all about character evolution and I think my character's constantly evolving," Stratus surmised.

With only a few women on the WWF's roster, Stratus has gotten a chance to face them all, and also had a run with the WWF Women's title in late 2001 and early 2002. The WWF marketing machine has also pushed the Canadian "diva" in various photo shoots and videos, something she is more than familiar with. "That's the easiest part of this whole thing. You know, my former career as a fitness model . . . It's funny, I say former, but I mean my 'other' career," she said. "So I was used to that, that was actually a comfortable environment."

TEST

Andrew Martin dreamed of becoming a pro wrestler while growing up in Whitby, Ontario, a suburb of Toronto. At the prompting of some buddies, he decided to explore the option and headed down to the SkyDome for a big WWF show. After the event, he got into the Planet Hollywood restaurant next to the 'Dome, and managed to meet Bret Hart.

"To make a long story short, he offered to train me," explained Martin. "Two weeks later I quit both my jobs, went down for eight months. He and Leo Burke trained myself and

TEST. PHOTO: MIKE LANO

a few other Canadian guys — Glenn Kulka, Adam Copeland [Edge] was there, Jay Reso [Christian Cage]. The four of us trained together and it was a good experience. He was very good to me."

After some initial training, Martin wrestled on small shows in Saskatchewan, working as T.J. Thunder and Martin Kane. A short while later, the WWF came calling and had him attend a training camp at the federation's headquarters in Connecticut. Under the guidance of Dory Funk Jr. and Tom Pritchard, Martin got better and was offered a deal with the WWF.

His first TV appearance was as a roadie when Motley Crüe played RAW. His ring debut came later, when he interfered on behalf of The Rock in a match against Hunter Hearst-Helmsley. The 6-foot-6, 320-pound Martin was dubbed Test.

Martin's biggest push came when he was paired romantically with Stephanie McMahon. The two appeared headed to the altar when McMahon married Triple H instead. Rather than starting a major feud between Triple H and Test, the WWF moved him downcard, in part because of injuries.

Test rebounded later in a tag team with Albert, under the management of newcomer Trish Stratus. The team, T&A, never won tag gold, but were solid competitors for a number of months.

As a single, Martin has captured the WWF's hardcore and European titles, but in doing so, the towering behemoth has drawn many comparisons to Kevin Nash. To Martin, the likenesses — similar heights, builds, their slower, power-move-based ring skills — are just a fact of life. "It doesn't bother me at all," he said. "People make comparisons to me and Kevin Nash all the time, and if my success is only as good as Kevin Nash's then I'm happy. I mean, the guy has done tremendously in the business, and I don't take that as an insult."

VAMPIRO

The lure of a rock 'n' roll lifestyle took Thunder Bay's Ian Hodgkison away from a promising hockey career, and later helped define his character when he became the pro wrestler El Vampiro Canadiense in Mexico. He's quick to point out that the goth look, complete with white face paint and spiky hair, is really him. "I've had this gimmick for 11 years now," he said. "It's who I am and it's my actual lifestyle. It's not just an image, it's really me."

VAMPIRO BEFORE BEING COMPLETELY COVERED IN TATTOOS ON HIS CHEST. PHOTO: MIKE LANO

VAMP IS SURROUNDED BY ADMIRERS. PHOTO: MIKE LANO

A hugely popular babyface and sex symbol in Mexico during his runs for EMLL and CMLL through the 1990s, Vampiro was on hardly any Canadian wrestling fan's radar until he was brought in to WCW in 1999. The 6-foot-1, 240-pound Vampiro had a rocky stay in WCW, bickering with management and fellow wrestlers. He had a memorable feud with Sting, and two less-than-successful runs trying to capitalize on his penchant for rock 'n' roll — one with the Insane Clown Posse and one with the Misfits.

Like his character, the rock 'n' roll aspect of his life is legit. Hodgkison was a doorman at Toronto's legendary Horseshoe club, and worked as a roadie for Teenage Head and Jack DeKeyzer. Vampiro also appeared onstage with ICP and the Misfits.

Vampiro eventually tired of the politics of WCW and headed off into the sunset, settling in Montreal while raising a family. He still hits the ring occasionally in Mexico and for bigger independents.

VAL VENIS

When he struts to the ring, where he proceeds to bump and grind while removing his towel in a suggestive manner for the ladies, it's easy to forget that Val Venis, or "the Big Valbowski," the WWE's "porn star," is actually Sean Morley, a politically active, wannabe helicopter pilot from Toronto.

After wrestling and playing football in high school, he trained with Dewey and Jason Robertson in Hamilton in 1991. In the summer of 1992, he worked in Britain as Scott Borders and saw for the first time what life could be like as a wrestler.

THE BIG VALBOWSKI VAL VENIS SAYS "BRING IT ON."
PHOTO: MIKE LANO

Morley passed on a chance to attend Colorado State University to study aeronautical science, and instead headed to the small Ozark Wrestling Federation with fellow Toronto-area native Shane Sewell, whom he actually faced on the football field in their local high school championships.

After eight months in the Ozarks, both headed to Puerto Rico to wrestle for the World Wrestling Council. The island became Morley's base for the next few years, with trips to Japan or Mexico for extended periods. "I just kept bouncing back and forth. I was really fortunate that I wasn't stuck on the independents too much. I worked mostly all small territories."

In Mexico, Morley worked as Steel. "The mask looked like steel, like I had metal on my face. It was totally unique, especially to Mexican standards. It got over really, really big in Mexico." For a time, he was even the CMLL World Champion.

The WWF came calling in 1997, and after a number of tryouts and a training camp at the WWF's headquarters, Morley got the call to come in and work as Val Venis. He was taken aback at first, partly because it was a controversial character bound to draw attention. But Morley is also a strong supporter of the Libertarian Party, which believes that people should be allowed to do whatever they wish as long as it is not detrimental to others. He even publishes a newsletter called *Hardball*, where he expresses his views in print. In the end, of course, Morley ran with the Val Venis character, to great success.

In the WWF, Venis has been prominent in numerous storylines, including feuds with Golddust over Marlena (Terri Runnels), Rikishi, and Kaientai. He has held the WWF Intercontinental and European titles as well. During the brief run of the mockingly titled Right To Censor, Venis did an abrupt change and joined the Stephen Richards-led band of baddies trying to clean up the WWF.

Off because of injury in late 2001, Venis returned early in the new year as his old character. No doubt he will continue to impress the ladies for years to come.

EDDIE WATTS

Eddie Watts gets no respect at home. A veteran of more than 17 years in the ring, when Watts comes back to Winnipeg, he won't work for the local promoters. "It's hard to justify promoters internationally paying me the money they do if I'm willing to go work for beans when I'm at home," Watts said. "They just don't draw substantial crowds to support me here. It's kind of tough, coming from a beautiful country like Canada, we just don't have the population like some of the countries. Mexico's not a rich country, but they pack the people in."

In 1986, Watts trained with Ernest Rheault in Winnipeg and was soon on the local scene. His first big break came with a tour of All-Star Wrestling in Vancouver with Al Tomko, who

WOLVERINE EDDIE WATTS (LEFT) AND VANCE NEVADA.
PHOTO: VERN MAY

billed him as Eddie "The Wolverine" Watts. Rheault's training was very old-school, and the 5-foot-8, 220-pound Watts found that he stood out. "People used to look at me, 'Whoa, take it easy, take it easy.' But I just like working tight. Even to this day, I have a bit of a reputation. They call me Cemento Eddie Watts because everything is snug. When I give you a tackle, I'm going to run right over you."

Besides Vancouver, Watts also worked for Stampede Wrestling and has done numerous tours of the Maritimes, including donning a mask as one of the Super Bees, with partner Carl Ouellet.

In Calgary, he made the connections for getting work internationally. It was Leo Burke who got Watts to Puerto Rico when he was booking there in 1990. Almost immediately, Watts won the wwc junior heavyweight belt. "From there, it just seemed to steamroll," Watts said. Back in Winnipeg, he hooked up with Rick Patterson, and together they drove to Mexico for his first tour. Watts has done four tours since.

Japan has been his favourite place to wrestle, because the money is great, but also because his tight-working style is appreciated there. He's hoping that Asian Sports Promotions, for whom he has been working recently, ends up being a regular gig. Between trips to Japan, Watts hopes to go to Europe to wrestle for the first time.

He's in the same boat as a few other Canadians who are well known abroad but not at home, like Shane Sewell and Patterson. "It's too bad that they don't know us. But in a way, they're only going to know us if we get on American tv," he said. Though encouraged by friends who work there, Watts has never worked a match for wwe or sent them a tape.

Selected Bibliography

Biographical Dictionary of Professional Wrestling, by Harris M. Lentz III (McFarland & Company Inc, 1997).

Bret "Hitman" Hart: The Best There Is, The Best There Was, The Best There Ever Will Be, by Bret Hart (with Perry Lefko) (Balmur Book Publishing, 2000).

Drawing Heat, by Jim Freedman (Black Moss Press, 1988).

Encyclopedia of American Wrestling, by Mike Chapman (Leisure Press, 1990).

Hey, Boy! Where'd You Get Them Ears?, by Paul Boesch (Minuteman Press Southwest, Houston, 1988, 2001).

Hommage aux célèbres frères Baillargeon, by Réjean Lévesque and Kathy Paradis (La Plume D'Oie, 1997).

Johnny Rougeau, by Johnny Rougeau (Les Éditions Quebecor, 1983).

Killer Pics, by Walter Kowalski (White-Boucke Publishing, 2001).

Les grand athlètes Canadiens, by S.F. Wise and Douglas Fisher (General Publishing, 1976).

The Montreal Forum: Forever Proud 1924-1996, by Chrystian Goyens (Les Editions Effix, 1996).

Of Mats and Men, by Glynn A. Leyson (Sports Dynamics, 1984).

Stu Hart: Lord of The Ring, by Marsha Erb (ECW Press, 2002).

Tributes: Remembering Some of the World's Greatest Wrestlers, by Dave Meltzer (Winding Stair Press, 2001).

Une vie de chien dans un monde de fous, by Maurice "Mad Dog" Vachon (with Louis Chantigny) (Guerin litterature, 1988).

Yvon Robert: Le Lion de Canada francais, by Pierre Berthelet (Editions Trustar, 1999).

Wrestling Real Names and Aliases, by Dominic Macika, Royal Duncan and Gary Will (Archeus Communications, 1996).

NOTES ON SOURCES

I have been writing about wrestling for 18 years now, and some of my interview material goes back almost that far. I have been fortunate to interview, either in person or over the phone, a good number of the men and women in this book and it's an experience that I wouldn't trade for anything. Many of the interviews took place during the course of my work for the SLAM! Wrestling web site, while others took place while working on magazine pieces or in person at great events like the annual Cauliflower Alley Club banquets. In a few specific circumstances, I have been permitted to use interview material from my former colleagues from the SLAM! Wrestling site, and I am greatly indebted to them.